Bloom's Modern Critical Views

Bloom's Modern Critical Views

Bloom's Modern Critical Views

DORIS LESSING

Edited and with an introduction by
Harold Bloom
Sterling Professor of the Humanities
Yale University

CHELSEA HOUSE
PUBLISHERS
A Haights Cross Communications Company
Philadelphia

©2003 by Chelsea House Publishers, a subsidiary of
Haights Cross Communications.

A Haights Cross Communications Company

Introduction © 2003 by Harold Bloom.

Printed and bound in the United States of America.
10 9 8 7 6 5 4 3 2 1

Library of Congress Cataloging-in-Publication Data

Doris Lessing / edited and with an introduction by Harold Bloom.
    p. cm. -- (Bloom's modern critical views)
Includes bibliographical references and index.
   ISBN: 0-7910-7441-2
   1. Lessing, Doris May, 1919--Criticism and interpretation. 2. Women
and literature--England--History--20th century. 3. Women and
literature--Africa--History--20th century. I. Bloom, Harold. II.
Series.
  PR6023.E833 Z597 2003
  823'.914--dc21
                                        2002154041

Chelsea House Publishers
1974 Sproul Road, Suite 400
Broomall, PA 19008-0914

http://www.chelseahouse.com

Contributing Editor: Camille-Yvette Welsch

Cover designed by Terry Mallon

Cover photo by ©Bettmann/CORBIS

Layout by EJB Publishing Services

Contents

Editor's Note

My Introduction centers upon "The Habit of Loving" and *The Golden Notebook*, and suggests that the crucial limitation in Lessing's work is her too-literal distrust of her own language.

James Gindin begins the chronological sequence of criticism with a study of Lessing's "intense commitment" to social justice in her earlier work. *The Golden Notebook*, still her best novel, is read by Paul Schlueter as an exercise in self-knowledge.

Phyllis Sternberg Perrakis examines Jungian and Sufi perspectives in Lessing's *The Marriages Between Zones Three, Four, and Five*, after which Robert Boschman discusses the excremental vision of "The Good Terrorist."

To Karen Schneider, Lessing is an authentic prophet against war and violence, while Sheila Roberts, comparing Lessing to Nadine Gordimer, finds social contradictions in both novelists.

Betsey Draine, commenting upon *The Four-Gated City*, sees Lessing's Martha Quest as a wise realist though a visionary, after which Claire Sprague finds in Lessing an heroic pattern of the "mother/daughter dialectic."

Lessing's mastery of "the poetics of change" figures in Gayle Greene's account of *Re: Colonised Planet 5, Shikasta*, while Roberta Rubenstein defends *Briefing for a Descent into Hell*, despite its palpably bad style of writing.

In a just estimate, Catharine R. Stimpson, looking at all the Martha Quest novels, sets aesthetic concerns aside as well as inadequate "politics of mind", yet still affirms that Martha's saga provides us with "goads to growth."

Introduction

I

The best known of Doris Lessing's short stories, "The Habit of Loving," still serves to introduce both her authentic virtues and her very severe limitations as a writer of fiction. George Talbot, a London theatrical personage (sometime actor, occasional producer, sporadic reviewer), is gently but firmly jilted by "the love of his life," who has been in Australia during the years of the Second World War. A youngish sixty, he grieves, fails to win back his divorced wife, catches severe influenza, and is nursed back to health by a song-and-dance performer, " a small, thin, dark girl," named Bobby Tippett. George and Bobby marry; at thirty-five, she seems childlike to him. But to herself, and to her youthful lover of twenty, she seems already past fulfillment. Two passages between George and Bobby are wholly representative of Lessing's strength and weakness, early and late. The first turns upon the fine phrase of the title, "The Habit of Loving":

> In the morning she looked at him oddly, with an odd sad little respect, and said, "You know what, George? You've just got into the habit of loving."
>
> "What do you mean, dear?"
>
> She rolled out of bed and stood beside it, a waif in her white pyjamas her black hair ruffled. She slid her eyes at him and smiled. "You just want something in your arms, that's all. What do you do when you're alone? Wrap yourself around a pillow?"
>
> He said nothing; he was cut to the heart.
>
> "My husband was the same," she remarked gaily. "Funny thing is, he didn't care anything about me." She stood considering him, smiling mockingly. "Strainge, ain't it?" she commented and went off to the bathroom. That was the second time she had mentioned her husband.

1

That phrase, "the habit of loving," made a revolution in George. It was true, he thought. He was shocked out of himself, out of the instinctive response to the movement of skin against his, the pressure of a breast. It seemed to him that he was seeing Bobby quite newly. He had not really known her before. The delightful little girl had vanished, and he saw a young woman toughened and wary because of defeats and failures he had never stopped to think of. He saw that the sadness that lay behind the black eyes was not at all impersonal; he saw the first sheen of grey lying on her smooth hair; he saw that the full curve of her cheek was the beginning of the softening into middle-age. He was appalled at his egotism. Now, he thought, he would really know her, and she would begin to love him in response to it.

Poor George is quite mistaken; he never will really know her, and she never will love him. He is the archetypal Lessing male, in the habit of loving even as he is in the habit of living. Shrewdly observed by Lessing, nevertheless he is not *there* sufficiently to bear observation. Like most "realistic" representations, he is a reduction, and so a caricature, though a very effective one. Bobby begins as a caricature also, but her final, self-willed transformation reverberates with a mimetic force beyond caricature:

One morning she announced she was going to have a birthday party; it would be her fortieth birthday soon. The way she said it made George feel uneasy.

On the morning of her birthday she came into his study where he had been sleeping, carrying his breakfast tray. He raised himself on his elbow and gazed at her, appalled. For a moment he had imagined it must be another woman. She had put on a severe navy blue suit, cut like a man's; heavy black-laced shoes; and she had taken the wisps of black hair back off her face and pinned them into a sort of clumsy knot. She was suddenly a middleaged woman.

"But, my darling," he said, "my darling, what have you done to yourself?"

"I'm forty," she said. "Time to grow up."

"But, my darling, I do so love you in your nice clothes. I do so love you being beautiful in your lovely clothes."

She laughed, and left the breakfast tray beside his bed, and went clumping out on her heavy shoes.

That morning she stood in the kitchen beside a very large cake, on which she was carefully placing forty small pink candles. But it seemed only the sister had been asked to the party, for that afternoon the three of them sat around the cake and looked at one another. George looked at Rosa, the sister, in her ugly, straight, thick suit, and at his darling Bobby, all her grace and charm submerged into heavy tweed, her hair dragged back, without makeup. They were two middleaged women, talking about food and buying.

George said nothing. His whole body throbbed with loss.

The dreadful Rosa was looking with her sharp eyes around the expensive flat, and then at George and then at her sister.

"You've let yourself go, haven't you, Bobby?" she commented at last. She sounded pleased about it.

Bobby glanced defiantly at George. "I haven't got time for all this nonsense any more," she said. "I simply haven't got time. We're all getting on now, aren't we?"

George saw the two women looking at him. He thought they had the same black, hard, inquisitive stare over sharp-bladed noses. He could not speak. His tongue was thick. The blood was beating through his body. His heart seemed to be swelling and filling his whole body, an enormous soft growth of pain. He could not hear for the tolling of the blood through his ears. The blood was beating up into his eyes, but he shut them so as not to see the two women.

One could read this as a parody, perhaps indeliberate, of a slogan in T.S. Eliot, thus rendered as: "Males cannot bear very much reality." Presumably Bobby's bitter self-reductiveness is Lessing's own. What is striking, and indubitably an aesthetic strength, is the extraordinary effect of the supposedly unbearable reality upon poor George. That is my second "poor George," reflecting the reaction of a fifty-five-year-old male literary critic to Lessing's "realistic" reduction of male attitudes. "Who is the interpreter and what power does he or she seek to gain over the text?" is a superb Nietzschean question. An answer, not un-Nietzschean, would be to remind the reader (and the critic) that the critic interpreting here is frequently assailed by feminist critics as "*the* patriarchal critic." Not un-Nietzschean also would be the related answer, reminding the reader that Doris Lessing is the interpreter, and that the power she seeks to gain over the

text of life is always reductive: tendentious, resentful, historicizing. Do we
know at the conclusion of "The Habit of Loving" what George Talbot is
really like, simply because Lessing has told us, so vividly, the very worst
things that can be said about him?

II

Lessing's one undisputable achievement remains her immensely influential
novel *The Golden Notebook*. The oddity of this achievement is that the book
is very much a traditional work, resembling neither her early social realism
nor her later, rather grim ventures into speculative fiction. *The Golden
Notebook* has mothered hordes of feminist novels, and yet it is hardly what
would now be considered "feminist" writing by most critics of that
persuasion. Not that Lessing is a contemporary version of George Eliot, a
woman so strong as a novelist and so majestic as a moralist that her vision is
not much more gender-oriented than was Shakespeare's. Critics who compare
Lessing to George Eliot or to Turgenev do her an ill service, as she simply is
not of that eminence. She is a contemporary of George Gissing or Olive
Schreiner, and inflating her importance, though inescapable in current
literary and sexual politics, finally may sink her without trace. *The Golden
Notebook* will survive, I think, because its rugged experimentation with form
rises out of socially realistic concerns, and is therefore undertaken against the
grain, as it were.

   At the center of *The Golden Notebook* is Lessing's assumption that her
Anna Wulf is the paradigm for all contemporary women. But is she? At one
moment Anna gives us her erotic credo, which is presumably Lessing's also:

> The closest of all bonds; neurotic, pain giving, the experience of
> pain dealt and received; pain as an aspect of love; apprehended as
> a knowledge of what the world is, what growth is.

Whether or not this is a universal experience, its equation of pain,
worldly knowledge, and growth is certainly the dialectic of experience in *The
Golden Notebook*. Someone as removed as I am from Lessing's stance is in no
position to challenge her dialectics, but only to wonder whether her own
rhetoric is adequate to her proclaimed vision. About twenty-five pages from
the end of the novel, Anna Wulf crawls into bed with the precise expectation
of a particular dream:

I also knew what I was going to be told. Knowing was an "illumination." During the last weeks of craziness and timelessness I've had these moments of "knowing" one after the other, yet there is no way of putting this sort of knowledge into words. Yet these moments have been powerful, like the rapid illuminations of a dream that remain with one waking, that what I have learned will be part of how I experienced life until I die. Words. Words. I play with words, hoping that some combination, even a chance combination, will say what I want. Perhaps better with music? But music attacks my inner ear like an antagonist, it's not my world. The fact is, the real experience can't be described. I think, bitterly, that a row of asterisks, like an old-fashioned novel, might be better. Or a symbol of some kind, a circle perhaps, or a square. Anything at all, but not words. The people who have been there, in the place in themselves where words, patterns, order, dissolve, will know what I mean and the others won't. But once having been there, there's a terrible irony, a terrible shrug of the shoulders, and its not a question of fighting it, or disowning it, or of right or wrong, but simply knowing it is there, always. It's a question of bowing to it, so to speak, with a kind of courtesy, as to an ancient enemy: All right, I know you are there, but we have to prevent the forms, don't we? And perhaps the condition of your existing at all is precisely that we preserve the forms, create the patterns—have you thought of that?

What this passage manifests (despite Lessing's intentions, I suspect) is that Anna Wulf is a failed writer, who cannot master "Words. Words." Lessing could be defended only by the assertion that Anna Wulf does not speak for the author, here or elsewhere, which is improbable. Certainly Lessing's speculative fiction *Canopus in Argos: Archives* perpetually relies upon the "terrible shrug" of saying:

The people who have been there, in the place in themselves where words, patterns, order, dissolve, will know what I mean and the others won't.

Novels, like poems, cannot be written with rows of asterisks, a circle perhaps, or a square. As a prophet of consciousness, Lessing increasingly is humanly impatient in regard to language, an impatience that sometimes she can render with poignancy. Ultimately, it is her refusal to sustain or be sustained by societal ideas of order that drives her on towards speculative fiction, and towards speculative doctrines, as in Martha Quest's reading preferences in *The Four-Gated City*:

> books on Rosicrucianism and the old Alchemists; Buddhist books
> ... Yoga ... Zoroastrianism and esoteric Christianity ... the I
> Ching; Zen, witchcraft, magic, astrology and vampirism;
> scholarly treatises on Sufism; the works of the Christian mystics
> ... everything rejected by official culture and scholarship.

The impulse is ancient and honorable, and recapitulates a tradition that goes from the Gnostics on through Blake and Yeats to such of our contemporaries as James Merrill and Thomas Pynchon. Yet Pynchon's Kabbalists, working out his doctrine of sado-anarchism, thoroughly exploit the limits of language, as do Merrill's occult personages and celebrants. Lessing's visionary fiction has some cognitive strength and considerable pathos, but the reader must fight through to them against Lessing's own language, which is, all too frequently, a kind of drab shrug. Doubtless the novel itself is a societal idea of order, a repressive convention that a prophet must transcend or circumvent in the struggle towards moral and spiritual liberation. Consider D.H. Lawrence, who achieved prophetic authority while remaining a strong novelist in *The Rainbow* and *Women in Love*, but who then became impatient, and so gave us *The Plumed Serpent* and other novels of his final phase. Lawrence was a great poet, with preternatural verbal gifts, and so a fairer comparison for Lessing is her exact contemporary, Iris Murdoch. How do Lessing and Murdoch compare, as novelists and as seers?

Both may be called Platonic novelists, though only Murdoch is actually a Platonist, while Lessing is a post-Marxist materialist who has wandered into Sufism in the honorable spirit of the firece Spanish anarchists who fought against Franco, while seeking a religion in Rosicrucianism and other assorted dank crankeries. Murdoch is a great storyteller, master of double plots and of endless surprises, while if you read even *The Golden Notebook* for the story then you may as well hang yourself. Neither Murdoch nor Lessing is proficient at depicting memorable personages, Murdoch because she runs to recurrent, set types, and Lessing because she cannot be bothered, since she has ceased to believe that we have (or ought to have) individual personalities anyway. Murdoch is an admirable comic writer, while there is not the slightest evidence that Lessing and her characters have any sense of humor whatsoever. The largest difference is that Murdoch trusts words, and has the discipline to order them.

Since both Murdoch and Lessing have the same underlying subject, which is the erotic war between men and women, Murdoch's superiority is palpable in representing the almost infinite nuances of the sexual agon. Men and women fall in love in Murdoch, as they frequently do in reality, but in Lessing they almost invariably deceive or are deceived, in a quest for power over others. Though clearly I prefer Murdoch, Lessing has the stronger extra-literary appeal in an age of ideologies, all of them promising liberation. Yet *The Golden Notebook* and certain moments in the Martha Quest novels should endure, because Lessing is very much a representative writer for our time. She has the spirit, if not the style, of the age.

JAMES GINDIN

Doris Lessing's Intense Commitment

Among young contemporary English writers, Doris Lessing is the most intensely committed to active persuasion to reform society. In a series of loosely connected essays, entitled *Going Home* (1957), published after she had returned to her early home in British colonial Africa for a visit, Miss Lessing frequently advocates direct participation in political action. She talks of the "sense of duty" that makes her join organizations, defends (on biographical rather than ultimate grounds) her own support of communism, and ends her essays by unfurling a qualified banner:

> In this book I have made various statements about the possibility of Communism becoming democratic. Since writing it the Soviet intervention in Hungary has occurred. It is hard to make adequate political assessments on notes added hastily to galley proofs as a book goes to press. But it seems to me that during the last three years the great words liberty, freedom and truth have again become banners for men to fight under—in all the countries of the world. It seems to me wrong that so many people should be saddened and discouraged by this sudden violent crisis we are all living through: it is a crisis in the battle of truth against

From *Postwar British Fiction: New Accents and Attitudes.* © 1962 by the University of California Press.

lies, of honesty against corruption, of respect for the goodness of
people against cynicism.   [Pp. 252–253.]

Miss Lessing's interest in the battle permeates most of her short stories and
novels. Frequently the theme of the work is whether or not, despite a hostile
or indifferent society, strong commitment to a particular cause or political
doctrine is justifiable.

The issue of commitment is most tersely stated in Miss Lessing's play,
Each His Own Wilderness (first presented in 1958). The play presents a violent
conflict between mother and son. The son, Tony Bolton, just discharged
from the army, returns to his mother's London home while she is preparing
for one of her frequent rallies to champion worthy causes. Tony, whose first
memory is the bomb that killed his father in World War II, is skeptical about
causes and rallies, bitter that so much of his mother's energy has been given
to Spain and Hungary and other world problems. In one argument he rails
at his mother: "You're so delightfully old-fashioned. Getting killed for
something you believe in is surely a bit of a luxury these days? Something
your generation enjoyed. Now one just—gets killed" (p. 15). His
contemporary, Rosemary, talks of six big men somewhere who could blow up
the world any time they wished, a concept that renders all protest against the
H-bomb useless. Tony is no closer to his mother on the subject of domestic
politics:

> Why are you sitting there looking so tortured? You've got what
> you wanted, haven't you? Well? You've spent your life fighting
> for socialism. There it is, socialism. You said you wanted material
> progress for the masses. God knows there is *material* progress.
> Hundreds of millions of people progressing in leaps and bounds
> towards a materially-progressive heaven.... Do you know what it
> is you've created, you and your lot? What a vision it is! A house
> for every family. Just imagine—two hundred million families—or
> is it four hundred million families? To every family a front door.
> Behind every front door, a family. A house full of clean, well-fed
> people, and not one of them ever understands one word anybody
> else says. Everybody a kind of wilderness surrounded by barbed
> wire shouting across the defences into the other wildernesses and
> never getting an answer back. That's socialism. I suppose it's
> progress. Why not? To every man his wife and two children and
> a chicken in the pot on Sundays. A beautiful picture—I'd die for
> it. To every man his front door and his front door key. To each his
> own wilderness.   [Pp. 50–51.]

The conflict between generations is not only political, for Tony, a highly Oedipal young man of twenty-two, becomes furious whenever his liberated mother mentions one of her love affairs. He shrieks that she lives "like a pig," yet he would rather live in her house than find a flat on his own. Similarly, the mother finds Tony a bore, a stupid "insufferable prig," yet she is willing to sell all her possessions to provide him with an allowance for self-discovery. The final exchange of the play summarizes both the political and the personal conflict, focuses on the issue of the sort of commitment a person ought to make. Tony's mother speaks first:

> I'm nearly 50—and it's true there's nothing much to show for it. Except that I've never been afraid to take chances and make mistakes. I've never wanted security and safety and the walls of respectability—you damned little petty-bourgeois. My God, the irony of it—that *we* should have given birth to a generation of little office boys and clerks and ... little people who count their pensions before they're out of school ... little petty bourgeois.
>
> [P. 94.]

After his mother leaves, Tony turns to Rosemary to deliver the final lines of the play:

> Rosemary, listen—never in the whole history of the world have people made a battle-cry out of being ordinary. Never. Supposing we all said to the politicians—we refuse to be heroic. We refuse to be brave. We are bored with all the noble gestures—what then, Rosemary? ... Leave us alone, we'll say. Leave us alone to live. Just leave us alone.
>
> [P. 95.]

Even though Tony is given the last speech, his point of view is not that of the author. Tony is made too childish, too petulant, to represent anything more than a contemporary phenomenon. Rather, the play simply states, without resolving, different attitudes toward political and social commitment.

Some of Miss Lessing's novels, however, develop these issues a good deal further. The series of novels that deals with Martha Quest's growing-up (a sequence, as yet unfinished, which includes *Martha Quest*, 1952; *A Proper Marriage*, 1954; and *A Ripple from the Storm*, 1958) demonstrates a strong endorsement of the heroine who is anxious to change society, to work actively for a more humane and just world. Martha, the heroine, encounters difficulty in attempting, within the severely restrictive society of colonial

Africa, to define herself both personally and politically. The books by
Havelock Ellis she has read as an adolescent do not square with the attitudes
toward sex she finds around her; the books about socialism and economics
have little to do with the problem of the color bar she sees every day.
Martha's books, her associations, her kind of perception, have all helped to
make her very different from her mother, the representative of conventional
colonial society.

The conflict between mother and daughter begins early, and, like the
conflict between mother and son in *Each His Own Wilderness*, covers both
political and sexual issues. Martha is disgusted with her mother's
combination of purity and calculation about sex, her mother's Victorian
propriety and constant assumptions concerning the laziness and the
dishonesty of all African natives. Her mother, on the other hand, finds
Martha blasphemous and immoral. But the two, like Tony and his mother,
cannot simply ignore each other. Mrs. Quest, though continually rebuffed,
keeps returning to her daughter, trying to help Martha and give her
unwanted advice, as if the bitter quarrels had never occurred. And Martha,
when seriously ill, wonders why her mother has never really loved her. Her
emotional attachment to her mother is deeper than that to either of the two
husbands she marries in unsuccessful attempts to discover herself.

Martha, in her quest for values, joins the Communist party early in
World War II, but finds the party, with all its interminable bickering and its
anxiety to remain a force within a hostile society, unable to do anything about
colonial Africa's principal problem, the division between white and black.
Yet, despite her many mistakes, Martha never retreats into the indifferent
complacency or the assumption of eternal rightness which she sees all around
her in colonial society. Martha searches for herself and battles for what she
believes.

Julia Barr, the young heroine in *Retreat to Innocence* (1956), represents a
more complex treatment of Miss Lessing's kind of commitment. In ways,
Julia, who frequents espresso coffeehouses and wears black sweaters, is like
Tony Bolton. Both are products of the new generation, born in the mid-
'thirties to liberal and aristocratic parents, handed educations their mothers
had to fight for, wanting only to find some personal meaning to hang on to.
Julia, too, fights the parents she cannot break from and bitterly opposes what
she calls her parents' "messiness" about politics and sex. Her desire for
stability and her wish to disassociate herself from political issues seem
priggish and selfish to her concerned father: "A more self-centred, selfish,
materialistic generation has never been born into this unfortunate old
country. All you want is to cultivate your own gardens. You really don't give

a damn for anyone but yourselves, do you?" (p. 195). Julia, who offers less childish defenses for her attitudes than Tony Bolton does, feels that her parents' political concerns have kept them from understanding and appreciating human beings. She recalls that on a trip through Spain with her mother, after a peasant had mended a puncture in their tire and they had spent several hours talking with the peasant's family, all her mother could speak of was the need for "a sensible English town Council and a birth control centre."

Julia, unlike Tony Bolton, develops as the novel progresses. She falls in love with a Communist refugee writer, Jan Brod, a man more than twice her age, long since defined by political forces Julia can barely comprehend. Julia, the product of a wholly different time and place, cannot share Jan's deep involvement in politics. But this involvement, this overwhelming concern, gives him an energy, a force, an attraction that Julia cannot find in any of the agreeable and socially acceptable young men she knows. Julia argues with Jan about politics, and makes him acknowledge his awareness of all the purges and iniquities the Communists have created. Yet she can also understand and feel the emotional force of Jan's ultimate defense of the Communists:

> But don't you see, when people formed themselves together in the Party, for the first time in history, without God, without excuses, relying on themselves, saying: We accept the responsibility for what we do, we accept all the good and the evil of the past, we reject nothing—then for the first time in history man became free; he became free because he rejected nothing.
>
> [Pp. 228–229.]

Jan's defense stands as the affirmative battle cry in the novel. Jan himself, however, cannot remain in England, for the established hypocrisy will not grant him citizenship. Julia is not sufficiently converted to follow him back to central Europe, for the affair with Jan is part of her means of self-discovery. But she is able to realize that her shelter and comfort have something hollow about them and that in losing Jan she has lost more than she has gained. Julia, being herself, has no genuine alternative. Still, Miss Lessing makes it clear that Julia and her generation are lesser beings than their predecessors because they lack the energy and the purpose of a Jan Brod.

Miss Lessing's commitment usually involves opposition to the reigning precepts of English or Anglo-colonial society. Both Julia and Martha Quest, despite their different political attitudes, are enormously attracted to an aristocrat, a representation of the society's model. Martha is fascinated by Mr. Maynard, the magistrate who, although reactionary, maintains a steady and biting wisdom about Africa. Julia is strongly drawn to her father, that liberal, tolerant, stable representative of the basic English virtue of fair play. Yet, in both instances, the aristocrat betrays the faith placed in him. Mr. Maynard runs a vigilant spy service directed against radicals which belies his pose of sardonic intelligence; more directly, he lies about Martha's close friend in order to cover up his failure to persuade her to lose by abortion the child fathered by Maynard's dissolute son. Julia, too, is betrayed by her father, the benevolent liberal and patron of the arts, living on the income earned in the family business now managed by a "competent commercial person from the Midlands." Julia asks her father to help secure British citizenship for Jan. Her father promises but, after making a casual inquiry, refuses to push the matter further and retreats into the shell of upper-class complacency, sure that the government must know what it's doing, confident of the judgment of the British Home Office. Julia's father's liberalism is hollow, despite the appearance he gives of genuine concern. Even Tony Bolton's mother, who had seemed fine and elegant and truly solicitous of others, stupidly wounds another person and betrays Tony by selling their house, his symbol of security and permanence. The liberals, the people who apparently manifest concern about social and political problems without objecting to the fundamental society itself, and the aristocrats, those sustained and honored by the society, stand revealed holding shoddy or dishonest poses.

Yet many of Miss Lessing's heroines, disillusioned by their own societies, can find themselves through an older person denigrated by most of society. Martha Quest, for example, has her first affair with a Jewish orchestra leader much older than herself, who is patronized with sneers by most of her colonial friends. His very difference, the fact that he cannot be defined in terms of the society, is part of his attraction for Martha. Similarly, the young actress in "The Habit of Loving" (a story in a volume of the same title, published in 1957) marries a much older actor who cannot understand the contemporary quality of her lost-gamin routine, who believes the theater should contain violent, bombastic gestures. The young actress requires definition outside the world by which she has been conditioned. Julia Barr, too, in loving Jan, has reached outside the society established for her, embraced the alien and the unexpected. Women define themselves through the sexual relationship, and Julia, Martha, and others all demonstrate their partial or essential rejection of their own societies by affairs with the ineligible and the unexpected. And conversely, in Miss Lessing's fiction, the aristocrats and the halfhearted liberals, those endorsed by the society, are apt to be worth little as men.

Doris Lessing has consciously sought the socially rejected. When she moved to England in 1949, her sense of social responsibility and her distrust of those who sanction and are sanctioned by the reigning society led her to search for her values and for her literary material among the working classes in London. As she herself explains in a recently published documentary (*In Pursuit of the English*, 1960):

> I propose to admit, and voluntarily at that, that I have been thinking for some time of writing a piece called: In Pursuit of the Working-Class. My life has been spent in pursuit. So has everyone's, of course. I chase love and fame all the time. I have chased, off and on, and with much greater deviousness of approach, the working-class and the English. The pursuit of the working-class is shared by everyone with the faintest tint of social responsibility: some of the most indefatigable pursuers are working-class people.   [Pp. 12–13.]

But the pursuit, as Miss Lessing describes it in her documentary, did not uncover any unanimity of repressed nobility among the London proletariat. Miss Lessing reports her difficulties in finding a place to live, her encounters with sharp operators and grasping landlords among the working classes. A poor clerk, Rose, finally helps her get settled, and the landlords, Dan and Flo, invite her to vast spaghetti suppers and round up the furniture she needs. Still, the same landlords are cruel to an old couple in the house, whom they want to evict, and neglect their own young daughter so badly that authorities threaten to take the child to a state home. Some of the people Miss Lessing encounters do reinforce conventional ideas of a concerned and humane working class:

> Two houses down on the opposite side lived an old man on the old-age pension, who was reading for the first time in his life. He was educating himself on the *Thinker's Library*. He had been a bricklayer, his wife was dead and he was now half-crazed with loneliness and the necessity to communicate what he had so slowly and belatedly learned. He lingered on the pavement at the time people were coming home from work, made a few routine remarks about the weather, and then whispered confidentially: "There's no God. We aren't anything but apes. They don't tell the workingman in case we get out of hand."   [P. 138.]

But few of the Londoners described would provide so fertile material for a potential uprising among the proletariat. In fact, most of them become capitalists themselves whenever they get the opportunity. Dan, the head of the household, first began to acquire extra cash in the war when he was personal servant to a surgeon commander and received tips for squiring the commander's mistress in and out of quarters. Right after the war he stripped washbasins and baths from bombed houses and sold them. With these two sources of income, he was able to buy and furnish the house he now owns. An enterprising capitalist, Dan has solid hopes of increasing his holdings and becoming a fairly wealthy landlord. Though able with his hands and skillful at remodeling furniture, Dan has no thought whatever of emulating William Morris.

Miss Lessing also shows the insularity of these people. They often hate the French and hate the Jews, and are aware of little outside their own corners of London:

> Flo's London did not even include the West End, since she had left the restaurant in Holborn. It was the basement she lived in; the shops she was registered at; and the cinema five minutes' walk away. She had never been inside a picture gallery, a theatre or a concert hall. Flo would say: "Let's go to the River one fine afternoon and take Oar." She had not seen the Thames, she said, since before the war. Rose had never been on the other side of the river. Once, when I took my son on a trip by river bus, Rose played with the idea of coming too for a whole week. Finally she said: "I don't think I'd like those parts, not really. I like what I'm used to. But you go and tell me about it after."
>
> [*In Pursuit of the English*, p. 104.]

These people have little respect for British institutions and the justice of the law courts. In one of the funniest episodes in the book, the family goes to court to evict the old tenants from their house. In the antechamber their lawyer coaches them to lie consistently, to make a coherent case out of a long history of mutual grudges, cruelty, and complaints about dirty bathrooms. They win the case only because the old couple are even more incoherent and gratuitously foul-mouthed than they. But the point of the scene is that all the parties—the family, the old couple, the lawyer, even the judge himself—make the whole notion of the supposed fair play of British courts seem ludicrous. The people from the working class are simply less verbally skillful, less proficient in handling the forms, less sophisticated versions of their counterparts who compose the Establishment. No one is adequate to carry the banner for the revolution.

In portraying the working class, Miss Lessing often uses women to present the argument in favor of restricting one's activity to the comfortable, the sheltered, the safe. In the short novel called "The Other Woman" (one of a series of short novels published as *Five* in 1953), a young working-class girl chooses to break her engagement when her mother is killed by a lorry just before World War II. She decides to stay with her father in the basement they have always known, rejecting any outside influence. She chides her father for wasting his time at political meetings where nothing is ever accomplished, berates Parliament periodically, and lumps Hitler, Churchill, Attlee, Stalin, and Roosevelt together as people who make her sick. Her small security is blown up when her father is killed in a bombing in the war. She clings to the demolished basement as long as she can, until a kind young man almost carries her out by force. Once out of the basement, she can live with the man quite easily, clinging to that which is most readily available. She discovers that her young man has been married before, and his attentions soon begin to wander toward a third woman. The girl and the young man's first wife, accepting the male's infidelity without scenes or recriminations, finally agree to start a cakeshop in another basement and leave the young man to his newest mistress. The heroine does not search for romance or for passion; she simply accepts conditions around her and tries to work things out as safely and securely as she possibly can.

Rose, one of the central figures in *In Pursuit of the English*, is much the same kind of person. A hard life has taught her to fend for herself, to value her daily round, her drop of tea, her security. She, too, is skeptical about and indifferent to political parties or slogans. Her view of political personalities has little to do with the policies or the programs the personalities supposedly represent:

> Rose would listen to Churchill talk with a look of devotion I entirely misunderstood. She would emerge at the end of half an hour's fiery peroration with a dreamy and reminiscent smile, and say: "He makes me laugh. He's just a jealous fat man, I don't take any notice of him. Just like a girl he is, saying to a friend: No dear, you don't look nice in that dress, and the next thing is, he's wearing it himself."
>
> "Then why do you listen to him?"
>
> "Why should I care? He makes me remember the war, for one

thing. I don't care what he says about Labour. I don't care who gets in, I'll get a smack in the eye either way. When they come in saying Vote for Me, Vote for Me, I just laugh. But I like to hear Churchill speak, with his dirty V-Sign and everything, he enjoys himself, say what you like."   [P. 121.]

Rose also objects to the false film versions of the Cockney and to any kind of slogan concerning brotherhood. Yet she sentimentally misses the warmth and the comradeship of the war when the usual class barriers were down and people all felt closer to one another. Rose's attitude toward politics, like that of the heroine in "The Other Woman," is handled somewhat sympathetically because she's had a hard life, she's a woman, and she's a member of the working class. Because of these, Miss Lessing can make Rose's insistence on her own narrow world and her rejection of all political questions both faintly comic and sympathetic.

People without Rose's warrant who still hold the same attitudes receive much more biting treatment. The younger generation has had a much easier time, and their choice in favor of limiting experience to the secure is made much more selfish and materialistic. In *Retreat to Innocence*, Julia is frequently labeled as selfish, and the young Cockney lad who tends the coffee bar is made to say:

My old man, he was a proper old Bolshie he was. I don't hold it against him, mind. They had it tough when he was young. And he was on to me when I was a nipper, giving me the *Herald* and all that. I've been raised on William Morris and Keir Hardie and all that lot. And I wouldn't say a word against them—grand old boys they were. But I says to my dad, I says, what's in it for me?
                                                           [P. 111.]

Yet Miss Lessing treats the middle-class woman of limited and nonpolitical interests with even more sharpness. Working-class people have, at least, the excuse of a certain amount of economic and educational deprivation. But the middle classes often receive no sympathy whatsoever. A middle-class couple spending a holiday abroad appear in "Pleasure" (another story in the volume called *The Habit of Loving*). The young couple are interested only in spear fishing, in impressing their neighbors with the fact that they've been abroad, in justifying everything English to themselves and to anyone else they happen to meet. Not a shred of sympathy enters the one-dimensional characterization of the empty couple in "Pleasure," and the woman seems singled out to bear the brunt of Miss Lessing's disapproval. This commonplace middle-class woman is treated with a fierce contempt, an attitude far more shrill than any leveled against stupid, materialistic Cockneys or patronizing and deceptive aristocrats or those nasty, bigoted, lonely colonial women on farming outposts in Africa.

Miss Lessing's commitment to a sense of social responsibility and to a pursuit of those oppressed by society also infuses her fiction about colonial Africa, where she spent most of her first thirty years. In Africa the pursuit centers on the color bar, and, in all Miss Lessing's fiction dealing with Africa—her first novel, *The Grass Is Singing* (1950); the three novels dealing with Martha Quest; a volume of short stories called *This Was the Old Chief's Country* (1951); and four of the short novels collected as *Five*—the division between white and black is central. Often, in Miss Lessing's fiction, the white man is an interloper, attempting to wrest independence or security from the African soil or asserting himself in a colonial office established to govern the alien country. The white man carries his European culture and attitudes with him, preserves his religion and his heavy oak Victorian furniture, and brings up his children as he would in England. The child, from whose point of view the story "The Old Chief Mshlanga" is told, is living in British Africa:

> This child could not see a msasa tree, or the thorn, for what they were. Her books held tales of alien fairies, her rivers ran slow and peaceful, and she knew the shape of the leaves of an ash or an oak, the names of the little creatures that lived in English streams, when the words "the veld" meant strangeness, though she could remember nothing else.
>
> Because of this, for many years, it was the veld that seemed unreal; the sun was a foreign sun, and the wind spoke a strange language.   [*This Was the Old Chief's Country*, p. 8.]

In many of the stories the white settler's assertion of his inherited culture is, in this new land, his means of establishing his difference from the black men all around him. Some of the white settlers, like Dick Turner in *The Grass Is Singing*, have been failures in English society and have come to Africa in order to reëstablish themselves; others, like the old farmer in "The De Wets Come to Kloof Grange," are motivated by an urge to bring new land into cultivation.

Most of Miss Lessing's alien white settlers, and their more shrill and insistent wives, regard themselves as sensitive, aware, and responsible, and look at the blacks as happy, amoral, and irresponsible. In one story in *This*

Was the Old Chief's Country, a black woman is missing and the clues surrounding her disappearance point toward possible suicide. But the whites hesitate to endorse this supposition: "Later, we talked about the thing, saying how odd it was that natives should commit suicide; it seemed almost like an impertinence, as if they were claiming to have the same delicate feelings as ours" (p. 73). Farmers and businessmen grumble about the useless and ignorant blacks as regularly as they discuss the crops, the weather, or the prospects of business; the women complain that the household blacks are lazy, dishonest, fully deserving of the cuffs they get, and then wonder why the blacks are not more grateful for their civilized servants' jobs. In *The Grass Is Singing*, a successful neighboring farmer helps Dick Turner, for whom he has little love and less respect: "He was obeying the dictate of the first law of white South Africa, which is: 'Thou shalt not let your fellow whites sink lower than a certain point; because if you do, the nigger will see he is as good as you are'" (p. 221). Any kind of human relationship between white and black, within the strictures of this environment, is impossible.

The Grass Is Singing traces the horror that can result from a subterranean relationship between white and black within colonial African society. Mary, a thirtyish office worker in an African town, marries as her last chance Dick Turner, the inept and inefficient farmer. Gradually Mary shrivels in the midst of their futile battle to achieve security from the land. Only the Negro houseboy has the energy and the skill to force Mary's attraction, yet she, having always lived in Africa, is also repelled by the sight of him. She cannot bear to look him in the eye, fears even talking to him, while she unconsciously reveres his competence, strength, and grace. Mary would like to preserve her sanity by discharging the boy, but she has been unable to handle servants before and her husband insists that she keep this one. The conflict within Mary, the alternating love and hate toward the Negro, the frightening awareness that she possesses the one emotion her society most violently condemns, leads to her murder. She is destroyed by her inability to reconcile a human emotion with her own deep commitment to the rigid line her society maintains between white and black.

Like Mary Turner, many of the colonials feel a deep fear, a constant emotional apprehension about living in Africa. They are aware that they are interlopers, white aliens in a black world. The little girl in "The Old Chief Mshlanga" fears the isolation of her whiteness as she walks through the brush to the native village. Her wealthy father can force the natives to move, but he cannot control the mounds of mud, the rotting thatch, the tangled growth of pumpkins, and the hordes of white ants which the natives leave behind them. And the girl is frightened. Most often it is the woman, like the poor farmer's wife in "The Second Hut," or the wealthy farmer's wife in "The De Wets Come to Kloof Grange," who feels this fear, this inability of the white man to control the black, lush growth around him, yet men, too, sometimes have these moments of perception. The able farmer in "'Leopard' George," a man who has never married because he thought himself in perfect control over his native mistresses, is surprised when a young, hitherto discreet mistress embarrasses him in front of white guests:

> In that moment, while he stood following the direction of his servant's eyes with his own, a change took place in him; he was gazing at a towering tumbling heap of boulders that stood sharp and black against a high fresh blue, the young blue of an African morning, and it was as if that familiar and loved shaped moved back from him, reared menacingly like an animal and admitted danger—a sharp danger, capable of striking from a dark place that was a place of fear. Fear moved in George; it was something he had not before known. [*This Was the Old Chief's Country*, p. 209.]

The apprehension that the sensitive white feels in Africa is the mark of his failure to impose himself and his standards completely on the dark, fertile continent he inhabits. The fear is also, simultaneously, the sign of his own awareness in contrast to his denser, more complacent fellow colonials. Martha Quest, the perceptive heroine of *A Proper Marriage*, who has made a bad, hasty first marriage with a young colonial, uses the black of the native as the image of her own awareness:

> There were moments that she felt she was strenuously held together by nothing more than an act of will. She was beginning to feel that this view of herself was an offence against what was deepest and most real in her. And again she thought of the simple women of the country, who might be women in peace, according to their instincts, without being made to think and disintegrate themselves into fragments. During those first few weeks of her marriage Martha was always accompanied by that other black woman, like an invisible sister, simpler and wiser than herself; for no matter how much she reminded herself of statistics and progress, she envied her from the bottom of her heart.   [P. 85.]

For Miss Lessing, the recognition of the black's simplicity and value is the admission of the white settler's failure to civilize Africa.

Not all the white settlers are identical in Miss Lessing's fiction. As in her work dealing with the English, her fiction about Africa frequently relies on a conflict of attitudes between different generations. In *Going Home*, Miss Lessing praises the motives of the older generation of white colonials:

> It seems to me that this story of the man who preferred to die alone rather than return to the cities of his own people expresses what is best in the older type of white men who have come to Africa. He did not come to take what he could get from the country. This man loved Africa for its own sake, and for what is best in it: its emptiness, its promise. It is still uncreated.
>
> [Pp. 14–15.]

Newer settlers, in contrast, are likely to be more dedicated to hard cash or to redeeming previous failures. The comparison between generations is not, however, always so one-sided. In "The De Wets Come to Kloof Grange," the older generation may have established a more comfortable and peaceful settlement, but the younger generation is more willing to try to meet Africa on its own grounds, to swim in its streams and talk to its natives. In another story, "Old John's Place," the newer generation is rootless, an example of those who use Africa to find a security they have been unable to find in Europe. Yet in this story the older community, dogmatic, sure of itself and its moral standards, can find neither room nor sympathy for the new, more morally flexible immigration. In a few isolated instances the new generation can even, personally and temporarily, break down the color bar. In "The Antheap," one of the short novels in *Five*, a white boy and a black boy, born on the same farm, manage to remain close friends despite the older generation's constant attempts to remind each that he owes allegiance only to his own color. The two boys finally win and go off to the university together. Martha Quest herself, brought up in Africa, tries to break through the color bar, an aim that appalls her parents. But Martha does not represent the majority of her generation. Her contemporaries rebel against their parents, but in a very different way. They build a club,

> and inside it, nothing could happen, nothing threatened, for some tacit law made it impossible to discuss politics here, and Europe was a long way off. In fact, it might be said that this club had come into existence, simply as a protest against everything Europe stood for. There were no divisions here, no barriers, or at least none that could be put into words; the most junior clerk

from the railways, the youngest typist, were on Christian-name terms with their bosses, and mingled easily with the sons of Cabinet ministers; the harshest adjective in use was "toffee-nosed," which meant snobbish, or exclusive; and even the black waiters who served them were likely to find themselves clapped across the shoulders by an intoxicated wolf at the end of the dance: "Good old Tickey," or "There's a good chap, Shilling," and perhaps even their impassive, sardonic faces might relax in an unwilling smile, under pressure from this irresistible flood of universal goodwill.   [*Martha Quest*, pp. 183–184.]

But clapping the waiters on the back is only part of the story. At a later party some of these drunken colonials try to force a Negro waiter to perform a "war dance," making rather malicious sport of him. Their parents engage in a different sort of cruelty, a more tight-lipped and morally defended white superiority. The younger generation never bothers to defend white superiority; the young club members simply, and casually, assume it.

Miss Lessing's African fiction, like her other fiction, often shows her scorn for the halfhearted liberal, the aristocratic do-gooder who does not really commit himself to the downtrodden. The newly arrived colonial woman in "A Home for the Highland Cattle" (one of the short novels in *Five*) is anxious to treat her native houseboy with justice and humanity. She is even willing to steal her landlady's huge picture of prize highland cattle so that the houseboy can legitimize his mistress by buying her as a wife. The white woman tries to understand the way black society operates, and the boy genuinely appreciates her efforts, but still, at the end of the story, the white woman, now no longer living in the rented flat, fails to recognize her former houseboy as she watches the police marching him off to jail. She is too busy buying a table for her new house, although her gifts have led to his prison sentence. In "Little Tembi," a white woman's special fondness for a black boy whose life she once saved turns the boy into a wheedling thief. The boy is unable to accept his position in the black society and yet he is not, despite the special favors, allowed full equality with the whites. His ambivalent position destroys him, while the kindhearted white woman sits by wondering what has happened. Both these women ultimately betray those they tried to help. But Miss Lessing strongly endorses those more systematically committed to working for the socially oppressed. In "Hunger" (another of the short novels in *Five*), a young Negro leaves his native village for the jobs and the lights of the large city. He is sent to some Communist whites who try to help him. But he neglects their advice; he lies, steals, falls in with prostitutes and professional thieves, and is finally carted off to jail for trying to rob the Communists' home. Yet the Communists stick with him and send him a letter, telling him so. From prison, the Negro returns the following message:

> Tell him I have read it with all my understanding, and that I thank him and will do what he says and he may trust me. Tell him I am no longer a child, but a man, and that his judgement is just, and it is right I should be punished.   [P. 364.]

The attempts of the person fully committed are apt to have impact and meaning.

Not all Miss Lessing's Communists are similarly effective. In *A Ripple from the Storm*, the third novel in the series dealing with Martha Quest, Martha's Communists, whose interminable debates take up about half the novel, are severely split over whether to follow their sympathies and fight the color bar or attempt to gain acceptance among the white population. What should be the crucial question for African reformers is abandoned as the party attempts to work its way into colonial society. The Communists' failure here is an example of the way history operates: the forces of time and place prevented the Communists from reconciling their beliefs with their possibilities. The same doctrine, carrying for Miss Lessing the same intrinsic worth, might well have succeeded somewhere else, at some other time, under different circumstances.

Miss Lessing maintains a consistent interest in time and place. Both the use of the social class as a significant part of the identity of the individual, and the fact that conflicts are so frequently depicted as conflicts between generations, between the products of one time and another, indicate Miss Lessing's addiction to historical categories. Frequent parenthetical historical references fill all the fiction. An attitude stemming from the 'twenties or from World War I is accurately pinned down and labeled. Martha Quest is characterized in terms of details relevant to her time and place; she categorizes herself, and is categorized by others, as a socialist and an atheist, labels that stick with her throughout the novels. Early in the first novel, *Martha Quest*, Miss Lessing fixes Martha:

> She was adolescent, and therefore bound to be unhappy; British, and therefore uneasy and defensive; in the fourth decade of the twentieth century, and therefore inescapably beset with problems of race and class; female, and obliged to repudiate the shackled women of the past.   [P. 20.]

Similarly, early in *Retreat to Innocence*, Julia is fixed as a young London girl of 1955 in terms of black sweaters, frequent attendance at espresso coffee bars, and constant objection to the "phony." Minor characters are also defined by time and place, often in an introductory biography that leaves little for the character to do or say once he appears on the scene. Willi, the haunted revolutionary in *Retreat to Innocence*, is fully explained as soon as he momentarily appears. The case history of Miss Privet's career as a prostitute is documented in *In Pursuit of the English* to an extent hardly merited by a minor character. This extensive detailing of character detracts from Miss Lessing's effectiveness in two ways: it sometimes breaks the fiction into a series of journalistic essays or case histories, and it limits the author to the view that all people are almost completely conditioned by time and place, by historical environment.

The historically conditioned character sometimes suggests the cause of an aesthetic shortcoming in Miss Lessing's novels. (The short stories, on the other hand, emphasizing a single relationship, a single conditioning, or the impact of a particular commitment, are often much more effective.) For example, *The Grass Is Singing*, the novel concerning Mary Turner's destruction, begins and ends with an account of Tony Marston, a young Englishman with the usual progressive ideas who has just come to Africa and finds his first job on the Turner farm. Tony serves a valid function in the plot, for he stumbles on a scene in which the Negro is dressing a strangely transfixed and hypnotized Mary. Mary cannot bear the white discovery of her fascination with the Negro, and this incident precipitates her destruction. Yet Tony himself reacts exactly as a young Englishman with vaguely progressive ideas, the product of his place and generation, might be expected to react: he falls right in with all the usual white clichés, sanctioned by the wisdom of experience, about maintaining the color bar. What might have been a device to extend the point of view, to provide additional insight toward the events of the novel, turns instead, because of the interest in fixing Tony, into the dullness of another case history. Historical accuracy, in this novel, cuts off a possible dimension of human perception.

Frequently, Miss Lessing's journalistic essays do not deal with specific characters but rather furnish sociological descriptions of what it was like to be in a specific place at a specific time. The Martha Quest series is full of such descriptions: the African legal office in the 'thirties; the change in the colonials' club at the beginning of World War II; the coming of British airmen to African bases, and the difference this creates in the town; the Communists' trying to sell their paper in the native quarter; the predictable seediness and irrelevance of the Left Book Club's meeting. A few of the short stories are entirely dependent upon this kind of sociological description. "The Eye of God in Paradise" (a story in *The Habit of Loving*) is an illustration, seen from the point of view of a pair of British doctors, of the various forms and echoes of Nazism still evident in Germany in 1951. Some of the sociological essays in *Going Home*, like the one defending the character of the Afrikander or the one pointing out that the Union of South Africa is no more discriminatory and at least more honest than is the British government of Southern Rhodesia, are both intelligent and unconventional. But essays are one thing and fiction is another. Too often Miss Lessing's fiction is dissolved in a long sociological or journalistic insertion, like the accounts of communistic tactics and wrangles in *A Ripple from the Storm* or the long, dull, clinical study of discovering that one is pregnant which takes up about seventy pages of *A Proper Marriage*. Her politics are one-sided, her characters are limited in conception, and her world revolves in a simple pattern.

The same flaw is evident in the first novel of another young author. Margot Heinemann, in *The Adventurers* (1960), carefully documents a good deal of history concerning the Welsh miners after World War II. Much of the sociological description carries enormous interest, but the character become simply sociological representations: the young miner's son who rises as a journalist and betrays his old tribal loyalties; the young miner, for whom force of character takes the place of education, who remains loyal to his fellows; the upper-class sympathizers who stick to a Communist ideal that is no longer relevant to conditions among the working class. All these characters are completely determined by the forces that have molded them, completely predictable once the background has been established. Then, the course set, the novel simply reports, with journalistic accuracy, what the conference or the strike or the industrial campaign was like. Miss Heinemann's novel, like some of Miss Lessing's, is not only rooted in the social scene but becomes, completely and merely, the reflection of that scene.

Doris Lessing's intense feeling of political and social responsibility is carefully worked into specific historical situations. But the positive convictions can become heavy-handed, and the specific situations journalistic, while the strict allegiance to time and place can limit the range of perception about human beings. Miss Lessing's kind of intensity is simultaneously her greatest distinction and her principal defect. She produces an enormously lucid sociological journalism, honest and committed, but in much of her work she lacks a multiple awareness, a sense of comedy, a perception that parts of human experience cannot be categorized or precisely located, a human and intellectual depth. Intense commitment can cut off a whole dimension of human experience.

PAUL SCHLUETER

The Golden Notebook

Mrs. Lessing's protagonists, as intelligent, sensitive women in the midst of racial and political turmoil, necessarily find two areas, the racial and political, occupying much of their thought and activity, and as a corollary to this preoccupation, they become increasingly aware of their status in an essentially masculine world. While Martha Quest is not "emancipated" in the trite and stereotyped sense (i.e., so concerned with sexual equality that it becomes a morbid, dehumanizing obsession blocking out all other considerations), she does manifest such a degree of personal integrity that she cannot look passively on injustice and prejudice, just as her acuteness of perspective gives her a far more coherent method of evaluating the conflict between her own generation and that of her parents than is true of most adolescents and young adults. But Martha Quest, in some ways, seems an apprenticeship-effort for the creation of Anna Freeman Wulf, Mrs. Lessing's protagonist in *The Golden Notebook* and by far one of the most consciously self-critical and analytical women in modern fiction.

Unlike Martha, though, Anna senses the incoherence in her life to such a degree that she attempts to compartmentalize it, thus giving the reader individual glimpses of several distinct and unique sides to Anna's psyche. Anna's method in detailing her own gradual mental and psychological disintegration takes the form of four separate notebooks in which she

From *The Novels of Doris Lessing.* © 1973 by Southern Illinois University Press.

systematically recounts the events and thoughts in four different time spans
or "moods" of her life: a black notebook (for the events in "black" Africa), a
red notebook (for her time as a Communist), a yellow notebook (a
fictionalized effort to see herself in perspective), and a blue notebook
(primarily a factual diary-account of her life). These are in turn succeeded
and superseded by another notebook, the golden one of the novel's title.

Thus while Anna, like her predecessors in Mrs. Lessing's fiction, finds
racial and political concerns forcing a personal commitment, each is
displaced by a successive commitment; only when the commitment that
seems also to be Mrs. Lessing's is recognized and adopted—the commitment
to individual artistic expression, such as through writing—does Anna achieve
emotional and personal equilibrium. Thereafter she does not lose her
concern for idealistic theory and practice, but she rechannels these drives
into personally satisfying public forms; no longer, for instance, does she work
surreptitiously and frustratingly for communism, but instead turns to more
publicly acceptable political expression, to the British Labour party. And by
turning from a private to a public use of language, she eliminates the
incoherence in her personal emotional life.

Mrs. Lessing had suggested some of the same character types and
emphases found in *The Golden Notebook* in a play produced at the Royal Court
Theatre in 1958, *Each His Own Wilderness.* A brief examination of this play, I
believe, can help lead to a greater understanding of the later novel. Two
middle-aged women named Myra and Milly, both evidently divorced or
widowed, work with high dedication in their particular social and political
realms, but both experience difficulty in achieving harmonious relationships
with their respective sons, who are alike in reflecting a malaise about life and
an indifference toward the issues that concern their mothers so deeply. Not
only is a conflict of generations present, but also a gulf that is never
satisfactorily breached: the mothers, as fairly typical women of the 1950s,
want their children to make up their own minds about life, while the sons
long for a serene, settled way of life. Tony, Myra's son, for example, says to
her,

> I've spent a good part of what are known as my formative years
> listening to the conversation of the mature. You set my teeth on
> edge. You're corrupt, you're sloppy and corrupt. I'm waiting for
> the moment when you put your foot down about something and
> say you've had enough. But you never do. All you do is watch
> things—with interest.[1]

Another statement, the source of the play's title, concerns the generation of Tony's mother and the special kind of world it has created for his generation:

> Do you know what you've created, you and your lot? What a vision it is! A house for every family.... A house full of clean, well-fed people, and not one of them ever understands one word anyone else says. Everybody a kind of wilderness surrounded by barbed wire shouting across the defences into the other wilderness and never getting an answer back. That's socialism. I suppose it's progress. Why not.... To every man his front door and his front door key. To each his own wilderness.[2]

Much of the play concerns Tony's gradual estrangement from his mother, as he first discovers her sacrifice in aiding his education and Myra's ultimately leaving the house to her son, discouraged as she is at her sense of having wasted her life. For she has been promiscuous, she has, really, little to show (both in life and in her son) for her efforts, and she is far more dedicated as a human being than her son. Perhaps the trouble, in a word, is that she believes too much and he believes nothing.

In 1962, another play, *Play with a Tiger* (also written in 1958), was produced in the Comedy Theatre in London, and is somewhat more explicit in its relationship to *The Golden Notebook*. This play, whose title gives the novel one of its central symbolic motifs,[3] again presents two people in an impassioned dialogue, an intellectual heroine and her younger American lover. The two are involved in the same kind of love-hate relationship Anna and Saul Green, the younger American writer with whom she for a time lives, have in *The Golden Notebook*; both are attracted to the other, but both realize the necessity of overcoming the other or of being overcome. While dramatically this play is no more satisfying than the other discussed,[4] it does show an organic and thematic similarity to the novel itself, and serves as a kind of trying-out of some of the character relationships and incidents of the novel.

Even without relying too heavily upon these earlier plays as possible sources for *The Golden Notebook*, one can easily see affinities between Mrs. Lessing's own life and the characters and emphases of the novel. Instead, one complaint Mrs. Lessing has continually voiced since the novel's publication has been the tendency of reviewers and critics to confuse the fictional protagonist and the author herself. In an interview in the *Queen*, a British magazine, Mrs. Lessing said she was "appalled" at the "frivolity" and "amateurishness" of the reviews, since they were mostly interested in seeing an alleged Marxist or sexual orientation for the novel as a whole, or, worse, in seeing the book on the "gossip-column" level,[5] with the author perfectly equated with the heroine. Indeed, as Mrs. Lessing said in another interview, some critics tried to turn the book into "The Confessions of Doris Lessing."[6] And in a letter, Mrs. Lessing goes even further by saying that

> this autobiographical approach by critics is a very bad and indeed a very frivolous one.... Like every other writer, my novels are a mixture of straight (as far as anything can be) autobiography, and creation.... A young lady came to interview me from the Observor [sic] recently, and I said: Well at least they can't say *Landlocked* is autobiographical. Her reply was: But of course they say it is. "Why?" I ask. Because it is so convincing, she replies.
>
> I thought it was the job of a writer to make things convincing.
>
> This annoys me not because it is personally annoying, but because it means people don't read what I've written in the right way. The right way to read a novel is as if its [sic] a thing by itself, with its own laws, with due attention to its shape, not with reference back to possible autobiographical incidents.[7]

One might go even further to say that *The Golden Notebook*, a book about a woman with a writer's block, could scarcely be the story of Mrs. Lessing herself, since she obviously has no writer's block. Hence one must consider the book not so much as an autobiographical or confessional novel, but more as a highly detailed examination of the forces which have gone into the complicated life of a real person who has some parallel characteristics with her fictional protagonist.

Mrs. Lessing has been keenly aware of the emphasis in twentieth-century literature on the artist's sensibility, and has singled out Thomas Mann as having devoted his entire life to an examination of this theme. But Mrs. Lessing says she has a "kind of hostility to the idea that an artist's sensibility should represent everyone," and that she wonders what, if anything, one could say about the theme after Mann's exhaustive examination. The "logical next step," she says, is that of a writer who cannot write. But this writer's block should result from "good intellectual reasons" such as political involvement; thus a development of such reasons, individually good as they are, would show how destructive they become when they lead to artistic inertia. In Anna Freeman Wulf, the protagonist of *The Golden Notebook*, Mrs. Lessing says, such a destructive emphasis causes the excessive "aggression, madness, cruelty, mixed up with love, kindness, and everything" that we find in the novel. "Not until the cruelty and aggression come out and are acknowledged," Mrs. Lessing adds, can Anna "start creating again." The writer's block itself, Mrs. Lessing says, is a way of saying something "about a certain way of looking at the world," a way which while not wholly Marxist is based in part on this political philosophy and such kinds of education as those assuming that "everything is of the best, justice will prevail, that human beings are equal, that if we try hard enough, society is going to become perfect, that people are fundamentally good." Thus *The Golden Notebook* is a novel about "certain political and sexual attitudes, that have force now; it is an attempt to explain them, to objectivise them, to set them in relation with each other. So in a way it is a social novel."[8]

More integrally important than the immediate stimulus for this novel, though, is Mrs. Lessing's deep concern over form. She has said that its "meaning is in the shape,"[9] and that the particular shape was chosen because she "wanted to write a short formal novel which would enclose the rest in order to suggest what I think a great many writers feel about the formal novel; namely, that it's not doing its job any more. So I thought that the only way to do this would be to write the short formal novel and put in the experience it came out of, showing how ridiculous the formal novel is when it can't say a damned thing.... So I put in the short formal novel and *all this*."[10] Indeed, so insistent was Mrs. Lessing in setting this short novel (i.e., the passages labeled "Free Women" taken collectively) apart from the rest of the book that it is even set in a different typeface from the rest of the novel—"in a rather old-fashioned print, with rather flowery chapter headings, to suggest that this kind of novel is old-fashioned."[11] Shape is, moreover, an integral part of the rest of the novel, since Mrs. Lessing says she "split up the rest into four parts to express a split person. I felt that if the artist's sensibility is to be equated with the sensibility of the educated person, then it is logical to use different styles to express different kinds of people.... Also this particular form enabled me to say things about time, about memory—which interests me very much; what we choose to remember—about the human personality because a personality is very much what is remembered.... If I had used a conventional style, the old-fashioned novel ... I would not have been able to do this kind of playing with time, memory and the balancing of people."[12] And elsewhere she has said that *The Golden Notebook* was a "very highly structured book, carefully planned. The point of that book was the relation of its parts to each other."[13] Finally, Mrs. Lessing, for the original British edition of *The Golden Notebook*, made this statement (quoted from the book jacket):

About five years ago I found myself thinking about the novel most writers now are tempted to write at some time or another—about the problems of a writer, about the artistic sensibility. I saw no point in writing this again: it has been done too often; it has been one of the major themes of the novel in our time. Yet, having decided not to write it, I continued to think about it, and about the reasons why artists have to combat various kinds of narcissism. I found that if it were to be written at all, the subject should be, not a practising artist, but an artist with some kind of a block which prevented him or her from creating. In describing the reasons for the block, I would also be making the criticism I wanted to make about our society. I would be describing a disgust and self-division which afflicts people now, and not only artists.

Simultaneously I was working out another book, a book of literary criticism, which I would write not as a critic, but as practising writer, using various literary styles, in such a way that the shape of the book would provide the criticism. Since I hold that criticism of literature is a criticism and judgement of life, this book would say what I wanted to say about life; it would make, implicitly, a statement about what Marxists call alienation.

Thinking about these two books, I understood suddenly they were not two books but one; they were fusing together in my mind. I understood that the shape of this book should be enclosed and claustrophobic—so narcissistic that the subject matter must break through the form.

This novel, then, is an attempt to break a form; to break certain forms of consciousness and go beyond them.

Quoting Mrs. Lessing's statements of intention regarding *The Golden Notebook* at such length, then, ought to indicate the degree to which her accomplishment in the novel is deliberate and self-consciously one in which both form and content are necessarily closely linked—perhaps more so than in most novels of our or any time—and that the novel is considerably more than mere self-confessional.

A brief statement about the exact ordering of the materials in *The Golden Notebook* would not, perhaps, be wholly out of place here. All four of the major notebooks are written in the first person, and cover roughly the years from 1950 to 1957, with the fifth notebook (the golden one) describing only events during 1957, the year of its composition, and with Anna's one successful novel, *Frontiers of War*, having been published during or shortly after World War II. There are also five sections labeled "Free Women," written in the third person and, as we discover toward the end of the entire novel, purportedly written by Anna. These "Free Women" passages also describe events during the last year covered by the notebooks, 1957. The book opens with the first of the "Free Women" sections, followed by the four notebooks, in succession, black, red, yellow, and blue, with this pattern repeated four times and with the individual notebook sections varying from one page to some eighty pages in length. After the fourth repeating of this pattern comes the section based on Anna's last, the golden, notebook, and with the entire novel then concluded with a final "Free Women" episode.

But since the "Free Women" passages (comprising the "short formal novel" mentioned earlier) are an attempt at describing the thoughts and activities of an alter ego of Anna's, there are of necessity a number of inconsistencies in detail. Most obvious of these is the choice of endings: if we are to believe the final notebook entry, Anna, after she is given the first sentence of a novel by her young American lover, starts to write the first of the "Free Women" passages, while the ending of the final "Free Women" section presents Ella, Anna's alter ego, planning to "join the Labour Party and teach a night-class twice a week for delinquent kids."[14] Furthermore, Tommy, Anna's son, is described in the opening "Free Women" section as being twenty years old in 1957 (p. 13) and seventeen years old in a notebook purporting to describe events in 1950 (p. 197); he later gets married, according to the notebooks (p. 468), or travels to Sicily with his father's wife (p. 554). While attempts at resolving such inconsistencies must ultimately be impossible, they seem to be part of the attempt on Anna's part to reflect and emphasize certain parts of life, not to mirror them perfectly in all respects. Thus one can read the "Free Women" sections as a kind of coda or variation on the themes emphasized in the notebooks, with Anna's controlled attempts at writing being the means by which she (but not necessarily her fictional alter ego) can achieve both a meaningful relationship with other people and an ordered personal identity. As a whole, then, these "Free Women" passages are a fictionalized effort by Anna to see herself in perspective, not a point-by-point parallel to her own life, and as such, their organic relationship to the story of Anna Wulf herself becomes clearer.

As has already been suggested, there is a pervasive awareness of the complex and constantly simmering racial struggle in central colonial Africa running throughout most of the writing of Doris Lessing. Even in those works, like *The Golden Notebook*, which are not directly set in Africa, there is a constant presence of Africa noticeable in many subtle but inescapable references and emphases. As was quoted earlier, Doris Lessing has said that she was brought up in Central Africa, which means that I was a member of the white minority, pitted against a black majority that was abominably treated and still is. I was the daughter of a white farmer who, although he was a very poor man in terms of what he was brought up to expect, could always get loans from the Land Bank which kept him. (I won't say that my father liked what was going on; he didn't.) But he employed anywhere from fifty to one hundred working blacks. An adult black earned twelve shillings a month, rather less than two dollars, and his food was rationed to corn meal and beans and peanuts and a pound of meat per week. It was all grossly unfair, and it's only a part of a larger picture of inequity.[15]

So explicit has Mrs. Lessing been in citing this injustice in detail, particularly (but not exclusively) in those works specifically concerned with Africa, that after a return trip in 1956 to Southern Rhodesia and South Africa, she found herself in the company of many of her friends in "being prohibited," as she has called it, that is, in being permanently exiled from the country in which she was raised. Thus she was not among those who were surprised at the dissolution of the Central African Federation in 1963, following a span of only a decade in which "the politics of partnership" was discarded as unworkable.[16]

Anna's own constant thinking about the African situation most often takes the form of entries in the black notebook, in which she describes memories and her own innermost thoughts and convictions about the black-white struggle. Toward the end of the black notebook entries, she describes a dream she has had, a recurring dream, about the individuals she had previously known in Africa. This particular entry contains a series of news items, every one of which refers to "violence, death, rioting, hatred, in some part of Africa" (p. 449). Anna dreams that a television film is to be made about the people she had known at the Mashopi Hotel in the colony. Although the director tells Anna in the dream that the script would be "exactly what [she] would have written [herself]," she soon discovers that his choice of shots and timing changes the "story" as she recalls it, that she no longer recognizes the lines spoken or even the relationships described, and that the technicians and cameramen, all black, alter the cameras into machine guns. The director defends his version of the incident because "it doesn't matter what we film, provided we film something" (p. 450). In short, Anna no longer remembers the "real" past, and cannot say exactly why the version being filmed is "wrong."

Anna also recalls in her notebook entries several Africans she has met and has talked with in an earlier day. Of these, Tom Mathlong and Charlie Themba are most prominent. Tom Mathlong especially becomes a kind of conscience for Anna, and even when not present except in her thoughts, his influence is pervasive and strong. When, for example, she and her friends, Marion and Tommy, express an interest in African nationalism, she tells them, first, that they must "stop this pretence of caring about African nationalism," and that they "both know quite well it's nonsense" (p. 436). She then immediately ponders,

> Well, what would Tom Mathlong say? She imagined herself sitting across the table in a cafe with Tom Mathlong telling him about Marion and Tommy. He would listen and say: "Anna, you tell me why these two people have chosen to work for African liberation? And why should I care about their motives?" But then he would laugh. Yes. Anna could hear his laugh, deep, full, shaken out of his stomach. Yes. He would put his hands on his knees and laugh, then shake his head and say: "My dear Anna, I wish we had your problems." [P. 436]

Indeed, Mathlong is a kind of saint, for he combines not only the idealism of the Communist party members mentioned above, but also an awareness of the ultimate rightness of his cause. He sees, in a word, not only the heights to which man's sense of ethicality can raise him, but also that sense of ethicality in perspective, in relation to those more sordid areas of life such as the inexorably slow progress visible in racial terms at any one moment. And although Anna, after pondering the meaning of the word, again says that Tom is a saint—"an ascetic, but not a neurotic one" (p. 440)—she recognizes, from his stoical acceptance of the inevitability of years in prison because of his nationalistic efforts, the degree to which he is perhaps too ideal for an imperfect world.

By contrast with Tom Mathlong, Charlie Themba, the other native discussed in detail in *The Golden Notebook*, demonstrates an opposite kind of character, one more approximating the opportunistic superiority of the whites in colonial Africa. No racial exclusiveness for him; he longs instead for political power as a means of personal aggrandizement and promotion. He had shown a similar high-mindedness to that of Mathlong's but ultimately becomes distrusted by his fellow natives. Anna describes Themba as a trade union leader,[17] "violent and passionate and quarrelsome and loyal" (p. 441), and recently "cracked up" because of the pressure of politics—"full of intrigue and jealousness and spite." Themba, evidently paranoid and even psychotic, believes that Mathlong and others are intriguing against him, so he begins writing bitter, fantastic letters to people like Anna who know him. These hysterical and incoherent communications show the degree to which a right-minded person, as a result of psychological and social pressures, loses not only his idealism but also his psychic balance.

But if Tom Mathlong represents the consistently ethical and trustworthy extreme, with Charlie Themba moving from that extreme toward one of opportunism and mental chaos, there is yet another type of native to be mentioned, the opposite extreme from Tom Mathlong. While this type is not singled out and named as an individual, he is described in terms generically applicable to purely opportunistic politicians the world around: "he's bombastic and rabble-rousing and he drinks and he whores around. He'll probably be the first Prime Minister—he has all the qualities— the common touch, you know" (p. 440).

These complicated and involved examples of the racial situation in Rhodesia show more than anything else the kind of commitment, admittedly a frustrating, futile one, that enlightened individuals like Anna Wulf dedicate themselves to during their African years. But just as the various natives described range from purely idealistic to purely opportunistic, so the whites too react in varying ways to the racial situation. Anna and others admit the wrongness of *apartheid* (even though this term is not used in the novel), but their ineffectual attempts at remedying the situation cause some to be so disillusioned that they give up, while others become cynically a part of the dominant power structure. As with both Mrs. Lessing herself and her earlier fictional creation, Martha Quest, Anna finds the frustrations and pressures too great to endure without signs of victory, so another commitment is made: to political action, particularly to Communist party activity.

In common with many other British and American intellectuals in the 1930s and early 1940s, Doris Lessing became a Communist as a result of sincere optimistic desires to see the world improved and to have the injustices of a supposedly inhuman competitive system of values eliminated. To a great extent, her decision to become a Communist appears now as naïve as many other youthful enthusiasms or commitments. She has said, for instance,

> when I became a communist, emotionally if not organizationally,
> in 1942, my picture of socialism as developed in the Soviet Union
> was, to say the least, inaccurate. But after fifteen years of
> uncomfortable adjustment to reality I still find myself in the
> possession of an optimism about the future obviously considered

jejune by anyone under the age of thirty.... Perhaps it is that the result of having been a communist is to be a humanist.[18]

For the writer, uniquely equipped to communicate the political tensions of an era, has as his "point of rest" his

> recognition of man, the responsive individual, voluntarily submitting his will to the collective, but never finally; and insisting on making his own personal and private judgements before every act of submission.[19]

Thus the same tension between the individual sense of responsibility and the collective emphasis on conformist thinking which has led so many idealists out of the party they considered a panacea for the world's economic and social ills is responsible for Mrs. Lessing's own disenchantment after some years' allegiance to the Communist party.

This allegiance, though, did not suddenly cease as if a radical experience such as a conversion had occurred. She has said that she

> decided to leave the party a good time before I finally left it. I didn't leave it when I decided to, because there was a general exodus, much publicized, from the British Party then, and the journalists were waiting for yet another renegade to publish his, her complaints against the C.P. [Communist Party]. To quote another old communist: "I find it nauseating when people who have been in the Party ten, twenty years, stagger out shouting and screaming as if they've been raped against their will." I left it because the gap between my own attitudes and those of the party widened all the time. There was no particular event or moment. The 20th Congress [in February, 1956, at which Khrushchev denounced Stalin] shocked me, not because of the "revelations" but because I thought the "revelations" were long overdue, pitifully and feebly put forth, and no one really tried to explain or understand what had happened.[20]

It is in Anna Wulf that Mrs. Lessing's subtle shifting of loyalty to communism is best illustrated, not only because of the later date of composition of *The Golden Notebook*, but also because of the fuller character portrayal we have of Anna than of earlier characters. Indeed, since *The Golden Notebook* is concerned most directly with the later stages in the political metamorphosis

of Anna Wulf, we are given far more to support a person's leaving the party
than his joining it. Anna once reflects that intelligent Communists believe
the party "has been saddled with a group of dead bureaucrats who run it, and
that the real work gets done in spite of the centre" (p. 137). Hence she and
most other Communists mentioned in the book suffer a profound
disillusionment, perhaps best illustrated by the bitter comment by Maryrose,
a young Communist Anna had known in Africa: "Only a few months ago we
believed that the world was going to change and everything was going to be
beautiful and now we know it won't" (p. 117). And Anna herself, in one of
her recurring dreams, tells about one particularly apocalyptic vision she has
in which she foresees an end to the Communist system, at the very least for
herself personally (pp. 256–57).

An end to communism, though, will result less from wishful dreaming
than from the weight of the party's own weaknesses—none of which, really,
have anything to do with party doctrine per se so much as the increasing
bureaucratization and narrowness of thinking Anna sees around her. Thus
the Communists portrayed in *The Golden Notebook* are consistently either
those like Anna and Maryrose, disillusioned and despondent, or like Willi
Rodde, who becomes part of the East German bureaucracy after the war;
there seems to be no middle ground, such as impassioned dedication to the
Communist cause, as can be found on occasion in Mrs. Lessing's earlier
books.

Anna in particular notices with increasing distaste and disgust the
official party falsification of truth whenever it seems expedient. Because of
her work for John Butte, a Communist publisher, she is in a unique position
to see at firsthand the exact ways in which such falsification takes place;
indeed, it is the world of publishing that first interests her in joining the
Communist party. But Anna soon finds out that the "truth" is not a very
highly prized commodity in Communist publishing. She, as an editor, is
given a novel by a faithful party member to consider for publication, which
she evaluates as follows:

> This novel touches reality at no point at all. (Jack described it as
> "communist cloud-cuckoo spit.") It is, however, a very accurate
> recreation of the self-deceptive myths of the Communist Party at
> this particular time; and I have read it in about fifty shapes or
> guises during the last year. I say: "you know quite well this is a
> very bad book." ... He [Butte] now remarks: "It's no masterpiece
> ... but it's a good book, I think." ... I will challenge him, and he
> will argue. The end will be the same, because the decision has

already been taken. The book will be published. People in the Party with any discrimination will be even more ashamed because of the steadily debasing values of the Party; the *Daily Worker* will praise it. [P. 296]

After Butte, exasperated, says, "Publish and be damned!", Anna says,

> What you've said sums up everything that is wrong with the Party. It's a crystallization of the intellectual rottenness of the Party that the cry of nineteenth-century humanism, courage against odds, truth against lies, should be used now to defend the publication of a lousy lying book by a communist firm which will risk nothing at all by publishing it, not even a reputation for integrity. [P. 297]

But Anna, herself sufficiently a person with integrity to admit the necessity of accepting her changing political views, can only protest; she cannot change the situation. For a time, though, she is temporarily recharged with enthusiasm and hope for the party, following the death of Stalin on March 5, 1953. Anna for a time believes that there is again a chance for a meaningful allegiance to communism. But the resurgence of hope does not last long; after she has been out of the party for over a year, she is invited back for a meeting at which the bureaucracy is supposedly to be removed and the party in Britain revitalized, "without the deadly loyalty to Moscow and the obligation to tell lies" (p. 382). But less than a year later, at another meeting, she realizes that she has accomplished nothing in all the "frenzied political activity" in which she has been involved. In short, Anna's renewed sense of purpose in the Communist party is short-lived, for she discovers that the situation she had sensed earlier, and which led her to her leaving the party, has not really changed at all.

Although Anna indicates at various times her reasons for leaving the party—its jargon, its dishonesty, its pettiness, and so on—she does specify in one passage in more detail her exact reasons for both becoming a Communist and for leaving the party. Jack, another party member, comments that society today is complex and technical that no one person can effectively understand it all. Anna answers him:

> "Alienation. Being split. It's the moral side, so to speak, of the communist message. And suddenly you shrug your shoulders and say because the mechanical basis of our lives is getting

complicated, we must be content to not even try to understand things as a whole?" And now I see his face has put on a stubborn closed look that reminds me of John Butte's: and he looks angry. He says: "Not being split, it's not a question of imaginatively understanding everything that goes on. Or trying to. It means doing one's work as well as possible, and being a good person." I say: "That's treachery." "To what?" "To humanism." He thinks and says: "The idea of humanism will change like everything else." I say: "Then it will become something else. But humanism stands for the whole person, the whole individual, striving to become as conscious and responsible as possible about everything in the universe. But now you sit there, quite calmly, and as a humanist you say that due to the complexity of scientific achievement the human being must never expect to be whole, he must always be fragmented." [Pp. 307–8]

Her sense of this fragmentation is such as to demand of her a more coherent, a more unifying life than has been possible through dedication to communism. Although party membership and activity can be a meaningful commitment, Anna discovers that it is too limited a commitment, too narrow in its rewards and too dishonest in its demands upon the individual, to remain for long the kind of commitment she needs for her own life. Again, she must move on to a further level of commitment, that of an open and free acknowledgement of her sexual nature, before she is able to move to what I believe is her ultimate and most lasting commitment, to verbal communication through writing for a public audience.

As Anna Wulf continues in her process of attempting to bring meaning into the chaos of her life, we see how she gradually but perceptibly moves from a purely objective area of concern (the racial), to an area with both objective theory and personal application (the political), and now to the more wholly subjective. That is, as an enlightened, liberal white, Anna is scarcely as involved in the fight for racial justice as, say, Tom Mathlong; as a sensitive, intelligent, and idealistic young woman, she cannot assimilate the inconsistencies and pettiness of communism; and now, we see another area of commitment in Anna's life, that collectively concerned with her views on sex and marriage, and, concurrently, her need of psychoanalytic counselling. This considerably more subjective commitment requires of Anna a correspondingly greater degree of insight into her own psyche and personality, as well as a frank admission of the exact kind of woman she is.

As we first meet Anna and see her in her milieu, we notice the extent to which she and her friend, Molly, seem conventionally "emancipated," particularly in the areas of sexual morality and their ability to move freely through what is always an explicitly masculine world. The term they use to refer to themselves, "free women," is itself the overall title for the short novel Anna writes about her alter ego, and thus it is no surprise that the concept of freedom occurs frequently in *The Golden Notebook*. But the concept itself changes as Anna step-by-step becomes more fully aware of her identity. Molly's statement early in the novel, "we're a completely new type of woman" (p. 10), is fairly typical of the self-conscious "emancipation" the two women adopt. Anna asks a bit later, "if we lead what is known as free lives, that is, lives like men, why shouldn't we use the same language?" Molly replies, "Because we aren't the same. That is the point." Anna's retort to this posits the essential contrast between the sexes evident throughout the book: "Men. Women. Bound. Free. Good. Bad. Yes. No. Capitalism. Socialism. Sex. Love" (p. 43). Despite this, Anna senses that women's "loyalties are always to men, and not to women" (p. 46); she painfully realizes she is approaching middle age, and recalls that when she was younger, twenty-three or so, she suffered "from a terror of being trapped and tamed by domesticity" (p. 114–15). Now, though, she realizes the extent to which she is lonely. Molly reminds her in these terms of her loneliness:

> You choose to be alone rather than to get married for the sake of not being lonely.... You're afraid of writing what you think about life, because you might find yourself in an exposed position, you might expose yourself, you might be alone. [P. 39]

And later, when Anna canvasses for the Communist party, she notices the many lonely women who long for an audience for their personal problems, "going mad quietly by themselves, in spite of husband and children or rather because of them" (p. 146). Much later, when Anna leaves her lover (as described in the final "Free Women" section), she recognizes the price she must pay for being as free and independent and intelligent as she is: "that will be my epitaph. Here lies Anna Wulf, who was always too intelligent. She let them go" (P. 562). For the toughness Anna so proudly claims for herself is seen to be more attitude than actuality, as when she tells Molly about the kind of life the two are living:

> Both of us are dedicated to the proposition that we're tough.... A marriage breaks up, well, we say, our marriage was a failure, too

bad. A man ditches us—too bad we say, it's not important. We bring up kids without men—nothing to it, we say, we can cope. We spend years in the communist party and then we say, well, well, we made a mistake, too bad.... Well don't you think it's at least possible that things can happen to us so bad that we don't ever get over them? ... Why do our lot never admit failure? Never. It might be better for us if we did. And it's not only love and men. Why can't we say something like this—we are people, because of the accident of how we were situated in history, who were so powerfully part ... with the great dream, that now we had to admit that the great dream has faded and the truth is something else—that we'll never be any use. [Pp. 50–51]

Indeed, Anna's American lover's charge that she has been trying to "cage the truth" (p. 563) is itself made near the end of Anna's series of notebooks and counseling sessions, and Anna, after the change is made, admits that "it's no good."

Anna's fictional alter ego, Ella, reflects, quite naturally, the same attitudes as her creator. We are told, for instance, of Ella's awareness that a free woman, having "positively disdained ordinary morality," is not acceptable to the majority of either sex (p. 150). Ella's lover, Paul, tells her that the real revolution of the day is that of women against men (p. 184). Ella herself realizes that her emotions are "fitted for a kind of society that no longer exists," a monogamous society, and that she ought to have been a man (p. 269). Even more self-consciously than Anna, Ella prides herself on her independence, and is repeatedly reminded of this by her lovers. Ella comments to her friend, Julia, that "we've chosen to be free women, and this [i.e., sexual double standards and male indifference] is the price we pay" (p. 392). Julia's reply indicates the desperation both women feel: "Free! What's the use of us being free if they aren't? I swear to God, that every one of them, even the best of them, have the old idea of good women and bad women" (p. 392). The price paid, though, does not only include frustration and doubt, for Ella realizes that by being a "free woman," she has an advantage over wives, simply because she "was so much more exciting than the dull tied women" (p. 388). But, like Anna herself, who ultimately realizes that she is not free (p. 237), Ella must accept responsibility to be either free or happy. Anna wishes she were married, for instance, saying that she doesn't like living the way she does (p. 237), and Ella herself, we are told, "after years of freedom, is over-ready for a serious love" (p. 394).

Parenthetically, it should be mentioned that neither Anna nor Ella, in their self-conscious celebration of being "free women," approximates Mrs.

Lessing's own attitude toward such freedom. She has said that she doesn't see herself as a "free woman" "only because I don't think anyone is 'free.'"[21] She also observed that "to imagine free man ... is to step outside of what we are," for

> There is no one on this earth who is not twisted by fear and insecurity, and the compromises of thinking made inevitable by want and fear.... Slaves can envy the free; slaves can fight to free their children; but slaves suddenly set free are marked by the habits of submission; and slaves imagining freedom see it through the eyes of slaves.[22]

Hence this imagined freedom of Anna's and Ella's, as this chapter suggests, is not so much a total lack of individual responsibility as a series of gradually more intense and personal commitments, culminating, as the next part of this chapter will indicate, in the commitment to writing. Prior to that, though, we must consider the exact ways in which Anna's "emancipation" is expressed, through sexual attitudes and behavior, and through an obsessive self-understanding gained through psychoanalysis.

Throughout her life as recounted in the notebooks, and in her past youth as occasionally recalled in moments of stress or reminiscence, Anna thinks of herself in sexual terms, ranging from the trancelike "sexual obsession" felt at age fifteen (and which she would not go through again for an immense amount of money; pp. 88–89), to her subsequent simultaneous fear of and appeal for sexual experience, when she is first aware of her "emancipated" state (pp. 114–15), to the steps leading up to her defloration: petting (p. 118) and the initial act of sexual intercourse (referred to on p. 66). In each of the several "lives" she experiences, she has lovers who more or less correspond in their meaning for her with the gradually changing sense of commitment she acknowledges. In colonial Africa, for instance, it is Willi (with whom Anna is sexually incompatible; pp. 66–67), a relationship that ends when Willi discovers that Anna has just had intercourse with another man and, full of hatred, forces her into one last act of intercourse (p. 133). Later, involved with Michael, Anna moves into a more self-assured, yet still somewhat guilty, sexual relationship. The relationship itself seems based more on sex than on love (p. 289), but does not last long. Then Anna meets the American Communist, Nelson, who has a "moral fear of sex," and who "could never stay inside a woman for longer than a few seconds" (p. 413). A friend of Molly's from Ceylon, DeSilva, further complicates Anna's wishes for a satisfactory sexual experience, for he, first, picks up a strange girl on the street with whom he wants only sex, no feelings, and, later, sleeps with Anna, who justifies the act on the grounds that "it didn't matter to me" (p. 428). This too ends, for DeSilva wishes to use one of Anna's rooms for sex with another woman, so that Anna could hear the couple in bed (p. 429). Meeting an unnamed friend of Nelson's, Anna thinks, "A normal man at last, thank God" (p. 465), but this relationship ends because of the lack of warmth the man felt and because of his fear of his wife back home. All the men in this promiscuous sequence, quite clearly, are desperate choices for a love-partner for Anna, so it is small wonder that all the affairs end in a futile and sterile way.

But when Anna meets Saul Green, the American writer who aids in Anna's ultimate self-knowledge, she finds an entirely different sexual experience, even though there are the inevitable conflicts and arguments that affect their sexual rapport. Saul comes to Anna's apartment to rent a room, and upon their first meeting, gives Anna a close sexual examination (p. 470). Their mutual attraction is shown in Anna's similar examination of Saul:

> I saw his pose, standing with his back to the window in a way that was like a caricature of that young American we see in the films— sexy he-man, all balls and strenuous erection. He stood lounging, his thumbs hitched through his belt, fingers loose, but pointing as it were to his genitals. [P. 473]

Green subsequently refers to a "friend" (evidently himself) and the friend's sexual problems, and in the process he and Anna discuss the language inevitably used in discussing sex, with Anna accusing Saul of having an unhealthy attitude toward sex and Saul retorting by stating that he doesn't agree with the typically masculine double standard; later the same day, they have their first act of sexual intercourse (pp. 478–80). Anna senses that sex for Saul is a combination of emotions, as it is for her: she sees him as making love out of fear (of being alone, p. 481), out of hatred (a hard, violent sex, p. 491; cf. pp. 500, 524), and out of an indifference toward Anna's feelings (after he has just returned from making love with another woman, p. 486). Anna realizes that Saul's lovemaking is not a sadistic act (p. 494), but that he does appear to be loving someone else while in the act (pp. 497, 515). But sex with Saul is warm and fulfilling, as it has not been with the other men in Anna's life, and, important for Anna's psychological well-being, occurs spontaneously and quickly (p. 539).

Anna's other self, Ella, goes through somewhat the same sequence of lovers and emotions prior to her achieving a fulfilling sexual experience. But since Ella is a fictional creation of Anna's, Anna can put into Ella's consciousness and words many of the secret thoughts and socially embarrassing ideas about sex that Anna does not mention. After her first act of intercourse with a lover, Paul, Ella critically examines him and finds the experience "beautiful" (p. 168), at least in part because he was the first lover she had had in two years (p. 170). They again make love, gradually more mechanically and less beautifully (p. 174), even though she still senses the "instinctive warmth" (p. 176) radiated by Paul. But Ella cannot accept statements made by Paul that make her unhappy, so she mentally rejects his statement, "Odd isn't it, it really is true that if you love a woman sleeping with another woman means nothing" (p. 177). Later, briefly separated from Paul, she casually spends time with Cy Maitland, an American businessman. She is immediately attracted to Maitland, but for reasons she cannot wholly analyze. His behavior in bed, though, is completely self-centered and unconcerned for her feelings. Rapidly reaching orgasm, he repeatedly exclaims "Boy, Oh boy!" and talks of his wife. His attitude is suggested by his statements to Ella: "That's what I like. No problems with you" (p. 277), and "That's what I like about you—let's go to bed, you say, and that's fine and easy. I like you" (p. 278). After the ending of this unsatisfactory affair, Ella realizes that there is no point in her going to bed with anyone but Paul (p. 283). Later, Ella has intercourse with Jack, the efficient type of man who "has learned love-making out of a book.... [He] gets his pleasure from having got a woman into bed, not from sex itself" (pp. 388–89). Ella's next step, the nadir of her erotic career, comes when feelings of despair hit her:

> Now something new happens. She begins to suffer torments of sexual desire. Ella is frightened because she cannot remember feeling sexual desire, as a thing in itself, without reference to a specific man before, or at least not since her adolescence, and then it was always in relation to a fantasy about a man. Now she cannot sleep, she masturbates, to accompaniment of fantasies of hatred about men. Paul has vanished completely: she has lost the warm strong man of her experience, and can only remember a cynical betrayer. She suffers sex desire in a vacuum. She is acutely humiliated, thinking that this means she is dependent on men for "having sex," for "being serviced," for "being satisfied." She uses this kind of savage phrase to humiliate herself.
>
> Then she realizes she is falling into a lie about herself, and about women, and that she must hold on to this knowledge: that when she was with Paul she felt no sex hungers that were not

> prompted by him; that if he was apart from her for a few days, she
> was dormant until he returned; that her present raging sexual
> hunger was not for sex, but was fed by all the emotional hungers
> of her life. That when she loved a man again, she would return to
> normal: a woman, that is, whose sexuality would ebb and flow in
> response to his. A woman's sexuality is, so to speak, contained by
> a man, if he is a real man; she is, in a sense, put to sleep by him,
> she does not think about sex. [P. 390]

But despite these thoughts, she again succumbs to the temptation of a brief
affair, this time with a Canadian scriptwriter; she again "feels nothing," and
believes that the act was "something he set himself to do and that's all" (p.
391), i.e., an act of accomplishment, not an act of feeling.

In these furtive acts of intercourse, Ella, like Anna, discovers that
although she can give pleasure, she does not receive it herself unless she has
a deep emotional commitment to the man; indeed, Ella reflects, when she is
with the Canadian writer, that she "has not had a real orgasm since Paul left
her" (p. 391), and with Maitland, she realizes that it is even more complicated:

> Ella was thinking: But with Paul, I would have come in that
> time—so what's wrong?—it's not enough to say, I don't love this
> man? She understood suddenly that she would never come with
> this man. She thought: for women like me, integrity isn't chastity,
> it isn't fidelity, it isn't any of the old words. Integrity is the
> orgasm. That is something I haven't any control over. I could
> never have an orgasm with this man, I can give pleasure and that's
> all. But why not? Am I saying that I can never come except with
> a man I love? Because what sort of a desert am I condemning
> myself to if that's true? [Pp. 278–79]

As an indication that the matter of orgasm is extremely central to the sexual
commitment made by both Anna and Ella, Mrs. Lessing provides one
lengthy passage in which both Anna and Ella occur. Anna mentions at first
that the "difficulty of writing about sex, for women, is that sex is best when
not thought about, not analyzed. Women deliberately choose not to think
about technical sex. They get irritable when men talk technically, it's out of
self-preservation: they want to preserve the spontaneous emotion that is
essential for their satisfaction" (p. 185). After reflecting about a broken
marriage, caused, as she was told, by the husband's too-small penis, Anna

begins describing Ella's and her own sexual experiences in as clinical a tone as elsewhere in the book is condemned by Anna:

> When Ella first made love with Paul, during the first few months, what set the seal on the fact she loved him, and made it possible for her to use the word, was that she immediately experienced orgasm. Vaginal orgasm that is. And she could not have experienced it if she had not loved him. It is the orgasm that is created by the man's need for a woman, and his confidence in that need.
>
> As time went on, he began to use mechanical means. (I look at the word mechanical—a man wouldn't use it.) Paul began to rely on manipulating her externally, on giving Ella clitoral orgasms. Very exciting. Yet there was always a part of her that resented it. Because she felt that the fact he wanted to, was an expression of his instinctive desire not to commit himself to her. She felt that without knowing it or being conscious of it ... he was afraid of the emotion. The vaginal orgasm is emotion and nothing else, felt as emotion and expressed in sensations that are indistinguishable from emotion. The vaginal orgasm is a dissolving in a vague, dark generalised sensation like being swirled in a warm whirlpool. There are several different sorts of clitoral orgasms, and they are more powerful (that is a male word) than the vaginal orgasm. There can be a thousand thrills, sensations, etc., but there is only one real female orgasm and that is when a man, from the whole of his need and desire takes a woman and wants all her response. Everything else is a substitute and a fake, and the most in-experienced woman feels this instinctively. Ella had never experienced clitoral orgasm before Paul, and she told him so, and he was delighted.... But when she told him she had never experienced what she insisted on calling "a real orgasm" to anything like the same depth before him, he involuntarily frowned.... As time went on, the emphasis shifted in their love-making from the real orgasm to the clitoral orgasm, and there came a point when Ella realized ... that she was no longer having real orgasms. That was before the end, when Paul left her. In short, she knew emotionally what the truth was when her mind would not admit it. [Pp. 186–87]

Just prior to the end of their time together, Paul leaves the country and Ella is thereafter incapable, as already mentioned, of achieving orgasm with any other lover. As she says later,

> And what about us? Free, we say, yet the truth is that they get erections when they're with a woman they don't give a damn about, but we don't get an orgasm unless we love him. What's free about that? [P. 392]

The "new mood or phase" in which Ella finds herself, she says, "is only the opposite side of being possessed by sex"; she now says she "cannot believe she will ever feel desire again" (p. 393).

The "Free Women" sections of *The Golden Notebook*, finally, suggests even more of Anna's deep concern with the inadequacies of a sexual commitment. Marion, Anna's friend in these sections of the book, tells Anna that she hates going to bed, even though it was once the "happiest time" of her life, when she was still a newlywed. She indicates that Richard, her lover, has to "make himself" have intercourse with her, and asks Anna if she had ever slept with a man when she knew he was forcing himself to do so (p. 238). Both Anna and Marion are concerned with what they call a "real man" (instead of the "little boys and homosexuals and half-homosexuals" in England; p. 245), and Anna goes so far as to wish for such a man for her daughter's sake (p. 334), evidently as a proxy father. Later Anna says to Milton, the American writer, that she has had her fill of "cold and efficient sex," after which he asks, "what's happened to all that warm and committed sex we read about in books?" He also says that "love is too difficult," to which Anna retorts, "And sex too cold" (pp. 560–61). As if to support this statement by Anna, Milton shortly thereafter abruptly asks her, "Want me to screw you?" (p. 564). Anna replies that "there's something about a man with a whacking great erection that it's hard to resist" (p. 565), but they nonetheless separate, for Anna has made the discovery that "committed sex," as Milton calls it, is too insubstantial and dissatisfying a commitment for either her emotional security or her sense of identity.

It is, in fact, her search for her identity that leads Anna to go to and depend upon a lay psychoanalyst[23] named Mrs. Marks, but who Anna usually refers to as "Mother Sugar." Anna recounts various dreams she has had to Mother Sugar, most of which are nightmares—of sheer terror (pp. 408–9), of sexual attack and sex-reversal (pp. 481, 516), of the mad Charlie Themba (pp. 506–7), of a film projectionist showing her own life (pp. 422, 525–29, 541–43), and of her own death (p. 512). The terrible dreams themselves parallel the emotional moods Anna experiences in her waking hours, and one dream in particular (in addition to the apocalyptic dream mentioned earlier of the Communist world) warrants fuller treatment:

> I dreamed I held a kind of casket in my hands, and inside it was something very precious.... There was a small crowd of people ... waiting for me to hand them the casket. I was incredibly happy that at last I could give them this precious object. But when I handed it over, I saw suddenly they were all business men, brokers, something like that. They did not open the box, but started handing me large sums of money. I began to cry. I shouted: "open the box, open the box," but they couldn't hear me, or wouldn't listen. Suddenly I saw they were all characters in some film or play, and that I had written it, and was ashamed of it.... I was a character in my own play. I opened the box and forced them to look. But instead of a beautiful thing, which I thought would be there, there was a mass of fragments, but bits and pieces from everywhere, all over the world—I recognized a lump of red earth, that I knew came from Africa, and then a bit of metal that came off a gun from Indo-China, and then everything was horrible, bits of flesh from people killed in the Korean War and a communist party badge off someone who died in a Soviet prison. This, looking at the mass of ugly fragments, was so painful that I couldn't look, and I shut the box. But the group of businessmen or money-people hadn't noticed. They took the box from me and opened it. I turned away so not to see, but they were delighted. At last I looked and I saw that there was something in the box. It was a small green crocodile with a winking sardonic snout. I thought it was the image of a crocodile, made of jade, or emeralds, then I saw it was alive, for large frozen tears rolled down its cheeks and turned into diamonds. I laughed out loud when I saw how I had cheated the businessmen and I woke up. [Pp. 215–16]

While a precise and full analysis of this dream is clearly impossible, there are several points that must be made. In the first place, this dream of Anna's parallels her own life in several points. Some of the men with whom Anna (and Ella) have had affairs have been businessmen, and these have uniformly been unresponsive to feminine needs; they have, in a word, treated that which is beautiful and prized as a mercenary thing. Anna's own fragmented life is also suggested by this dream. And the crocodile is suggested by the letter from Charlie Themba, referred to above, in which he insanely envisions a crocodile devouring him. Thus this dream contains in capsule, symbolic form the several elements of Anna's own life, focused as they are in terms of a film or scenario with Anna as the author. Evidently death is the outcome of all the various earlier struggles—racial, political, sexual—that Anna has experienced, if, that is, she is able to "cheat" the "businessman." And this is, I believe, suggested by Anna's final dream, described in the last "Free Women" section of the novel:

> One afternoon she went to sleep and dreamed. She knew it was a dream she had often had before, in one form or another. She had two children. One was Janet, plump and glossy with health. The other was Tommy, a small baby, and she was starving him. Her breasts were empty, because Janet had had all the milk in them; and so Tommy was thin and puny, dwindling before her eyes from starvation. He vanished altogether, in a tiny coil of pale bony starving flesh, before she woke, which she did in a fever of anxiety, self-division and guilt. Yet, awake, she could see no reason why she should have dreamed of Tommy being starved by her. And besides, she knew that in other dreams of this cycle, the "starved" figure might be anyone, perhaps someone she passed in the street whose face had haunted her. Yet there was no doubt she felt responsible for this half-glimpsed person, for why otherwise should she dream of having failed him—or her?
>
> After this dream, she went feverishly back to work, cutting out news items, fastening them to the wall. [Pp. 556–57]

This dream appears to suggest that Anna's fragmented self has extended to her two children in the dream, with the "starved" one being any person with whom she comes in contact. Her sense of responsibility is focused on this "starved" person, whoever it might be at the moment, but responsibility, at this point, can only take the cathartic form of the frantic newspaper clipping and pasting discussed in the last section of this chapter; it is, in brief, a preliminary step in Anna's ultimate self-knowledge and acceptance of both herself and the world around her. It is significant, also, to note that there is one child in this dream that is "plump and glossy with health"; the obsessive terror and wasteland effects of most of her other dreams are ameliorated slightly by this image of fertility and plenty.

Mother Sugar's counseling of Anna is thus the specific means by which Anna is gradually able to see herself in perspective and to gain control of her own life. One lengthy exchange between the two women (pp. 402–5) is central to any complete understanding of the forces that effect such a change in Anna, and is especially concerned with Anna's leaving the relative safety of her dreams and the world of "myth" they contain, and going forth on her own. No matter how horrible the dreams, Anna says, "all the pain, and the killing and the violence are safely held in the story and ... can't hurt me" (p. 402). Anna sees that "the individual recognizes one part after another of his earlier life as an aspect of the general human experience" (p. 403), and (further supporting the obvious Jungian emphasis) that

> What I did then, what I felt then, is only the reflection of that great archetypal dream, or epic story, or stage in history, then he is free, because he has separated himself from the experience, or fitted it like a mosaic into a very old pattern, and by the act of setting it into place, is free of the individual pain of it. [P. 403]

After Anna says that she is "living the kind of life women never lived before" (p. 403), Mother Sugar asks,

> In what way are you different? Are you saying there haven't been artist-women before? There haven't been women who were independent? There haven't been women who insisted on sexual freedom? I tell you, there are a great line of women stretching out behind you into the past, and you have to seek them out and find them in yourself and be conscious of them. [P. 404]

After raising several objections, Anna says that she wants "to separate in herself what is old and cyclic, the recurring history, the myth, from what is new, what I feel or think that might be new.... Sometimes I meet people, and it seems to me the fact they are cracked across, they're split, means they are keeping themselves open for something" (pp. 404–5). Mother Sugar's technique, quite clearly, is to ask Anna probing questions which force her to see herself in perspective and to see what she really is in the deepest recesses of her psyche. She does not leave Anna in the fragmented chaotic past, but instead, by the "shock of recognition," forces her to see the present and future as they really are, potentially coherent and ordered and fruitful.

Anna, though, cannot receive this ordered existence vicariously from Mother Sugar; she must work it out for and by herself, and this is done through her obsessive concern with language and with putting on paper the ordered language constituting human discourse. Paralleling her sessions and conversations with Mother Sugar are Anna's frantic efforts to record, in fragmented form, all the experiences of her several disparate "selves," in the notebooks that constitute the bulk of *The Golden Notebook*, and gradually to go beyond the limitations of private communication to express to others, through a novel, her affirmation of ongoing life and structured personal existence.

As Mrs. Lessing says in her personal credo, "The Small Personal Voice," commitment to writing is necessary because of today's confusion of standards and values; because of the compassion, warmth, humanity, and love of people to be found in the truly great novels; because the writer has a responsibility as a human being to choose for evil or to strengthen good; and—most important of all—because the writer's recognition of man as an individual is necessary if the novel as a genre is to regain greatness. To achieve greatness, Mrs. Lessing states that the novelist's "small, personal voice" must re-create "warmth and humanity and love of people,"[24] especially if a "great age of literature" like the nineteenth century is to result. Such a credo does not, Mrs. Lessing believes, necessarily become "propagandizing" for a cause, political or otherwise; nor does the novelist necessarily regress by so committing himself. Rather, the novelist "must feel himself as an instrument of change for good or bad," as an "architect of the soul."[25] Not only can such ideas be said to apply to Mrs. Lessing herself, they also apply quite well to her protagonist in *The Golden Notebook*, Anna Freeman Wulf.

As *The Golden Notebook* opens, Anna Wulf is living as a divorcée in London, supporting herself and her daughter by the residual royalties from a successful novel, *Frontiers of War*, which is in turn based on Anna's earlier life in colonial Africa. As Anna attempts to make sense of her life, she puts down in four notebooks—black, red, yellow, and blue—her memories and feelings. In the black notebook, Anna writes her own account of her time in Central Africa during World War II, and the events leading up to the writing of *Frontiers of War*. Anna's feelings concerning this book are equivocal: she simultaneously depends upon the book's earnings, and knows it to be a failure (pp. 59–60). And later, when the many financial solicitations for her novel by film companies pour in, Anna's feeling of revulsion against the world of communism is made all the more pronounced (p. 243). She ultimately does sell the film rights—three times, in fact—but never with any conviction that the book would be filmed (p. 464); and on one occasion she refuses a studio's offer when the representative arrives (pp. 471–72). And, finally, when Anna does again write (the autobiographical novel called *Free Women*), she conceives of herself as being glad when one of her lovers said he did not like *Frontiers of War* (p. 562).

As already mentioned, Anna's black notebook deals with her life in Africa and the red her life as a Communist. The yellow notebook, by contrast, is Anna's novelistic attempt to see herself in perspective, by means of a thinly disguised fictional alter ego, Ella, whose circumstances and personal life are quite like Anna's. Anna had mentioned earlier, in discussing the Communist party, that the ogre of capitalism—from a Communist viewpoint—could be "supplanted by others, like communist, or woman's magazine" (p. 296). It is no surprise, then, that Ella works for a woman's magazine, nor that she had written part of a novel (p. 149). This fictional work in which Ella appears is entitled *The Shadow of the Third*, a reference, as Anna later explained it, to "the woman altogether better than I was" (p. 545). But this woman does not remain static; she is at first the wife of Paul, Ella's lover; then she becomes "Ella's younger *alter ego* formed from fantasies about Paul's wife," and she finally becomes Ella herself (pp. 384–85). The bulk of the yellow notebook, however, concerns Ella's gradual completion of her novel (it is barely half-finished as the notebook begins; p. 151). The initial idea, she says, came "when she found herself getting dressed to go out to dine with people after she had told herself she did not want to go out" (p. 152). The difficulty she has with the writing, though, is not technical; we are told that "it was as if the story were already written somewhere inside herself" (p. 152). Just as Ella is Anna's alter ego, so Ella conceives of her novel as a reflection of herself, as "carrying on conversations with one's image in the looking-glass" (p. 153). Similarly, just as Anna can "read" Ella's story, so Ella sees her own novel as being already written and with herself reading it (p. 182). Ella's novel is accepted for publication, and Ella sees it as having the same basic quality that Anna had earlier wished the Communist novels would have: honesty (p. 184). For, as Anna herself says later concerning the yellow notebook,

> It frightens me that when I'm writing I seem to have some awful second sight, or something like it, an intuition of some kind; a kind of intelligence is at work that is much too painful to use in ordinary life; one couldn't live at all if one used it for living. [P. 489]

And just as those in Anna's Communist period who had experienced the most loneliness frequently turned to writing for meaning in an otherwise meaningless existence, so Ella too discovers that, for herself as well as for others, writing is a kind of therapy. Ella discovers, for instance, that her father, "alone, withdrawing from his wife into books and the dry, spare dreams of a man who might have been a poet or a mystic" (p. 398), is in fact both; but, significantly, his poems are about "solitude, loss, fortitude, the adventures of isolation" (p. 398).

For Ella, though, this isolation continues beyond the vicarious act of writing out, as a form of therapy, her emotions and sense of isolation. After the conversation with her father, she looks "for the outlines of a story" and finds, "again and again, nothing but patterns of defeat, death, irony." She refuses these; she fails to force "patterns of happiness of simple life"; but she finally finds it possible to "accept the patterns of self-knowledge which mean unhappiness or at least a dryness," and which could be twisted into a victory. That is, by searching in the negative "patterns," she can, she hopes, twist a positive "pattern" into shape. And by conceiving of a man and a woman, "both at the end of their tether," "both cracking up because of a deliberate attempt to transcend their own limits," a "new kind of strength" is found. She waits, we are told, "for the images to form, to take on life" (pp. 399–400). But instead of "life," we are given a series of nineteen synopses of short stories or short novels, all of which are counterparts or summaries of events in the four notebooks or in the "Free Women" sections of *The Golden Notebook*, and all of which are expanded in the final portion of the yellow notebook, in the comments Anna makes (Ella has now been completely dropped from the narrative) about her relationship with Saul Green, an American. Saul is quite like Anna in his sense of defeatedness and spiritual and emotional isolation, and closely approximates Paul, in the earlier portions of the yellow notebook. He is particularly and acutely aware of Anna's attempt to make notations in a series of fragmented diaries (the four notebooks) a substitute for a direct encounter with her problems, with life, with her need to write. He asks, on one occasion, "Instead of making a record of my sins in your diary, why don't you write another novel?" (p. 516). Anna's retort that she has a "writer's block," of course, neither deters nor persuades Green; his comment has sufficiently disturbed Anna that she decides to begin a fifth notebook (the golden one mentioned in the novel's title), which Saul requests of her.

Instead of giving away the new notebook, Anna decides to pack away the other four notebooks and to start the new one—"all of myself in one book" (p. 519). In this golden notebook, the relationship between Anna and Green continues and is finally broken off, but with each providing the first sentence for a novel by the other; Green's finished novel, we are told, "was later published and did rather well" (p. 550). But Anna's initial sentence serves as the beginning of the *Free Women* novel which, like the four major notebooks, is divided into parts; the fifth and last of these parts concludes *The Golden Notebook*, and is her primary method of using writing as a therapeutic measure.

The blue notebook, about which little has been said thus far, is primarily a factual diary-account of Anna's experiences in analysis and of her near-madness and is designed to be a contrast to the "fictional" qualities found in the other notebooks. Anna Wulf is forced in this notebook to face her nearly overwhelming fear of war and "of the real movement of the world towards dark, hardening power" (p. 503), and as a result provides the novel's most searing criticism of society. The diary entries run from 1950 to 1956 without major omissions, but the eighteen months from March 1956 to September 1957 are described without dates and concern Anna's initial experiences with Saul Green.

The "Free Women" portions of *The Golden Notebook* are in some respects more enlightening than anything else in the book, and are certainly to be considered an integral part of the major narrative of the novel, since the events described in these portions (occurring in 1957) are chronologically the closest to the present. Evidently ironically, Mrs. Lessing has said, "The structure of the whole book says that this little novel (i.e., "Free Women") came out of all that mass of experience."[20] But since the point of *The Golden Notebook* is, as Mrs. Lessing has said elsewhere,[27] "the relation of its parts to each other," the "Free Women" sections must be considered as relevant, even if ironically so, as the notebooks themselves.

The first four (of five) parts entitled "Free Women" closely match what is known of Anna from the notebooks, with the difference, as was mentioned above, primarily one of chronology. These portions of the book deal particularly with a friend of Anna's, Molly Jacobs, and her son, Tommy, who is closest to Anna in the sense that he knows her better than anyone else. Molly's former husband (and Tommy's father), Richard, knows Anna well enough to allude to her "complicated ideas about writing" (p. 38), and he also points out that she is afraid of writing what she really thinks about life, since this would make her expose herself emotionally and thus lead to isolation (p. 39). Anna says to Molly that her notebooks are "chaos" (p. 41), but to Tommy Anna admits much more. To his question about her four notebooks ("Why not one notebook?" p. 226), Anna replies, "Perhaps because it would be such a—scramble. Such a mess." And Tommy, aware of the pressures at work in Anna's mind (evident primarily because of similar pressures which lead to his own futile suicide attempt later), asks the question no one can state without self-incrimination: "Why shouldn't it be a mess?" (p. 226). Tommy also examines Anna's four notebooks, an act no one but Saul Green otherwise is described as doing. Anna explains her notebook habit by saying that she keeps "trying to write the truth and realising it's not true" (p. 233), to which Tommy retorts, "Perhaps it is true; perhaps it is, and you can't bear it, so you cross it out" (p. 233). Later, in an exhausted, near-delirious state, Anna sees herself,

> seated on the music-stool, writing, writing; making an entry in one book, then ruling it off, or crossing it out; she saw the pages patterned with different kinds of writing; divided, bracketed, broken—she felt a swaying nausea; and then saw Tommy, not herself, standing with his lips pursed in concentration, turning the pages of her orderly notebooks. [P. 332]

The ironic word "orderly" is of course unintentional because of Anna's mental condition at the time it was uttered, for if any one point is made repeatedly, it is that Anna's diaries (unlike Saul Green's, for example, which run chronologically; p. 448) are chaotic, like her life. And when Saul later asks her the same question Tommy had asked earlier, about her four notebooks, she replies (putting away three of the four while speaking), "Obviously, because it's been necessary to split myself up, but from now on I shall be using one only" (p. 511). Anna had neglected her notebooks after Tommy's attempted suicide, and had wondered if his attempt had been "triggered off by reading her notebooks" (p. 566). But Anna herself has been reading Saul's diaries, until the moment when she knows she will never again do so (pp. 540–41; but see also p. 460), primarily because she has been able to manipulate the tangled lives of two isolated people, herself and Saul, and to find some meaning in life itself.

It is in Anna's frenzied efforts to find meaning in life that the most chaotic expressions of her obsession with writing and with words are to be found. Shortly after she was first advised to keep a diary, in 1950 (p. 205), Anna began the practice of cutting out and pasting—in the notebooks or on the walls of her room—carefully dated newspaper clippings. Seven years later, toward the novel's conclusion, Anna is still, and perhaps even more so, concerned with such clippings (pp. 555–56). Anna once again turns to her notebooks, neglected since Tommy's accident, but she feels alien to them, so, faster than ever, she cuts out newspaper clippings. Even though Anna, in these frenzied activities, approaches a psychotic state, she has always had the same obsession with masses of newspapers and magazines. But all these hysterical episodes with newspapers are but a prelude to the ultimate experience, which occurs toward the book's end.

After having missed the newspapers for a week (significantly, the things Anna realizes she has missed are "a war here, a dispute there"; p. 502), Anna moves "forward into a new knowledge, a new understanding" based on her fear (p. 503). In brief, this entire newspaper obsession serves as contrast or perhaps counterpoint to the major concern Anna senses with regard to her sanity, namely, the use and effects of written words. And while Anna's ultimate "cure" (if such is the word) for her malaise is her writing the novel entitled *Free Women*, such of the mental calm she achieves obviously comes through the medium of newspapers. For after she satisfactorily resolves her feverish obsession with newspapers, Anna looks at the blue notebook, in which these events are recorded, and thinks, "if I could write in it Anna would come back, but I could not make my hand go out to take up the pen" (p. 511). But after she discovers who she is, with the help of Saul Green, who is also lost and isolated, she is able to write again, with the result being, of course, the "Free Women" passages. Previously, Anna had turned "everything into fiction," which she then concluded was "an evasion" (p. 197). She also asks herself why she can not put down, simply, the real events in her life and in others' lives, with the answer that such fictionizing is "simply a means of concealing something" from herself (p. 197). But after her return from the world of insanity and chaos, she finally does become capable of stating, through the medium of fiction, her true feelings and experiences.

The self-knowledge which seems to be at the heart of Mrs. Lessing's theme in *The Golden Notebook* is clearly, then, necessary for mental equilibrium and emotional stability, and is, at least in the case of Anna Wulf, capable of being gained through a psychological and mental descent into hell. But the written and printed word is especially important for Anna; hence the ultimate resolution of her particular mental and emotional problems is necessarily bound up in and with and through writing. Through writing—public writing, such as a novel, not private writing, such as the notebooks—Anna is able to relate meaningfully again to the world and to those she knows. Just as the earlier commitments Anna had made have proven false or insufficient or inadequate, so her final commitment proves true and sufficient and adequate. Although others can be committed to other causes, writers like Anna must, in Mrs. Lessing's words, re-create "warmth and humanity and love of people" in their writing. No longer can Anna remain neutral, uninvolved in the lives of others (as she certainly is in much of this book, particularly in the case of her passivity and unconcern at

Tommy's attempted suicide), or unattached. She must become, again in Mrs. Lessing's terms, an "instrument of change for good or bad," an "architect of the soul." And since Anna, primarily through her commitment to writing, does find it possible to become these things, one can say with little hesitation, because of the personal struggle in which the protagonist is involved and the satisfactory victory that protagonist gains over her weaker self, that *The Golden Notebook* is very much in the line of the memorable nineteenth-century novels Mrs. Lessing cites as being the "highest point of literature"[28]—those by Tolstoy, Stendhal, Dostoevsky, Balzac, Turgenev, and Chekhov.

Anna Wulf, then, is herself no more "free" than those she knew in the Communist party or in Africa or in any of several other earlier commitments; indeed, her very name suggests this symbolically, for she has ceased to be a "Free/man" when she married; then she became a "Wulf," not unlike the wolves of destruction she had earlier envisioned in her nightmares. But if absolute "freedom" is not possible in this world, then commitment is, and on this point Mrs. Lessing has been most explicit:

> The act of getting a story or novel published is an act of communication, an attempt to impose one's personality and beliefs on other people. If a writer accepts this responsibility, he must see himself ... as an architect of the soul.[29]

And in so communicating, Anna is paradoxically exercising the very quality mentioned above as impossible in our world, the freedom of the individual—the freedom to fight, to "push boulders," to write for others, to work responsibly to improve the world, to try to eliminate personal and social chaos, to see ourselves as we really are. The "commitment to freedom," then, is both relative and continually in need of reexamination and modification as life goes on. Even if such "freedom" is never attained, it is the goal which keeps us sane and able to handle the many pressures of human life responsibly. Mrs. Lessing has referred to a "resting-point, a place of decision, hard to reach and precariously balanced." She goes on to say:

> It is a balance which must be continually tested and reaffirmed. Living in the midst of this whirlwind of change, it is impossible to make final judgements or absolute statements of value. The point of rest should be the writer's recognition of man, the responsive individual, voluntarily submitting his will to the collective, but never finally; and insisting on making his own

personal and private judgements before every act of submission.[30]

Certainly Mrs. Lessing, in and through such profound and rich works as *The Golden Notebook*, has made this "recognition of man, the responsive individual." This is no small task for any writer, and Mrs. Lessing has generally succeeded in demonstrating in her longer fiction the extent to which she has mastered it. To be sure, there are points on which Mrs. Lessing can be criticized, as in her handling of character and situation, but these are, I believe, of less significance than her accomplishment in detailing the experiences and development of such highly sensitive, intelligent, and self-analytic women as Anna Wulf.

NOTES

1. *Each His Own Wilderness*, in *New English Dramatists*, ed. E. Martin Browne (Harmondsworth, Middlesex: Penguin Books, 1959), p. 41.

2. Ibid., p. 50.

3. Toward the end of Anna's delirious descent into nightmare, she dreams of a tiger crouched to attack her. Unlike her other nightmares, though, Anna is able in this one to fight back and to realize that she has nothing to fear from the tiger. Half awake after this realization, Anna decides to write a play about herself, Saul, and the tiger (pp. 525–27).

4. For an intelligent brief discussion of Mrs. Lessing's several plays and their relationship to the works of other contemporary British playwrights, see John Russell Taylor, *Anger and After* (Baltimore: Penguin Books, 1963), pp. 195–96.

5. "Footnote to *The Golden Notebook*," interview with Doris Lessing by Robert Rubens, *Queen*, 21 August 1962, p. 31.

6. Interview in *Counterpoint*, ed. Roy Newquist (Chicago: Rand McNally, 1964), p. 418.

7. Personal letter from Doris Lessing to Paul Schlueter, 24 July 1965.

8. The points and quotations in this paragraph are summarized from the interview with Mrs. Lessing in the *Queen*, p. 31.

9. Ibid., p. 32.

10. Ibid.; italics are Mrs. Lessing's.

11. Personal letter from Doris Lessing to Paul Schlueter, 24 July 1965.

12. "Footnote to *The Golden Notebook*," *Queen*, p. 32.

13. Interview in *Counterpoint*, p. 418.

14. Doris Lessing, *The Golden Notebook* (New York: Simon and Schuster, 1962), p. 568. (Since the three most common editions of *The Golden Notebook* currently available in English [the British edition, published in London by Michael Joseph in 1962, the Simon and Schuster edition, 1962, and the first American paperback edition, published in New York by McGraw-Hill in 1963] are photographic facsimiles and have exactly the same pagination, references can apply to any of the three. Page references will hereafter be inserted parenthetically following quotations or allusions.) The first published reference to this seeming discrepancy of endings, incidentally, appeared in Granville Hicks's review of the novel, *Saturday Review*, 30 June 1962, p. 16. Since the McGraw-Hill paperback was issued, the novel has also been issued by Ballantine in a mass-circulation reprint edition.

15. Quoted in *Counterpoint*, p. 422.

16. The best brief, recent discussion of the background and subsequent history of Rhodesia is Patrick Keatley, *The Politics of Partnership* (Baltimore: Penguin Books, 1962).

17. But on p. 83 we are informed that there were no black trade unions.

18. "The Small Personal Voice," in *Declaration*, ed. Tom Maschler (London: MacGibbon and Kee, 1957), p. 26.

19. Ibid., p. 20.

20. Personal letter from Doris Lessing to Alfred A. Carey, 10 March 1965.

21. Personal letter from Doris Lessing to Paul Schlueter, 24 July 1965.

22. "The Small Personal Voice," *Declaration*, p. 17.

23. Mrs. Marks is evidently a Jungian therapist, although this is not specified; psychoanalysts in England need not be physicians.

24. "The Small Personal Voice," *Declaration*, p. 27.

25. Ibid., p. 16.

26. Ibid.

27. Interview in *Counterpoint*, p. 418.

28. "The Small Personal Voice," *Declaration*, p. 14.

29. Ibid., p. 16.

30. Ibid., p. 20.

PHYLLIS STERNBERG PERRAKIS

Sufism, Jung and the Myth of Kore: Revisionist Politics in Lessing's Marriages

In a 1980 interview, Lessing observed of her literary career: "I always write about the individual and that which surrounds him" ("Interview" 1). This comment, of course, echoes her well-known 1950s declaration that her novels are about "the individual conscience in its relations with the collective" (*Voice* 14). What Lessing does not highlight in her 1980 interview, however, is how much her conception of the relationship between the individual and his/her world has changed over the years. In her early realistic novels Lessing presents individuals trying to relate themselves to a fragmented social reality, trying to find social and political ways of healing that fragmentation, whereas in her space-fiction *Canopus in Argos* series she places fragmented individuals and societies in a galactic context which reveals their egoism and disunity as aberrations from the integrity and wholeness which are their true states and which reflect the essential unity and order of the cosmos. I wish to trace this change in Lessing's vision by relating it to her encounter with Jungian psychology and Sufi mysticism and to show how her assimilation of these philosophies/psychologies provides the informative power of *The Marriages Between Zones Three, Four, and Five*, the second volume of the *Canopus* series.

Although critics like Evelyn J. Hinz and John J. Teunissen and Roberta Rubenstein have previously dealt with Jung's influence on Lessing's fiction,

From *Mosaic* 25, 3 (1992). © 1992 by *Mosaic*.

and although Nancy Shield Hardin pioneered studies of Lessing's use of Sufism, there has been little attempt to relate the two, especially in the more recent space-fiction. Lorelei Cederstrom's recent Jungian study does briefly discuss the *Canopus* series, including *Marriages*, but her focus is on the earlier evolution in Lessing's fiction from "Marxist and feminist ideas to psychological patterns" (3) and she shows little interest in the post-Jungian development in Lessing's fiction. To Betsy Draine *Marriages* may be read as a "metaphor of the mystical path" (163) to enlightenment, and she explicitly relates Lessing's concerns to Sufi, as well as Gnostic and Christian, mystic traditions. As she sees it, however, the novel evades the problem of evil found in other works in the *Canopus* series and concludes that its formal clarity is the result of a "simplicity of moral vision" (168).

I wish to argue that while, on one level, *Marriages'* vision does reflect the integrated self as defined by Jung, that is not *all* it reflects; in this novel Lessing incorporates her Jungian insights into a larger whole stemming from her encounter with Sufi teachings. Lessing herself briefly discusses what I am calling her "post-Jungian" thinking in an introduction to a book on Sufi psychology and spirituality by Idries Shah. Commenting on the West's arrogance and insularity regarding ideas from outsiders, she notes that "Jung acknowledged his debt to the East. Is it not remarkable that his disciples are not curious about what else there might be?" (Introduction 4). In *Marriages* Lessing portrays "what else there might be," creating a holistic universe that finds a source of power outside the psyche (as well as in it), and revealing how this external power both awakens and empowers the receptive soul to begin the difficult process of inner growth.

Marriages' referential richness seems to derive from Lessing's response to the emphasis in Sufi teachings on the need to embrace seemingly contradictory or disparate aspects of experience. Hardin, writing in 1974 of the Sufi influence on Lessing's writings, notes that they "partake of the two worlds—of real life on the one hand and of mental processes on the other. The secret is that Lessing, as the Sufis, does not see the two as separate: 'it isn't either or at all, it's and, and, and, and, and, and.... Your dreams *and* your life'" ("Lessing" 571). *Marriages'* narrative embodies this "and." It is not only an allegory of Jungian rebirth or mystical ascent; nor is it merely a sexual-political dialectic, as Katherine Fishburn reads it. Like a dream or visionary myth *Marriages* integrates all these levels of meaning and reference with a resonance and clarity found nowhere else in Lessing's writings.

A brief look at the development of Lessing's novels will reveal how *Marriages'* integration of psychic, social and spiritual elements is the culmination of a gradual thematic movement from individual and social fragmentation toward first internal and then external integration. In the first four volumes of *Children of Violence*, Martha Quest is presented as a rebellious adolescent at odds with herself, her family and the values of the white colonial society of the southern African country where she is raised. As the Second World War begins, Martha immerses herself in radical politics, finding a new sense of identity and commitment as a member of a small Communist group, marrying its leader to prevent his deportation. Again, however, Martha gradually becomes aware of discrepancies between her personal feelings, political beliefs and impulsive behavior.

In *The Golden Notebook*, written between volumes three and four of *Children*, Lessing's protagonist moves deeper within, realizing that there will be no cure for the external fragmentation undermining her until she deals with the inner disunity that both mirrors and contributes to it. Anna Wulf's breakdown, after her lover leaves, not only destroys the careful partition of her consciousness into various notebooks but also forces her to confront the parts of herself that this fragmentation had obscured, including her fear of her own anger. Lessing's "preoccupation with fragmentation" (Vlastos 128) continues in *The Four-Gated City*, the final volume of the *Children of Violence* series. In this novel, Martha Quest, now living in England and having spent years mothering the unnurtured children of her employer and his relatives, has discovered and acknowledged the self-hater deep within her and "has learned to trust her capacity to grow and learn from any situation" (Christ, *Diving* 69). As reflected in the futuristic ending of the novel, her now more fully integrated self has equipped her to deal with a social milieu which combines catastrophic destruction with hints of an emerging new world containing children with more evolved powers.

Increasingly, in the subsequent novels, Lessing looks for different structural means to convey what seems to be a new vision of the possibility of both inner and outer unity. In novels like *Briefing for a Descent into Hell* and *Memoirs of a Survivor* she portrays protagonists with increasingly rich inner worlds that become more real and powerful than their everyday lives. In her recent *Canopus in Argos* series, however, Lessing adopts a different strategy, housing different levels of consciousness in separate external worlds in a vast galactic system. Each of the five volumes in the series records the efforts of Canopus, the most advanced star in the galaxy, to raise the level of understanding and assist the evolutionary growth of both her own colonies and those of the other two galactic empires, Sirius and Puttoria. Repeatedly narrators from one world and level of understanding retell the story of their relationship with other worlds and, in the retelling, discover how, without realizing it, they (and the other worlds) have been transformed.

With one exception, all the volumes in the *Canopus* series use the science-fiction apparatus of star systems and their colonies and of near immortal inhabitants who interfere in the fates of their earth-like colonies. This science-fiction machinery, while clearly designed to undermine readers' habitual assumptions and to encourage new ways of seeing, has had at times the opposite effect; for example, Carey Kaplan, who reads the Canopean series as "depersonalized" autobiography, dismisses the Canopean Empire as essentially a benevolent space-fiction version of an imperialistic British Empire (150). In *The Marriages Between Zones Three, Four, and Five*, however, Lessing dispenses with the use of other planets and near immortal colonizers, and as a result this novel enables us to appreciate what she was really trying to accomplish in this series.

In *Marriages* Lessing focuses on one small portion of her vast fictional galaxy—four of the six concentric zones around the planet Shikasta. Narrated with parable-like simplicity, *Marriages* recounts the legendary story of how the queen of the peaceful and idyllic Zone Three, Al•Ith, is ordered by higher powers to go down to the militaristic and patriarchal Zone Four and marry its king, Ben Ata. Al•Ith herself does not understand what is happening to her as she and Ben Ata begin the painful and disorienting process of overcoming their initial antipathy and adjusting to their vast cultural and psychological differences. The deep love they eventually come to share makes all the more poignant their grief when they are at last ordered to part.

Returning to Zone Three, Al•Ith finds her own people fat and complacent; awakened to the need to search for a meaning to her own difficult experiences, she settles near the border of Zone Two. Her strangeness and dissatisfaction with Zone Three frighten her sister Murti, the Zone's new queen, who places a guard in front of Al•Ith's shed on the border to prevent her from spreading contaminating ideas. She is eventually freed by a visit from her former husband Ben Ata who, in the meantime, has also lived out the new understanding engendered in him by his marriage to Al•Ith. After Ben Ata returns home, Al•Ith, now free to share her ideas with Zone Three friends, eventually crosses over to Zone Two and does not return. The novel ends with a "continuous movement now, from Zone Five to Zone Four. And from Zone Four to Zone Three—and from us, up the pass .... and a lightness and freshness ... where there had been only stagnation. And closed borders" (198-99).

In *Marriages* Lessing seems to be consciously counteracting the fragmented vision of her earlier novels by offering a parable of integration and union. While the fragmentation of the pre-Canopean novels grew out of the individual's or society's need to protect itself by excluding whatever seemed threatening—even other parts of the psyche—*Marriages* is based on the acknowledgment, exploration and, finally, acceptance of otherness, both in the self and in society. Lessing has described *Marriages* as being "full of forgiveness" (qtd. in Bigsby 192), and this forgiveness is part of the healing of wounds and integrating of fragments that characterize the story.

The uniquely integrated vision of *Marriages* may be traced to a perception that came to Lessing at the time she was composing *The Golden Notebook*: "writing that book" in the form I did forced me to examine myself in all kinds of ways" (qtd. in Bigsby 200). Realizing that her ideas and her philosophy were totally inadequate to the new thoughts and experiences she was then having, she began to investigate alternative ways of viewing reality, culminating in her study of Sufism in the early 1960s. A mystical movement originally founded within Islam in Iran in the ninth century, the Sufi Way has for its goal the attainment of the presence of the Divine. While mystical in goal, the Sufi vision is all-encompassing, relating every aspect of an individual's life to his/her spiritual growth; this integration includes the erotic, as Draine points out (164), just as it also involves the correlation of the stages of inner spiritual development with external cosmic reality. One particular aspect of the Sufi way emphasized by Lessing's Sufi mentor, Idries Shah, is the acquisition of detachment. Almost all of Shah's *Learning How to Learn* is devoted to awakening his readers to the understanding that their usual way of thinking and feeling are based on an all-pervasive conditioning. He explains that beneath people's emotions and socially-conditioned ideas of themselves there is a deeper self that puts them in touch with a source of transcendental power in the universe (292). In more traditional Sufi writings the ability to detach oneself from one's body and ego sufficiently to become aware of and in touch with spiritual phenomenon is what raises the human spirit above the first level of existence which is associated exclusively with physical reality (Chittick 30-31). While Lessing herself does not think that *Marriages* is "a description of Sufi attitudes," she nevertheless does not deny the possibility of their presence, but actually goes on to explain how this might happen: "unless what I have learnt has become very unconscious and has come out differently" (qtd. in Bigsby 203).

In Lessing's own 1980 account of the origin of *Marriages* she brings up rather casually the other major source of her vision: "When I was in my late thirties and early forties my love life was in a state of chaos and disarray.... Unconsciously I used a certain therapeutic technique which just emerged from my unconscious." She describes how she invented an ideal landscape in which she placed a strong man and an equally strong woman, each responsible and autonomous in their own way. Lessing explains that she later read that this was a Jungian technique—to "take some part of you which is weak and deliberately fantasize it strong, make this part different, make it as you would like it to be." She went on doing this "for some years in fact.... So this book has come out of years of the closest possible work of the imagination" (qtd. in Bigsby 204).

In a lecture in New York City in 1984 Lessing amplifies this explanation of the genesis of *Marriages*. Originally, she explains, she created

> two ideal landscapes, male and female.... They were equally strong, very different, operating from strength.... When I fished that story out of my unconscious and looked at it, it had become different. The two original landscapes were both my favorite landscapes... high, dry, mountainous, cool with a clear sky.
>
> What came out of my unconscious was that the male realm, which is a highly exaggerated sort of Prussian realm or British public school, had become low, flat and watery. (qtd. in Tiger 222)

In the finished version of *Marriages* there are three zones: Three, Four and Five. These zones obviously correspond to Lessing's imaginative landscapes. The zones are clearly geographical locales and modes of life closely connected with so-called masculine and feminine qualities. Yet they are also suggestive of different stages in an individual's life, different levels of spiritual awareness, and even of different historical periods.

From another perspective the zones tie *Marriages* to the other books in the series, particularly to *Shikasta*. In that first volume, the zones are defined as concentric circles around the planet Shikasta. The only zone we see in detail in the first volume is Zone Six—the home of unhappy Shikastan souls who have not met the challenges of life on their planet and are therefore doomed to go back and endure another life there. Presumably those who do successfully complete their lives on Shikasta without succumbing to its absorbing but chimerical attractions (sex, money, fame, even romantic love) go on to the other zones. Thus Zones Three, Four and Five are populated by those who have already learned the painful lesson of detachment from the obsessions that overwhelm most of Shikasta's inhabitants and prevent them from knowing their own selves.

As a result of their detachment, the inhabitants of Zones Three, Four and Five in *Marriages* are able to respond to the hidden messages of the cosmos symbolized by an order from the Providers, a definite but unknowable source of authority. This order provides the framework for the entire fiction. Unlike the other books in the *Canopus* series, *Marriages* does not focus on the mechanism by which this order is given, or on who gives the order (although we can assume from the other volumes in the series that the Providers are Canopeans). Rather *Marriages* focuses on the effect of the "message" on the people to whom it is given, especially Al•Ith and Ben Ata. Thus, whereas *Shikasta* is about the way that individuals become aware of deeper forces at work in the universe, *Marriages* is about how these forces affect people who are able to "hear" and respond to them.

In *Marriages* not only the implicit way of relating to the world but also the very structure of the zones is also highly suggestive of Sufi influence. Just as the zones are defined as concentric circles around Shikasta, so Sufi cosmology posits nine concentric spheres surrounding the earth. On one level these spheres are identified with literal planets and reflect the old Ptolemaic system: the Moon, Mercury, Venus, The Sun, Mars, Jupiter, Saturn, the fixed stars, and the starless heaven. These spheres, however, are also "the outward manifestation" of ascending spiritual worlds and "correspond to the ascending stages of the spiritual journey" (Chittick 73, 72). According to Islamic cosmology, the individual spirit is thought to begin in the realm of the Divine and then at conception to descend symbolically through the various spheres or spiritual worlds until it reaches the level of being manifested as a physical body, at which time the human being begins life consciously at the level of the "animal spirit or ego." "All of the directives of religion and the spiritual life are aimed at releasing it from this prison and taking it back to its original home" (Chittick 74). To do this, however, requires conscious understanding and effort.

The process of spiritual change is described symbolically as "an ascent by means of the ladder of the heavens" (Chittick 75), i.e., at the higher levels of spiritual transformation the soul is described as symbolically passing through the ascending spiritual worlds identified with the spheres. Thus the macrocosm and the microcosm are identified, "the concentric spheres acting as a most powerful and efficient symbol for the states of being which man must traverse to reach Being itself" (Nasr 31).

Like the planets in Sufi cosmology, the zones in *Marriages* also function on the physical and the spiritual level. The geography of the zones suggests the marriage of physical and metaphysical reality. The mountains of Zone Three are a physical symbol for the spiritual attribute of grandeur and for the human need to aspire and ascend. The low, watery, flat land of Zone Four suggests the bogged down state of the patriarchal system of that Zone—a state where the heavy wet earth of the military hierarchy holds down peoples' aspirations in the way that the punishment helmets hold down their heads. The mists, so prevalent in Zone Four, reflect the clouding of the inhabitants' understanding of the purpose and meaning of their existence. The dry, gritty desert land of Zone Five mirrors the meagreness of this level of civilization. Yet everywhere the gritty sand drives people to move about, ride fast, test themselves. Their restlessness suggests their anarchic energy which can lead to the adoption of new challenges or to the destructive pilfering of settled villages.

Besides the symbolism of the zones, the other key metaphor in Lessing's novel is that of marriage itself. Where in the earlier and later novels in the series we have the model of psychic and spiritual growth through the interaction between a teacher and a pupil (Canopus and Shikasta, Klorathy and Ambien II, etc.), in *Marriages* we have instead the interaction, the marriage, between equals as the impetus for inner and outer growth. It is specifically the interaction, the give and take, between male and female equals that stimulates the growth and development of each partner and of his and her worlds.

In order for the literal marriage to take place, Al•Ith must go down to Zone Four and marry its king, and this descent will force both Al•Ith and her zone to come to terms with feelings and experiences not previously accepted or valued. We quickly get an idea of what kind of feelings these will be from Al•Ith's response to the order to marry Ben Ata. She puts on dark blue mourning clothes and her actions express a sense of grief. The Zone Three chronicler of the tale notes that "Emotions of this kind are not valued by us…. As individuals we do not expect—it is not expected of us—to weep, wail, suffer" (13-14). Al•Ith's descent to Zone Four does, in fact, expose her to many "negative" emotions, including the domination and subsequent feelings of inadequacy experienced by women in that Zone; she also experiences the joy and pain of "marriage," of a long term commitment between two people who possess very different strengths and weaknesses. Through the dynamics of this marriage Al•Ith descends internally as well as externally, encountering in the militaristic Zone Four the dark side of her own psyche as well.

Seen in this light, Al•Ith's journey becomes highly suggestive of the kind of powerful, inner experiences described by Jung as leading to a transformation and enlargement of the personality, an experience of rebirth. In "Concerning Rebirth" Jung analyzes the process by which this kind of change takes place. In particular he links the personality's transformation to an encounter with the unconscious and a new integration of the conscious and unconscious aspects of the psyche. The result is the birth of the "self"—by which he meant "a psychic totality and at the same time a centre, neither of which coincides with the ego but includes it, just as a larger circle encloses a smaller one" (142). Because this new center is not accessible to the ego it can feel like an alien being. Thus the "self" is sometimes personalized as a separate being or force.

In the eighteenth Sura of the Koran, Jung finds a telling example of how the "self" can feel like an alien being. This Sura consists of two parts: the first recounts a legend about seven sleepers in a cave who sleep for 309 years; the second part describes a meeting first between an immortal guide and Moses and then between the guide and Alexander the Great. While "this entire Sura is taken up with a rebirth mystery," according to Jung (135), it is the second part of the Sura that is most relevant to Lessing's fiction. It concerns a quest by Moses, accompanied by a servant, to find the place where two seas meet. Jung notes that such a landscape suggests a deep place within the psyche, the unconscious. When Moses and his servant reach this special place, they forget the fish they had brought along for nourishment and it miraculously jumps back into the sea. In its place they meet Khidr (an immortal spiritual guide akin to Elijah) who leads Moses through an inexplicable series of events, including the boring of a hole in the bottom of a ship belonging to a group of poor men. When Moses protests, Khidr explains that he damaged the men's ship because "in their rear was a king who was taking every ship by force" (138). Jung identifies the fish and Khidr with the "self" and interprets the "incomprehensible deeds" of Khidr as actions "which show how ego-consciousness reacts to the superior guidance of the self through the twists and turns of fate" (141).

Jung's interpretation of the story of Moses's quest in Sura Eighteen fits Lessing's parable very well up to a point. The Providers can be interpreted, like Khidr in the Koran legend, as symbols of the self, and their command that Al•Ith go to Zone Four and marry its ruler resembles the inexplicable actions of Khidr in destroying the boat. The command, based on an awareness of a malaise of which the inhabitants of the zones are not consciously aware, initiates a set of actions which seem at first incomprehensible to the conscious mind of Al•Ith and Ben Ata. Each of them responds differently to the command according to their capacity for rebirth, and this also is anticipated in Jung's commentary on the Koran legend. Jung notes that "those who cannot be reborn themselves ... have to be content with moral conduct, that is to say with adherence to the law. Very often behavior prescribed by rule is a substitute for spiritual transformation" (136-37). In his first unpleasant encounters with Al•Ith, Ben Ata can endure his anxiety and disorientation only through his rigid adherence to the law commanding them to be married. Yet from the beginning Al•Ith, while also obedient, recognizes that there must be a deeper meaning to their situation, and she searches for the new understanding that it will initiate. Her greater openness to the process of spiritual transformation allows her to function as a guide and aid for Ben Ata (somewhat like Khidr) in what is for him a very frightening and foreign process.

Al•Ith also functions as guide and friend to Dabeeb and the other women of Zone Four. This role throws some light on Lessing's explanation that the idea for *Marriages* developed from a series of fantasies about a strong, independent woman and man. She had noted how this fantasy had helped her deal with her own sense of dependence and weakness at a difficult time in her life. We now see that in creating Al•Ith, Lessing was, from a Jungian perspective, imagining her own potential source of strength, opening herself up to a friend or guide who was also a personification of her own self.

Furthermore, the mountains of Zone Three and the blue clearing between the mountains that is all that can be seen of Zone Two, like the place where the two seas meet in the Koran legend, both function as deep unconscious places within for Ben Ata and Al•Ith. For Al•Ith, however, the path to this deep level is more complex than for Ben Ata. He has the advantage of having Al•Ith there to help him aspire to the mountains of Zone Three and to a deeper level of himself, whereas for Al•Ith, the marriage to Ben Ata plunges her into an outer region of the unconscious filled with negative attitudes toward women—a region similar to what Jung called the personal unconscious. Al•Ith does not experience the deeper plunge into the unconscious until she leaves Zone Four. No longer satisfied with Zone Three, she travels with only her horse Yori as a companion to the edge of Zone Two and tries to enter it. She is not yet, however, ready to cross over into this non-material realm: her physical self is a barrier. Returning to Zone Three, she spends a strange dreamed-filled night imagining all kinds of mythological shapes associated with ancient tales. Lusik, the narrator, explains that the shapes Al•Ith encountered in her dream were also the visions of storytellers, and Al•Ith, imagining these shapes, was herself at that moment a storyteller and a chronicler. Thus Al•Ith, after integrating into herself her experiences in Zone Four, was able to gain access to a collective realm available to both artists and those who descend imaginatively deep inside themselves.

Al•Ith's descent into this realm in her dream is like Jung's interpretation of Moses's discovery of the place where the two seas meet in the "Sura of the Cave." She has an encounter with a deeper place within. Here, however, Lessing's fiction goes beyond Jung's interpretation of these experiences as symbolic encounters with the self. Her protagonist does not finally enter Zone Two until she has sufficiently advanced spiritually to leave her physical self behind. Thus the deep level of self or integration suggested by Zone Two in Lessing's parable is associated with a spiritual dimension beyond the physical world and forces us to take into consideration the Sufi element in Lessing's novel.

What Jung defines as a psychological change is seen by Sufi teachings as a transformation of the spirit or heart. Furthermore, what Jung calls a recentering of the personality around the self is explained by Sufi writings as the individual's ascent to a higher spiritual stage. For the Sufis, however, such an ascent is not the result of human endeavor only. Its ultimate source lies in the Divine and, more specifically, in God's revelation of His laws and teachings through His Prophets. Hence from a Sufi perspective, Moses, in the "Sura of the Cave," is changed not merely by a contact with his own unconscious knowledge and strength. He is assisted by a higher being (Khidr) who teaches him the ways of God. As a result of this encounter, for the Sufis as for Jung, Moses undergoes a process of rebirth and transformation. For the Sufis, however, this transformation is the result not only of being aided by an outside spiritual power. Moses's transformation also depends on his response to that power, his willingness to trust and follow Khidr even when his actions seem to violate Moses's understanding of spiritual behavior. Thus from a Sufi perspective, Khidr, whom Jung identifies with the tendency of the self to be seen as an alien being, is the representative or image of a Divine source. The resulting change in Moses's personality is due to the purifying of his soul or heart through its efforts to understand and follow the teachings of the Divinely sent helper.

In *Marriages* Lessing creates a universe that, like the Koran tale, possesses both an inner and outer spiritual dimension. The Providers are presumably sent from a Divine source and reflect an outer spiritual dimension. The initial response that Al•Ith and Ben Ata make to the Providers' order represents their acknowledgment of and obedience to that Divine source. It marks them as having attained the second level of spiritual awareness, of being conscious, aware human beings. Their subsequent efforts to discover the meaning of the order in terms of their own lives— what is the purpose and meaning of their lives—begins them on the path of spiritual search and growth. Thus they become spiritual pilgrims, and Al•Ith's final entrance into Zone Two marks her ascent to a spiritual stage beyond the physical.

For Western readers, however, the psychological dimension of Al•Ith's progress is more accessible and familiar than the Sufi element. Her journey to Zone Four has much in common with the inward journeys found in other novels of rebirth and transformation by women. In such novels, as Annis Pratt has observed, the protagonist usually starts off in the world of everyday society and is led deeper into her psyche by a token or lover connected with the green world; this is an archetypal realm of oneness with nature in which women are free to experience themselves fully, feeling no division between mind and body, nature and psyche. Zone Three, however, where Al•Ith begins, is already reminiscent of the green world defined by Pratt. Similarly, although Pratt associates this green world with the development of a young girl to maturity, and although Al•Ith begins as a mature woman and the mother of five children, she incorporates into herself the role of the young maiden.

In fact, Al•Ith, who at the beginning of *Marriages* is at one with herself and nature and comfortable with her eros ("one of the skills of her zone" she later tells Ben Ata), seems to be reminiscent of the archetypal earth goddess Kore, or the "lady of the beasts." This aspect of Al•Ith is emphasized in the early pictures done by Zone Three artists, showing Al•Ith on horseback, escorted by the soldiers of Zone Four to their land. The soldiers are angry and impatient to be out of the uncomfortable foreign Zone Three; the wind is bitter and Al•Ith's horse droops his head from the difficult ride. Added to this realistic depiction, however, is an emblematic element: "All kinds of little animals have crept into this picture. Birds hover around her head. A small deer, a great favourite with our children, has stepped on to the dust of the road, and is holding up its nose to the drooping nose of Al•Ith's horse.... Often these pictures are titled 'Al•Ith's animals'" (19).

As much as Al•Ith functions as the archetypal wise woman, witch or earth goddess, at home with herself and nature, however, so much is the realm into which she descends emblematic of the corrupted world of male power, military violence, abuse of nature and denigration of women. This world functions as both a social criticism of the values of patriarchy and, on a deeper level, as an analogue of that part of the unconscious, that Jung calls the "shadow," the home of ideas and feelings unacceptable to the ego. It is also the realm of the animus, of the woman's personal and cultural expectations about men. Al•Ith's exposure to the painful domination experienced by the Zone Four women, their obdurate survival and her own loss of independence and self sufficiency, allow her to experience and come to terms with the common negative experiences of women in patriarchal cultures.

Here Al•Ith seems to be undergoing an experience that is common in women's rebirth fiction: an encounter with the shadow that seems to have no parallel in men's corresponding encounters. For women, instead of embodying elements that are antisocial and opposed to societal gender norms, the shadow seems "to bring with it from the social world the opprobrium for womanhood associated with sexism, infusing characters with self-loathing." The result of this combination of animus and shadow is a "gynophobia" coupled with "such 'masculine' impulses as logic, aggression, and power struggles" (Pratt 141). Although Ben Ata initially functions as such a shadow/animus figure, Al•Ith herself lives out some of the self-loathing associated with the shadow after her child is born, feeling unattractive, jealous and needy. At this point, she needs to make love with Ben Ata "as if she were drowning and could only be saved by his driving body" (223), otherwise she fears she will "go crazy, explode" from tension. Yet this stage too must be passed through if she is to acquire her full development. Similarly, in a highly Freudian scene in which Al•Ith lovingly inspects her naked baby, her husband is overwhelmed with jealousy. This leads to a new equilibrium between them, which signals the end of their marriage. On leaving Zone Four, Al•Ith is finally able to assimilate these experiences into a new whole which will put her on the path to Zone Two and a deeper self.

Lessing's narrative differs from the usual rebirth pattern, however, in that the narrator also focuses on Ben Ata's perceptions, sees into his fears and limitations and "marries" him to the tale of descent and growth. Ben Ata, too, descends into unknown and undeveloped parts of his psyche and, through his marriage to Al•Ith, encounters the despised and discarded possibilities within him. He must come to terms with the feminine, with his anima, and the meeting with Al•Ith also signals his encounter with a repressed or despised other. He is immediately repulsed by her seriousness, independence and lack of flirtatiousness: "She was not unbeautiful, with her dark eyes, dark hair, and the rest of the usual appurtenances, but there was nothing in her that set out to challenge him physically, and so he was cold" (45). He becomes even more uneasy when he learns that she does not sleep much, is at home in the night, and can speak to her horse. He thinks of her as a witch, instinctively fearing and hating the feminine, intuitive power she represents to him, the part of himself, that like the dark he has always managed to avoid. Lessing's detailed account of the descent and transformation of both her protagonists makes *Marriages* a unique story of rebirth.

At the same time, Lessing's novel can be seen as a revisionist account of the Demeter/Kore (or Persephone) myth discussed by Jung in relation to women's individuation and identified by Pratt as common to women's rebirth fiction. In the classical version of the myth, Persephone, who has wandered away from her mother, Demeter, to gather flowers, is raped by Pluto and abducted to the underworld to live there as his wife. Demeter, grief-stricken, searches everywhere for her daughter, finally going to Zeus to ask for Persephone's return.

In Lessing's story Al•Ith plays the role of both Demeter and Persephone. Like Persephone, she is forced to go down to the underworld, where she is raped and married by Ben Ata, playing the role of Pluto. Through her marriage, however, she rescues various other Persephones (Dabeeb and the other Zone Four women) and is herself transformed. Because she is Ben Ata's equal, their marriage leads to both of them acquiring aspects of the other's strength. As a result Ben Ata and his realm are transformed, and the underworld becomes peaceful and verdant. In the end Al•Ith does leave her daughters behind, but not before helping them acquire some of her power so that they can live in equality with the Plutos of the transformed underworld. Furthermore, when she returns to Zone Three, Al•Ith confronts and is imprisoned by a symbolic repressive mother in the person of her sister Murti, although because of the inner strength and perseverance, learned from her experience in the underworld of Zone Four, she is able to withstand imprisonment by this "mother" and her maternal society. Her eventual rescue by her transformed husband brings the energy of the androgynous lover to help overcome repressive "mothers" and leads to the growth and transformation of Zone Three and even of Murti herself. Thus Al•Ith's mythic descent and return involves mothering adequately herself and others, and then—with the new strength acquired from that role and from her equality with her husband—she is able to master the challenges of playing the role of daughter to herself and others.

Jung notes that the configuration corresponding to the Kore aspect in a woman is generally a double one, i.e., a mother and a maiden. He further notes that "Demeter and Kore, mother and daughter, extend the feminine consciousness both upwards and downwards"; they "widen out the narrowly limited conscious mind bound in space and time, giving it intimations of a greater and more comprehensive personality which has a share in the eternal course of things" ("Kore" 188). Kérenyi, in his study of the Eleusinian Mysteries surrounding the Demeter/Kore myth, dwells even more suggestively on the unity of Demeter and Kore. He notes that "a Great Goddess" could combine "in a single figure which was *at once* Mother and

Daughter ... the motifs that recur in *all* mothers and daughters, and she could combine the feminine attributes of the earth with the inconstancy of the wandering moon" (32). Kérenyi also notes that Demeter, as the goddess of grain, is associated with the earth and earthiness while Persephone, who wanders off to pick flowers, is associated with the moon and spirituality. Finally, he suggests that the Eleusinian Mysteries included a new vision of the possibility of birth in death. In sacred reenactments of the myth, Persephone is supposed to give birth to a child in the underworld, and this new birth is equated with the possibility for mortals of discovering life in death. Furthermore, Persephone herself is, of course, reborn for two-thirds of the year and spends this time in the upper regions of earth. In conjunction, Demeter—the more earthy figure—and Persephone—the more spiritual— suggest the gift to human kind of "food and wealth" on the one hand and "birth under the earth" on the other (Kérenyi 94).

In Lessing's revision of the myth, Al•Ith in her role as wife combines the qualities of mother and daughter and serves as a source of both physical and spiritual enlightenment to Ben Ata and Zone Four. Through her influence, Ben Ata sees for the first time the poverty of his zone and eventually dismisses three-fourths of his army. The new manpower and resources now available lead to a new flourishing of the practical arts in Zone Four. Spiritually, too, the influence of Al•Ith on Zone Four is profound. After Ben Ata assimilates what he has learned from her, it becomes acceptable to look up to the mountains of Zone Three, her home, which before had been a forbidden sight. This activity brings with it a new respect for the women's ceremonies which had kept alive the understanding of the need to look up and aspire. A new appreciation of women's values brings a whole new climate of peace and cooperation to Zone Four.

* * *

Another way of looking at the mythic union of the earthly (represented by Demeter) and the spiritual (represented by Persephone) in Al•Ith's journey to Zone Four is to correlate it with both a social quest and a spiritual quest. Socially, Al•Ith learns to integrate herself into the world of Zone Four and, spiritually, she acquires a deeper level of selfhood on her subsequent return to Zone Three. Furthermore, both are interrelated. Al•Ith needs to incorporate into herself the new strength and understanding that she gains from interacting with Ben Ata and the women of Zone Four in order to recognize and move beyond the stagnant atmosphere of Zone Three.

This correlation between spiritual and social, inner and outer quests is already at work in the protagonist of Lessing's *The Four-Gated City*. As Christ has noted: "Whatever she initially experiences as alien to herself is gradually understood to be as much internal as external, and conversely as much external as internal. For Martha there is no radical duality between the self and the world" ("Quest" 14). Christ also notes that the possibility for the kind of self discoveries that Martha makes in *The Four-Gated City* had been available in earlier books, but Martha had not been able to take advantage of them because "she drifts, moved by forces she does not comprehend. She looks to something outside herself to establish meaning and transcendence in her life. Yet at each stage of her life she is in touch with a source of transcendence within herself which she recognizes only momentarily, then forgets" ("Quest" 8). We are reminded of the moment on the veld, early in *Martha Quest*, when Martha has a mystical sense of oneness with the whole, an experience which she soon forgets, but which is reenacted in a more all-encompassing way during her love affair with Thomas in *Landlocked*.

What is new in *Marriages* is that Al•Ith is in touch with a deep level of herself from the beginning, and this puts her in touch with a source of transcendence that is both within her and without and which she does not forget. Al•Ith is Lessing's first heroine to begin in this state of inner and outer wholeness. Earlier heroines had acquired varying degrees of integrated selfhood, from the purely psychological integration achieved by Anna Wulf at the end of *The Golden Notebook*—which allows her to "feel separate from others but also have a sense of kinship with them that doesn't overwhelm her own sense of identity" (Perrakis, "Notebook" 426)—to the more transcendent wholeness struggled toward by Martha Quest in *The Four-Gated City* (as noted by Christ and Pratt). The survivor in *Memoirs of a Survivor*, as Cederstrom has argued, seems to acquire an even more all-encompassing integration by the end of that novel (169-90). Al•Ith, however, begins in the state that is only slowly worked toward and/or painfully achieved by these earlier heroines.

The other powerfully original element of Lessing's myth is her integration of the detailed account of her female protagonist's descent, change and ascent with the parallel journey of her male counterpart. Because Lessing can forgive the male patriarchal world that has imprisoned so many Dabeebs and forgive her own subjection to that world, she can accept her male protagonist's equal need to grow and change. Similarly, she portrays a world where neither male nor female can reach their full potential without interacting, "marrying," or balancing each other. Hence in order for Al•Ith to free her more dependent "daughters" in Zone Four (symbolically her weaker self), and to stand up to Murti's repressive behavior in Zone Three (symbolically her repressive "mother"), she needs to incorporate the androgynous elements (the perseverance and determination) she gained from her relationship with Ben Ata.

Furthermore, Al•Ith's final rescue and the opening up of Zone Three is due to the intervention of the now more androgynous Ben Ata. His new sensitivity and thoughtfulness (gained from his relationship with Al•Ith) allow him not only to help Al•Ith but to aid Vahshi and Zone Five in their transformation. Hence it is the balance of equally strong women and men and their interaction that leads to the social transformation of all three zones. Lessing has thus added a third factor into her revision of the Demeter/Persephone myth: she has positively incorporated Pluto, the male lover, into the story. Whereas previously the male had no part to play in the myth except "that of seducer or conqueror" (Jung "Kore" 184), in Lessing's version he both acts and is acted on by Demeter/Persephone. This new interaction is possible only because Demeter/Persephone and Pluto are presented as equals. More specifically, the marriage of Al•Ith and Ben Ata is successful only because right from the beginning Al•Ith feels and acts as her husband's equal. When Ben Ata, feeling insecure and threatened at their first meeting, carries her to the bed and rapes her, she reacts by being surprised, interested and a little afraid. Unlike Dabeeb and the other women of Zone Four, she is not reduced to subterfuge and ironic submission to safeguard her identity and existence. Her self-confidence and independence throw Ben Ata off balance psychologically and eventually force him to seek new ways of interacting with her. Thus through their interaction both of them become involved in a reciprocal process of change and growth.

Whereas the classical Greek myth is based on a duality of mother and daughter, in *Marriages* we have a trinity of mother, daughter and lover, and, if we take into account the transformed Al•Ith who enters Zone Two, we ultimately have a quaternary—mother, daughter, lover, and androgynous soul. Furthermore, we have four zones and four spiritual states that Al•Ith and Ben Ata pass through. In another sense, however, we have a new duality because mother and daughter fuse into one strong woman, Al•Ith, and it is her marriage to her equal but opposite partner, Ben Ata, that creates the new mystery—the possibility of inner and outer transformation.

This inclusion of Pluto into the story is Lessing's most significant deviation from the original myth. It also distinguishes her work from the pattern of rebirth in the novels discussed by Pratt. This difference in Lessing's vision seems to stem not only from her earlier psychological investigation of her feelings of dependence on men (the Jungian influence), but again from her assimilation of Sufi elements that emphasize the correlation of the psychological and the social, of internal growth and external behavior and attitudes.

Furthermore, *Marriages* not only correlates Al•Ith's growth with that of Ben Ata but also connects the inner transformations of both to the outer transformations of their respective zones. Because she is the embodiment of Zone Three, Al•Ith's immersion in and integration of the repressed parts of her psyche through her marriage to Ben Ata is also an integration by Zone Three of its darker side. In fact, what we gradually come to realize is that Zone Three is listless and lacking in vitality because it has split itself off from its own shadow. It has dissociated itself from all kinds of emotions and experiences, now associated with Zone Four.

One of the most direct ways that Zone Four functions as the forgotten or repressed side of Zone Three may be seen in the descriptions of the song festivals held by the two zones. The festival of songs and tales held by Zone Three at Al•Ith's specific request was designed as a way to stimulate the memory of forgotten ideas that might be a clue to Zone Three's malaise. Although the attempt does not succeed—"Each song, each set of verses, each tale, came out so pat and smooth and smiling"—Lusik, the chronicler, realizes that "this was at least partly because it [the festival] had already taken place—but elsewhere." Identifying the improved condition of Zone Three with the secret ceremonies of the Zone Four women, he notes: "When those women strove and struggled to lift their poor heads up so they could see our mountains towering over them it was as if they were secretly pouring energy and effort into springs that fed us all" (176-77). He therefore concludes with one of his most explicit statements about the significance of Al•Ith's trip to Zone Four: "When Al•Ith made her forced descent to that dreary land it was for us all."

Because Al•Ith descended to places and feelings not accepted by her zone, it is not surprising that she is quickly forgotten by her people. Lusik tells us that "she is connected in the general mind with that [past bad] time"; her visits home "made her sound bizarre.... As it were tainted and contaminated." Finally, he explicitly identifies her with "those who represent places in ourselves we find it dangerous to approach" (177). Such dark places, however, are also accessible to the storyteller, and while this ability to evoke them is frightening, it is also necessary. Thus Lusik concludes: "there is a mystery here....without the sting of otherness, of—even—the vicious, without the terrible energies of the underside of health, sanity, sense, then nothing works or *can* work....the ordinary, the decent—these are nothing without the hidden powers that pour forth continually from their shadow sides. Their hidden aspects contained and tempered" (243). These energies of the shadow must be acknowledged and incorporated by both Al•Ith and her zone into their overall sense of self.

I have earlier noted that both Al•Ith and Ben Ata are able to endure their initial conflicts and a highly disorienting time of change because of their equality and their openness to a source of power both outside them (the order of the Providers to marry) and within them (their confidence and sense of responsibility as rulers). According to the narrator: "If they were nothing else, these two, they were representatives and embodiments of their respective countries. Concern for their realms was what they were" (61). Without their obedience to a higher authority and their sense of responsibility to their zones, they could never have stayed together, much less overcome their initial antipathy. Yet almost from the beginning, while finding each other repugnant, they are able to feel a bond in terms of their commitment to a higher ideal—their gradual awareness that something is wrong with their realms.

Their first real moment of communication comes when Al•Ith confronts Ben Ata with the fact that the animals are despondent and that the birthrate among both animals and people is falling: "I think that things are very serious. Very bad. Dangerous. They must be! ... for us to be together, like this. Ordered to be. Don't you see?" (58). Instead of simply dwelling on their personal situation in all its frustrating and unpleasant detail, Al•Ith assumes that because they have been ordered to come together there must be some larger purpose or significance which makes sense of their own personal troubles, and she begins to search for that larger meaning. When she returns to Zone Four, after her first visit home to Zone Three, she is able to state explicitly, "We are here for a purpose—to heal our two countries and to discover where it is that we have gone wrong, and what it is we should be doing, really doing" (97).

* * *

The ability of Al•Ith and Ben Ata to place their unhappiness in a larger context, to connect it to a purpose and meaning beyond their personal situation, is one of the major differences between *Marriages* and *Shikasta*. The people on Shikasta lack the ability to search beneath their personal pain for some deeper truth that will both make sense of their unhappiness and give them the strength and vision to deal with it. The whole purpose of Canopus's intervention in Shikasta's history is to stimulate Shikastans to make this search. As Rachel's experience shows, however, it is not that easy for Shikastans to gain this kind of detachment.

This ability to detach themselves enough from their feelings to become open to other influences (an ability which is the basis for the process of change that both Al•Ith and Ben Ata and their zones undergo) is one of the most powerful examples of how Lessing's study of Sufi principles has affected *Marriages*. In fact, we can see now that Lessing's whole mythic fiction is based on a Sufi-like vision of correspondences between the individual and the world, the internal and external, the physical and the spiritual.

From a psychological perspective, we can now see that the Zones function as psychic entities. For Al•Ith, Zone Three represents the ego, and Zones Four and Five constitute the personal and the collective unconscious respectively. Her movement toward Zone Two suggests her gradual movement toward the "self," toward a new integration of the conscious and unconscious parts of her personality. From a mystical perspective, the zones can be understood as different spiritual states as defined in Sufism. Zone Five suggests the animal spirit—the body without awareness or consciousness. Ben Ata awakens Zone Five to the human spirit, the condition of Zone Four. Here human beings have the power of consciousness; they are able to discern truth from error, good from evil, etc. Zone Three suggests the greater consciousness of a more fully realized human spirit, while Zone Two hints at the angelic spirit, a higher level of spirit now completely free of the outer form of the body. Zone One is mentioned only once in *Marriages* and we have no information about it. Presumably it represents a still higher spiritual state.

From a historical perspective, the zones can be seen as analogues for the different ways that human kind has related to the cosmos in different eras. Zone Five may be equated with the simple sense of oneness with the forces of nature of primitive peoples. Zone Four evokes the new sense of separateness from the rest of nature that came with the scientific revolution; here the inhabitants, like modern industrial societies, stress their ability to control and manipulate others and their separation from nature. Zone Three suggests the near future in which an integrated and mature humanity will recognize its unique powers of consciousness, but at the same time be aware of its unity with the rest of creation and of the need to cooperate with the natural world. Finally, Zone Two functions as that timeless state beyond death in which the understanding of oneness learned in the physical world (through the marriage of the zones) prepares the soul for another state of union, when the physical body has been shed.

We can also correlate the changes that Ben Ata and Al•Ith undergo in their adjustment to each other with the spiritual transformations described in a classic Sufi text. Al•Ith and Ben Ata's spiritual growth corresponds remarkably closely to the first four of seven valleys which had to be crossed by Sufi Pilgrims seeking the Lord of Creation in a twelveth-century allegorical poem by the Sufi poet Attar, entitled *Colloquy of the Birds*.

The first of these is the "Valley of The Quest" in which the spiritual traveler must learn to "detach [his] ... heart from all that exists" in order to give himself up totally to "the quest symbolized by this valley" (Masani 85). Al•Ith and Ben Ata must also search for the meaning of their forced marriage when they first meet and must detach themselves from their old ways of thinking and behaving in order to open themselves up to the new experiences and understandings that their marriage will bring.

In the next valley in Attar's poem, the "Valley of Love," the true lover is "plunged in fire"; "He must not for a moment think of consequences" but be willing to endure anything to draw near his beloved (Masani 87). Similarly Al•Ith and Ben Ata, when they are reunited after their period of separation and search, now enter fully into their marriage, submerging themselves in their love without reservations or thoughts of consequences. In Attar's "Valley of Knowledge," the third of the series, "the progress of each individual will depend on the degree of perfection that each will have attained, and the approximation of each to the goal will be in accordance with the state of his heart and the strength of his will" (Masani 91-92). Thus Al•Ith, following her marriage and her return to Zone Three, will have a new understanding of the complacency of her people and will now long for Zone Two. Similarly Ben Ata, following his visit to Zone Five and meeting with Vahshi, will now understand what Al•Ith was trying to tell him about his zone being poor.

"Complete detachment from the world, which in this place is not worth a straw," is the essence of Attar's fourth valley, the "Valley of The Detachment"; Attar's guide tells his pilgrims: "Sacrifice your soul and your heart in this road. If not, they will turn you away from the path of Independence" (Masani 97, 99). Similarly, in their own ways Al•Ith and Ben Ata must each become independent of all they knew and loved. Al•Ith comes to dwell in a little shack at the edge of Zone Two, cut off from all contact with others, longing only to be allowed to cross into that other zone and world. Ben Ata, who has spent all his life as a soldier, must dismiss most of his army and help his country acquire the ways of peace and prosperity. He must detach himself from his love for Al•Ith and involve himself with Zone Five and marry its Queen. He must forget his own training and teach his people to look up to the mountains of Zone Three. Finally, he must be sensitive enough to Al•Ith's needs to be able to go to Zone Three and rescue her from her imprisonment.

In another sense, however, the zones themselves correspond to the first four valleys of Attar's journey. Vahsti and her people in Zone Five in their restless wanderings are symbolic of the "Valley of The Quest." Ben Ata and his people dwell in the "Valley of Love" and Ben Ata's love for Vhasti awakens her to this spiritual stage while Al•Ith's love for Ben Ata gradually draws him closer to her realm, Zone Three, the "Valley of Knowledge." It is only after Al•Ith has taken the secrets of love learned from Zone Four back with her to Zone Three and assimilated them into a deeper knowledge of who she is that she can gradually approach Zone Two, the "Valley of Detachment." Thus the zones can be seen as symbolic of the stages the soul needs to pass through in it movement toward union with the Divine. It is only when all the physical zones (and the spiritual qualities associated with them) have been assimilated and married that the soul is prepared to enter Zone Two and acquire transcendence. We might also note that Attar's fifth valley, the "Valley of Unity," seems to correspond to Zone One. This valley is "the region in which everything is renounced and everything is unified, where there is no distinction in number and quality"; because here "all ... individuals ... compose only one, this group is complete in its oneness" (Masani 101).

* * *

Part of the rebirth process involves storytelling itself, and Lessing seems to emphasize this deliberately in *Marriages*. She specifically makes the narrator a chronicler and singer of songs and at various places in the narrative relates how the different zones turn the facts of Al•Ith and Ben Ata's marriage into story, song and art. As she says in her 1980 interview, "We never stop telling ourselves stories; it is the way we structure reality" (qtd. in Bigsby 206). What makes *Marriages* particularly innovative is that Lessing seems intent on providing women with a new way of structuring their reality. As Christ has pointed out, not only have "WOMEN'S STORIES ... not been told," but also "women often live out inauthentic stories provided by a culture they did not create" (*Diving* 1). In *Marriages* Lessing offers women an authentic new story, embodying new possibilities for them and for "us all." It is a story of such resonance and power as to suggest a new myth—the myth of a strong woman who faces the negative forces around her (embodied in her marriage to a strong but wholly patriarchal man) and within her (suggested by her descent into feelings of dependence and jealousy). The balancing of her powers against those of an equally strong man creates a new synthesis, their marriage (and their son) and both are changed in the process—each incorporating some of the other's strengths. Furthermore, their transformation leads to the transformation of the social world around them, which now mirrors the new synthesis created by their marriage.

Some of the consequences of Lessing's myth for our cultural future are suggested by Riane Eisler in *The Chalice and the Blade*, a multi-disciplinary study of the implications of "a gender-holistic perspective" (xvii) for cultural evolution. Eisler not only gathers together the evidence supporting the existence of a partnership mode of relations between women and men in pre-history, but she also traces the emergence of a new contemporary thrust toward this cooperative mode of interaction, after millennia of rule by male domination. For Eisler, our choice of partnership or dominator modes of social interaction will determine the "direction of our cultural evolution, particularly whether it will be peaceful or warlike" (xix).

Marriages seems to trace this movement, within individual zones and between the zones, from patriarchal and matriarchal modes to a new partnership model of social relations between women and men. The novel also provides a rethinking of Lessing's earlier works and our own recent history, suggesting that the fragmented identities and relationships which characterized both were the inevitable consequences of dominator modes of thinking and relating. *Marriages'* new story suggests that women are now strong enough and men are sufficiently openminded to begin the exciting, although at times disorienting, task of learning to live and work together as equals, both for their mutual development as individuals and for the future of the world.

To the same effect, by conjoining Jungian and Sufi insights and grounding them in social realities, Lessing not only makes available to the West previously unexplored or ignored ways of knowing, but in the very act of "marrying" Eastern and Western thought is offering a model for cooperation and interchange between nations. From this perspective, Zones Four and Five can easily be seen to suggest aspects of the underdeveloped and undeveloped world, while Zone Three might be the West's own perception of its ideal self. Her parable, then, suggests that we have some vital things to learn from as well as much to offer to those less well off than ourselves. In fact *Marriages* reminds us that our very futures depend on our discovery of this mutual interdependence.

As much as Lessing seems to argue for an interdependent universe in which politics, religion and cultural and sexual equality must be directed toward furthering a holistic balance, however, so much does she seem to have doubted that modern individuals were ready to exercise the kind of detachment needed to achieve it. Thus after *Marriages* she returns again to a more complex narrative structure and to a concern with the fragmentation and obsessive egoism that characterize much modern thinking. The times, however, may be changing, and perhaps Lessing's own poignant comments on *Marriages* will provide the necessary stimulus for readers who appreciate her achievement: "this book goes right down into me pretty deep. How and why I really don't know.... It will never happen again" (qtd. in Bigsby 204).

Works Cited

Bigsby, Christopher. "Interview with Doris Lessing." *The Radical Imagination and the Liberal Tradition. Interviews with English and American Novelists.* Ed. Heide Ziegler and Christopher Bigsby. London: Junction, 1982. 190-208.

Cederstrom, Lorelei. *Fine-Tuning the Feminine Psyche: Jungian Patterns in the Novels of Doris Lessing.* New York: Lang, 1990.

Chittick, William. *The Sufi Path of Love: The Spiritual Teachings of Rumi.* Albany: SUNY P, 1983.

Christ, Carol. *Diving Deep and Surfacing: Women Writers on Spiritual Quest.* Boston: Beacon, 1980.

———. "Spiritual Quest and Women's Experience." *Anima* 1.2 (1975): 4-15.

Draine, Betsy. *Substance under Pressure: Artistic Coherence and Evolving Form in the Novels of Doris Lessing.* Madison: U of Wisconsin P, 1983.

Eisler, Riane. *The Chalice and the Blade: Our History, Our Future.* San Francisco: Harper, 1987.

Fishburn, Katherine. *The Unexpected Universe of Doris Lessing: A Study in Narrative Technique.* Westport: Greenwood, 1985.

Hardin, Nancy Shields. "Doris Lessing and the Sufi Way." *Contemporary Literature* 14 (1973): 565-81.

———. "The Sufi Teaching Story and Doris Lessing." *Twentieth-Century Literature* 23 (1977): 314-25.

Hinz, Evelyn J., and John J. Teunissen. "The Pieta as Icon in *The Golden Notebook." Doris Lessing: Critical Studies.* Ed. Annis Pratt and L.S. Dembo. Madison: U of Wisconsin P, 1974. 40-53.

"Jung, Carl. "Concerning Rebirth." *Archetypes and the Collective Unconscious.* Trans. R. F. C. Hull. Vol. 9, part 1 of *The Collected Works of C. G. Jung.* Bollingen Series XX. Princeton: Princeton UP, 1969. 113-47.

———. "Psychological Aspects of the Kore." *Archetypes and the Collective Unconscious.* Trans. R. F. C. Hull. Vol. 9, part 1 of *The Collected Works of C. G. Jung.* Bollingen Series XX. Princeton: Princeton UP, 1969. 182-203.

Kaplan, Carey. "Britain's Imperialist Past in Doris Lessing's Futuristic Fiction." *Doris Lessing: The Alchemy of Survival*. Ed. Carey Kaplan and Ellen Cronan Rose. Athens: Ohio UP, 1988. 149-58.

Kérenyi, C. *Eleusis: Archetypal Image of Mother and Daughter*. Trans. Ralph Manheim. London: Routledge, 1967.

Lessing, Doris. *Briefing for a Descent into Hell*. London: Cape, 1971.

———. *The Four-Gated City*. 1969. New York: Bantam, 1970.

———. *The Golden Notebook*. 1962. New York: Bantam, 1973.

———. "Interview." *Doris Lessing Newsletter* 4.2 (1980): 1.

———. Introduction. *Learning How To Learn: Psychology and Spirituality in the Sufi Way*. By Idries Shah. San Francisco: Harper, 1981. 6 unnumbered pages, of which pages 3 and 4 are reversed.

———. *Landlocked*. 1965. London: Granada, 1967.

———. *The Marriages Between Zones Three, Four, and Five. Canopus in Argos: Archives*. 1980. London: Grafton, 1981.

———. *Martha Quest*. 1952. London: Granada, 1966.

———. *Memoirs of a Survivor*. 1974. New York: Bantam, 1976.

———. *Re: Colonised Planet 5. Shikasta*. 1979. London: Granada, 1981.

———. *A Small Personal Voice: Essays, Reviews, Interviews*. Ed. Paul Schleuter, 1956. New York: Vintage, 1975.

Masani, R. P. *Persian Mysticism*. New Delhi: Award Publishing House, 1981.

Nasr, Seyyed Hossein. *Sufi Essays*. London: Allen, 1972.

Perrakis, Phyllis Sternberg. "Doris Lessing's *The Golden Notebook: Separation and Symbiosis*." *American Imago* 38.4 (1981): 407-28.

———. "The Marriage of Inner and Outer Space in Lessing's *Shikasta*." *Science-Fiction Studies* 17.2 (1990): 221-38.

Pratt, Annis. *Archetypal Patterns in Women's Fiction*. Bloomington: Indiana UP, 1981.

Rubenstein, Roberta. *The Novelistic Vision of Doris Lessing: Breaking the Forms of Consciousness*. Urbana: U of Illinois P, 1979.

Schimmel, Annemarie. *Mystical Dimensions of Islam*. Chapel Hill: U of North Carolina P, 1975.

Shah, Idries. *Learning How to Learn: Psychology and Spirituality in the Sufi Way*. San Francisco: Harper, 1981.

Sprague, Claire, and Virginia Tiger, eds. *Critical Essays on Doris Lessing*. Boston: Hall, 1986.

Tiger, Virginia. "Candid Shot: Lessing in New York City, April 1 and 2, 1984," Sprague and Tiger 221-23.

Vlastos, Marion. "Doris Lessing and R. D. Laing: Psychopolitics and Prophecy." Sprague and Tiger 126-40.

ROBERT BOSCHMAN

Excrement and "Kitsch" in Doris Lessing's "The Good Terrorist"

Behind all the European faiths, religious and political, we find the first chapter of Genesis, which tells us that the world was created properly, that human existence is good, and that we are therefore entitled to multiply. Let us call this basic faith *a categorical agreement with being*.

The fact that until recently the word "shit" appeared in print as s–has nothing to do with moral considerations. You can't claim that shit is immoral, after all! The objection to shit is a metaphysical one. The daily defecation session is daily proof of the unacceptability of Creation. Either/or: either shit is acceptable (in which case don't lock yourself in the bathroom!) or we are created in an unacceptable manner.

It follows, then, that the aesthetic ideal of the categorical agreement with being is a world in which shit is denied and everyone acts as though it did not exist. This aesthetical ideal is called *kitsch*.

"Kitsch" is a German word born in the middle of the sentimental nineteenth century, and from German it entered all Western languages. Repeated use, however, has obliterated its original metaphysical meaning: *kitsch* is the absolute denial of shit, in both the literal and figurative senses of the word; *kitsch* excludes everything from its purview which is essentially unacceptable in human existence.
—Milan Kundera, *The Unbearable Lightness of Being*

From *Ariel* 25, 3 (July 1994). © 1994 by The Board of Governors, The University of Calgary.

Like Swift's Gulliver, Alice Mellings, the bifurcated protagonist of Doris
Lessing's *The Good Terrorist* (1985), has her own "strict rules of decency"
(Swift 19). The result of a comfortable middle-class childhood, these rules
are ironically seen as "shit" by the other members of the revolutionary group
which she calls her family. Alice, in fact, is caught between two opposing
kinds of kitsch: between the British middle-class kitsch that in her mind
represents decency and cleanliness, and the terrorist kitsch that stands for the
ruthless destruction of that middle-class. Besides Kundera's definition-by-
negation, kitsch is more simply a word for pretension, and pretension is
Alice's forte. According to *The Good Terrorist*, the contradictory roles that
Alice adopts are equally mendacious. The point is that Alice and her friends
cannot finally escape kitsch at all; they need it to conceal and deny the
various kinds of "shit" that attend their existence even on the margins of
society.

Applied to Lessing's novel, Kundera's shit/kitsch paradigm is useful in
much the same way that Norman O. Brown, over thirty years ago, found
Freud's theory of sublimation useful for discussing Swift's penchant for the
scatological: "Swift's ultimate horror ... was at the thought that
sublimation—that is to say, all civilized behavior—is a lie and cannot survive
confrontation with the truth" (188). Brown's thesis derived part of its
impetus from a rigorous psychoanalysis of (or Gulliverian surgical procedure
on) earlier Swiftian critics, such as Aldous Huxley, Ricardo Quintana, and
Middleton Murry, who had managed either to evade or to sublimate the
unpalatable truth that Swift obsessively presents in terms of excrement. The
irony that Swiftian critics should "prove incapable of seeing what there is to
see" (180) was not lost on Brown. He wrote, "It is a perfect example, in the
field of literary criticism, of Freud's notion that the first way in which
consciousness becomes conscious of a repressed idea is by emphatically
denying it" (181).[1] Nevertheless, even Brown's iconoclastic criticism bows to
Gulliver's "strict rules of decency." With its series of dashes to conceal the
word *shit*, Brown's essay in *Life Against Death* itself formally bows to the
universal human neurosis, just as Gulliver, disrobing before his Houyhnhnm
master to reveal his Yahoo-like torso, refuses—with post-Edenic
furtiveness—to uncover his genitals (Swift 191).[2]

It has taken the passage of another quarter century since *Life Against
Death* for a writer like Doris Lessing to expose unabashedly our continuing
desire to hide shit behind aesthetical and political ideals. Lessing, in fact, uses
the words *shit*, *shitty*, and *bullshit* over fifty times throughout the novel.
Together with synonyms such as *excrement* and *faeces*, shit and its variants
gather such force that terms like *muck*, *rubbish*, *waste*, *trash*, *garbage*, the

euphemistic *matériel*, and even (in a manner that Freud would appreciate) *money* reverberate with excremental meaning. By thus employing scatalogical terminology and imagery, Lessing takes up Swift's desire to disclose the ways in which kitsch is used to conceal the unacceptable reality of the body's excretory functions, as well as how, on metaphorical levels, shit becomes a rhetorical device for denouncing the enemy. The first part of this essay therefore focusses on demonstrating how in *The Good Terrorist* excrement functions both literally and figuratively as a symbol of all that is deemed unacceptable by various individuals, fringe groups, and established institutions within society, whose definitions of what precisely constitutes *shit* or *waste* are often conflicting. Part Two examines Lessing's project from a more general historical and theoretical perspective; lastly, Part Three looks at how Lessing's radical characters are caught up in the machinations of a kitsch culture, even while they stridently claim to have freed themselves from it.

Like Brown (but with none of his refinement), Lessing shows us how persons from *all* levels of society closet the truth of the body behind aesthetical ideals. She understands how a so-called subversive like Alice Mellings will sublimate the truth as much as, say, her father Cedric, who occupies what Defoe's Crusoe calls "the middle station of life" (32). What Alice does in the novel, with her tormented attitude toward money, property, and sexuality, is to make this disagreeable fact indisputably obvious. Through Alice, Lessing's whole thrust seems to be to expose the excremental truth that lurks behind the images on which our civilization is built. About excrement Brown states:

> Excrement is the dead life of the body, and so long as humanity prefers a dead life to living, so long is humanity committed to treating as excrement not only its own body but the surrounding world of objects, reducing all to dead matter and inorganic magnitudes. Our much prized "objectivity" toward our own bodies, other persons, and the universe, all our calculating "rationality," is, from the psycho-analytical point of view, an ambivalent mixture of love and hate, an attitude appropriate only toward excrement, and appropriate toward excrement only in an animal that has lost his own body and life. (295)

I

If Alice and her radical colleagues view the system in excremental terms, the system's representatives, particularly the police, neighbours, and Alice's middle-class parents, associate the crew of squatters with trash and faeces. Similarly, individuals within and on the periphery of Alice's group who differ ideologically comment on each other using scatological language, and several group members' personal histories are also described in terms of shit. With the "middle-class expertise" which she despises and yet employs, Alice perceives the condemned house in which she lives as unclean and wasted (102), its top-floor room "a scene of plastic buckets, topped with shit" (6). The group itself, however, is clearly portrayed as divided over what, concerning the condition of the house, is acceptable and what is not. Finally, from the narrative point of view, the novel's sustained irony implies that the group's squalid revolutionary politics and Alice's putative middle-class expertise are themselves kinds of excrement.

Alice refers to her mother, Dorothy, as a "shitty old fascist" (407) with "shitty rich friends" (22). She also scorns her father, Cedric, for

> printing fucking garbage for this or that bloody faction in the fascist bloody Labour Party, printing dishwater newspapers for bloody liberals and revisionists, sucking up to shitty politicians on the make and bourgeois trash anyway doomed to be swept into the dustbins of history. (248)

Alice objects to her parents' complicity in what she sees as a corrupt social order: "This shitty rubbish we live in" (406). With its "shitty great enormous buildings" (20), modern Britain is condemned by Alice and her co-conspirators as a wasteland worthy only of destruction. One group member, Caroline, "saw the light—that is, that the System was rotten and needed a radical overthrow—when she was eighteen" (354). More violently, Faye "want[s] to put an end to this shitty fucking filthy lying cruel hypocritical system" (129). Jocelin takes several of the group members on a neighborhood practice bombing run to blow up "Something absolutely shitty" (359). They eventually destroy a cement bollard, its bases "stained with dog urine and shit" (361), and Alice views the bollard as "some kind of invincible stupidity made evident and visible." Alice, moreover, is enraged not just by the rubbish and excrement collected in and around a house cast off by the establishment, but also by the "sordid piles" of junk in the attic, evidence of "Bloody filthy *accumulating* middle-class creeps" (193).

Dorothy Mellings, for her part, views her daughter and the group as "rotten" (399) and "just peasants" (406), "full of rubbish and pretensions" (398). Cedric calls Alice "some sort of wild animal.... beyond ordinary judgement" (250). The squatters' neighbours are infuriated by these "Nasty dirty people" (76), and when Alice and Jim bury the buckets of excrement in the garden "shouts of 'Pigs!'" come from the garden opposite (79). Unable to hide their hatred, the police eventually knock on the door to fling a plastic bag of faeces into the hall, yelling "shit to shit" (387). Yet here the narrator also implies a kind of excremental correspondence between the revolutionaries and the police that is reminiscent of an observation by the Professor in Conrad's *The Secret Agent:* "Like to like. The terrorist and the policeman both come from the same basket. Revolution, legality—counter moves in the same game; forms of idleness at bottom identical" (94).

Ideological differences within the loosely-knit group itself are also portrayed in terms of excrement and refuse. Bert and Jasper call a meeting of "the real revolutionaries, not the rubbish" (337). With their "Furniture, pretty curtains, and a large double bed" (168), Reggie and Mary are far too "sensible" (344) and middle-class to be included in the revolutionary agenda. Indeed, Reggie's profession as a chemist suggests the kind of polluting activity which the group vehemently opposes with pickets and, ironically, spray paint (344). Solid Greenpeace members, Reggie and Mary, in turn, display contempt and loathing for their more subversive housemates. As Faye states, "We're just shit to them, that's all" (390). Yet she rejects the radicals squatting next door as "just amateurish rubbish" (130), and "shitty Comrade Andrew and his works" (346) are eventually perceived as too closely linked to corrupt Russian Communism.

The two brown cases of guns euphemistically called *matériel*, which Andrew's associates try to force Alice to keep in the house, are dumped by the group in a scrap metal yard "where every kind of rubbish had found a place" (382). Lessing's irony is unmistakable when Bert exclaims, on opening the packages to discover an arms cache: "You'd think we were scared shitless—and I believe I am. Suddenly, it's all for real" (379). This irony— that the revolution is itself a kind of excrement—becomes heightened when Bert and Jasper beat "the sleek brown monsters" to make them look "just like all the other rubbish lying around":

> Jasper, deadly, swift, efficient, was rubbing soil into the smooth
> professional surfaces of the packages, and scarring them with a bit
> of iron he had snatched up from a heap, working in a fury of
> precise intention and achievement. That was Jasper! Alice

thought, proud of him, her pride singing through her.... Why, beside him Bert was a peasant, slowly coming to himself and seeing what Jasper was doing. (383)

The usually indolent Jasper is portrayed as a man who has wasted his adult life feeding off Alice's efforts, which he occasionally rewards by taking her out for an intoxicating evening of spray-painting slogans. Besides preying on others, Jasper can only deface and pollute the environment, and almost everyone in the novel finds him repulsive. His act of pissing on suburbia, which Alice witnesses, aptly evokes his nature: "From the top of her house a single yellow jet splashed onto the rubbish that filled the garden" (27). The irony here applies exclusively to Jasper and Alice: Jasper because he is thoroughly duplicitous and unaware of his own stupidity, and Alice because she continually rationalizes her association with a man she knows is a "rat." She sublimates the truth about Jasper in the same way that she buries the squat's buckets of shit in the back garden. Even more than Gulliver (who urinates on the Lilliputian Palace in order to save it from destruction by fire and thereby undermines the form or face of government) Jasper unwittingly satirizes himself and Alice by pissing out the window on a yard full of trash. As Gulliver discovers in Lilliput, the Body Politic has its own legal dress or fictive covering; and by undermining *polity* (through pissing on the Palace and outraging the Queen), his act demonstrates the conflict between truth, as represented by excrement, and kitsch, as represented "by the *fundamental* laws" that his saving action transgresses (Swift 45; emphasis added). Jasper, on the other hand, sees himself as a ruthless, cunning terrorist when, in fact, he is a poseur much like Conrad's Verloc in *The Secret Agent*. Although Jasper does not "wallow" or possess Verloc's "fat-pig style" (Conrad 52), his laziness evokes the earlier character: he "lounge[s], drinking beer" (86) while Alice feeds him, clears the squat of rubbish and excrement (62), and finances his sexual liaisons with other men.

What Alice witnesses when she sees Jasper pissing out the window can be interpreted as another instance of "shit to shit," and, to be sure, *The Good Terrorist* is full of such excremental correspondences. Despite the "terrorist" kitsch that motivates her existence as a squatter, Alice is solidly middle-class as she defends and forgives Jasper because he has "had a shitty family" (254). Glib psychological summaries like this are given to rationalize the actions of several members of the group, like the violent, suicidal Faye, who has had, according to Roberta, "an awful shitty terrible life" (128). Not only are the group members' "shitty" histories portrayed as spilling over into a destructive, violent present, but their inability to face and to deal with their own "shit," in Alice's view, indicates a lack of middle-class expertise. Alice, in fact, with her ability to put all kinds of shit in the appropriate place, fits Freud's profile of the anal erotic. Such personalities are

> remarkable for a regular combination of the three following combinations: they are exceptionally *orderly, parsimonious,* and *obstinate.* Each of these words really covers a small group or series of traits which are related to one another. 'Orderly' comprises both bodily cleanliness and reliability and conscientiousness in the performance of petty duties: the opposite of it would be 'untidy' and 'negligent.' 'Parsimony' may be exaggerated up to the point of avarice; and obstinacy may amount to defiance, with which irascibility and vindictiveness may easily be associated. The two latter qualities—parsimony and obstinacy—hang together more closely than the third, orderliness; they are too, the more constant element in the whole complex. It seems to me, however, incontestable that all three in some way hang together. (Freud 45-46)

Later in his essay, Freud goes on to say that "The cleanliness, orderliness, and reliability give exactly the impression of a reaction-formation against an interest in things that are unclean and intrusive and ought not to be on the body ('Dirt is matter in the wrong place')" (48).[3]

Indeed, readers of *The Good Terrorist* can easily imagine Alice saying "Dirt is matter in the wrong place" at many points in the novel, but particularly as she and Jim bury the buckets of excrement in the garden. The cockney (and black) Jim is frightened by the thought of "how much shit we all make in our lives": "they say our sewers are all old and rotten. Suppose they just explode?" (80). For Jim, the public sewer-system's fragility has metaphorical implications that are both private and public: "'I mean, we just go on living in this city,' he said, full of despair" (81). According to Alice, Jim's sense of helplessness stems from his lack of middle-class expertise (198), and it is this lack of expertise (or plain bad luck, helped by Alice) that also gets him fired from his job by Cedric. Confronting her father later on, Alice typically calls this firing "a shitty, bloody fascist thing to do" (244), knowing that she rather than Jim is guilty of stealing money from Cedric's office. The connection between money and excrement has, of course, been made by Freud and will be examined further on in this essay, but suffice it to say, as Brown quotes Ferenczi, that "[Money] is seen to be nothing other than odourless dehydrated filth that has been made to shine. *Pecunia non olet*"

(Brown 287). Alice's middle-class know-how enables her not only to steal her father's money but also to bury the shit, "have a cup of tea and forget it," all of which makes the blue-collar Jim incredulous. From his perspective, Alice's "know-how" amounts to denial, and the garden becomes a symbol of both private and public repression: "You say, Come and have a cup of tea. And that's the end of it. But it isn't the end of it, not on your life it isn't" (81).

The narrative suggests that Alice tries to bury her own unacceptable past in a manner that parallels the garden scene with Jim. She gets the idea to dig the pit at the same time as she recalls the harsh political argument between Dorothy and her mother's leftist friend, Zoë (75). Their conflict suggests Alice's own divided sensibility, her two worlds (313)—the middle-class, on the one hand, and the marginalized group with idealized proletarian pretensions, on the other—which she straddles irresolutely. The memory makes her feel like vomiting (75) just before she begins the "loathsome" task of burying the excrement—"in a miasma that did not seem to lessen but, rather, spread from the house and the garden to the street" (79). Alice, in fact, cannot repress her past any more than she can bury and forget about the faeces, which the police feel duty-bound to dig up again (316-17). The "explosion of order" (49) that she brings to the household stems from her repressed middle-class background, a background which is largely unacceptable to her as well as to the group's would-be ideologues, although they take advantage of her while they can.

Alice's background compels her to see the squat as "Waste. All this *waste*" (102), and to deal with "the weight of that vandalised house" (45) by manipulating the system which has allowed it to become unsanitary (66). While her efforts to clean and reorganize the house attract Mary and Reggie and impress Comrade Andrew (obviously for different reasons), they do not so easily win the approval of others in the house, and the ideological reasoning behind the others' scepticism is something to which, paradoxically (and hypocritically), Alice herself is committed. "We are not here," states Jasper when he and Alice first inspect the derelict squat, "to make ourselves comfortable" (6). Later, after Alice has made them comfortable, Jasper chides: "You are making us all sick.... We all think you've gone rotten. All you care about is your comfort" (241). Faye scathingly denounces Alice: "Any minute now we are going to have hot running water and double glazing, I wouldn't be surprised. For me this is all a lot of shit, do you hear? *Shit!*" (127). And, in terms of one part of Alice's bifurcated sensibility, the part that wants to be a genuine revolutionary, Faye may be right. In terms, however, of that part of Alice which yearns for middle-class order, it is Faye who, together with Roberta, is wasted and excremental: "They like it ... like living in filth.... They need it" (197).

Next door, Andrew tries to resolve Alice's inner rift by telling her that "there is nothing wrong with a comfortable life" (203), for he is also acutely aware that Alice's middle-class efficiency and sense of loyalty make her less prone to the "stupid silly mess[es]" that are the result even of "KGB plots" (312). (Indeed, "plump, healthy" Caroline, who "[exudes] physical enjoyment" [310], refuses to participate in Alice's group's bombing foray against the Kubla Khan Hotel, calling it "All amateur rubbish" [446].) Andrew sees Alice as potentially "pure" because she has a fierce need for order and organization coupled with a hatred of the status quo. But Alice, who takes part in the badly bungled bombing, rejects Andrew's complimentary insight: "You couldn't use the word 'pure' like that in Britain now, it simply wasn't on, it was just silly" (280). Caught at the end of the novel between the sinister O'Leary, looking for his *matériel*, and Peter Cecil, of "MI-6 or MI-5 or XYZ or one of those bloody things" (453), Alice is certainly not pure. She is sandwiched too much between conflicting types of excrement to see Andrew's point.

II

At the close of the novel, the narrator significantly refers to Alice as "the poor baby" (456), suggesting her stunted development and seeming therefore to preclude the possibility of change. The narrator stresses that, because Alice is sandwiched between ideologies, her own personal development, has been stunted: "Alice was stocky, and she had a pudgy, formless look to her" and a "plump childlike formless face" (11, 59). The "grublike" Jasper is "the meaning and purpose of [Alice's] life" (91) because he permits her to cultivate her middle-class "good-girl" virtues and to believe that she is a genuine revolutionary at the same time. Thus, on one level, the novel's oxymoronic title suggests both sides of Alice's contradictory personality. She is torn between "doing good" and terrorizing her family and society, between rebuilding the vandalized house where the would-be revolutionaries squat and tearing down the social order that she sees in excremental terms.[4]

Freud's profile of the anal erotic is once again helpful to us in coming to terms with Alice's divided character; and, to be sure, the issues that Lessing explores via Alice—issues of sexuality, excrement (waste management), and money—are precisely the issues articulated by Freud as most crucial in the makeup of the anal-erotic personality. In his essay "On the Transformation of Instincts with Special Reference to Anal Erotism" (1916), Freud states:

> To begin with, it would appear that in the products of the unconscious—spontaneous ideas, phantasies, symptoms—the conceptions *faeces* (money, gift), *child* and *penis* are seldom distinguished and are easily interchangeable....these elements in the unconscious are often treated as if they were equivalent and could replace one another. (166)

From this perspective, which, as Freud himself notes, is not easily sorted out (Freud 169), it is possible to see how Alice might, for instance, view Jasper's penis as a form of shit, which she does not have to consider putting inside her vagina, since Jasper is a homosexual. If the child-like Alice is as alienated from her own adult body as the novel indicates (Lessing 243), then vaginal "cleanliness" would be as important to her as rectal cleanliness. "Faeces, penis and child," says Freud, "are all three solid bodies: they all three, by forcible entry or expulsion, stimulate a membranous passage, that is, the rectum and the vagina, the latter being as it were 'rented' from the rectum, as Lou Andreas-Salome remarks" (Freud 171).

Further, according to Freud, money is merely the point of transference for shit as gift in early personal development. "It is probable," he writes, "that the first significance which faecal interest develops is not 'gold— money', but 'gift.'" On this subject, Brown adds: "Money is inorganic dead matter which has been made alive by inheriting the magic power which infantile narcissism attributes to the excremental product.... Money inherits the infantile magic of excrement and then is able to breed and have children: interest is an increment" (Brown 279). In other words, the toddler's faeces has value in his or her eyes because the excrement is viewed as a parcel delivered from the body to the parent, which the parent, in turn, disposes of and thus rejects; later on, the mysterious value attached to shit is transferred to money, which the child learns is emphatically not rejected by the parent. In this connection, it is worthwhile to note that Alice herself is rejected by various colleagues, friends, and family members as a kind of shit, as one who has wasted her life. Interestingly, Freud also argues that the child who decides against offering up his or her faeces consequently chooses "defiance (obstinacy), a quality which springs, therefore, from a narcissitic clinging to the pleasure of anal erotism" (Freud 168).

Such "narcissistic clinging" is evident throughout *The Good Terrorist* and is directly related to Alice's rage for order, her deep desire to control and contain all the various kinds of excrement around her and yet at the same time remain defiant. By moving the buckets of shit from the squat's top floor to the pit in the garden, Alice simply qualifies her obstinacy, thus satisfying (at least temporarily) the demands of both her radical friends and her conventional past. She rids the house of excrement but still withholds it in such a way that the police and neighbors are outraged: for, in the final analysis, Alice does not part with her shit via conventional means, that is, the public sewer system. At the same time, her frenetic attempts to meet these conflicting requirements are also motivated by guilt, which Brown (among others) has shown to be inextricably involved with the money/excrement complex (Brown 290).

But such a complex surely includes the act of writing as well. A bill of any kind is also a written note, ascribing a unit of value to the bearer; similarly, the literary manuscript constitutes a composition, a putting together of words into a potentially valuable body of work that may be granted a high place in the civilized world or may also become mere compost. Brown is clear on this point when he states that "there is no aspect of higher culture uncontaminated by connections with anality" (199); and again, in connection with the death instinct, which plays a critical role in the formation of the anal character, Brown writes:

> Civilized economic activity has this death-defying and deadening structure because economic activity is sustained by psychic energy taking the form of sublimation. All civilized sublimation, and not only the pursuit of money, has this structure. Thus in the first of his odes Horace sees poetry as a career, like all careers (trader, soldier, athlete, etc.), basically characterized by self-sacrifice and instinctual renunciation; it is nevertheless worth while if success will enable him "to strike the stars with head sublime." And at the end of the third book he celebrates his success: "I have wrought a monument more enduring than bronze, and loftier than the royal accumulation of the pyramids. Neither corrosive rain nor raging wind can destroy it, nor the innumerable sequence of years nor the flight of time. I shall not altogether die." (287)

By contrast, the pilfering Jasper is viewed by Dorothy as a wastrel who "loathes anything decent, and he once wrote a terrible novel he couldn't get published" (407). Here Lessing's narrator not only follows Swift's strategy by implying a link between the acts of writing and defecation but also comes close to fulfilling one of Swift's own fears: that ultimately his work would be good only as a bum wipe (Flynn 209). Similarly, Ashraf H. A. Rushdy states: "For Swift, like Bacon, the reading of bodily functions was the best analogy for the reading function. The difference between them is that whereas Bacon began by noting how reading was akin to ingestion, Swift begins by noting how writing is akin to elimination" (Rushdy 3).

Discarding the convention of dividing the text into carefully-crafted chapters, Lessing gives her novel its own plump formlessness, which both evokes the characterization and strongly suggests "how writing is akin to elimination." Hence, this unbroken narrative of over 400 pages formally implies Jasper's "grub-like" character as well as Alice's inability to shape her experience into meaningful, manageable episodes. But more than that, the novel structurally mimics its content (which recounts a tale of human *waste* on several levels—physical, psychological, spiritual, and intellectual) so that together form and content constitute a process analogous to the act of physical elimination.

The Good Terrorist's formal stance toward bodily functions (especially the excretory function) is, in point of fact, an ironic comment on the kind of civilized activity, whether commercial or artistic, outlined and analyzed by Brown; and, like her predecessor Swift, Lessing often appears provoked by the ironic implications of her own words. Carol Houlihan Flynn's recent description of the eighteenth century as one of consumption, guilt, and ambivalent attitudes toward bodily functions could also describe the period portrayed by Lessing. Swift's age, writes Flynn,

> became, by necessity, a time of greed, for if one is material, one can never get enough, and a time of guilt, for if one is even remotely conscious, one can see the unfairnesses implicit in the distribution of goods both physical and sexual. "We are all Adam's children," went the proverb, "But Silk makes the Difference." Within such a context of desire indulged and held in check, the body becomes a site of confused attempts at ordering what gets in the way, an appetite that can never, given the conditional uneasiness of its owner, be satisfied.
>
> ... In an attempt to achieve stability in a complex, modern world of patterns threatening to break down, theorists put their minds to material at hand, material guaranteed not to go away, the body itself. It could be crammed, purged, overfed, or starved, serving

as an index for outside ills more difficult to resolve. As Lord Hervey ... complained, all physicians "jog in one beaten track; a vomit to clear your stomach, a glister to give you a stool, laudanum to quiet the pain, and then a purge to clear your bowels, and what they call 'carry it off' ". (Flynn 94-95)

Flynn rightly wonders what "it" is: "When Moll, the *Jade*, lets 'it' fly, she is letting loose the same symptoms of repletion that Swift attempts to modify and displace" (95). Whatever name we give such "symptoms of repletion," they are found everywhere in Lessing's novel: "it" is constituted by the various forms of literal and figurative shit which threaten to overwhelm civilization, and Alice is the frenzied agent who attempts "to modify and displace" them. Not surprisingly, then, *The Good Terrorist* is also "postmodern" in so far as it denies the possibility of bringing conventional modes of order to bear on certain kinds of experience. At the same time, however, Lessing portrays Alice as both desiring and rejecting such modes, with consequences that are nothing short of pathological. Perhaps the novel's most potent irony resides in its portrayal of the self-abortive character of revolution in the late twentieth century. Indeed, behind the facade of Alice's desperate activism are the familiar prostration and deadlock associated with *aporia*.

III

In poststructuralist terms, Alice's situation is "undecidable" (Eagleton 146-47) since she has adopted roles that violently contradict one another. This "undecidability" or aporia, which Samuel Beckett explored forty years ago in *The Unnamable*, repeatedly surfaces in her compulsion to switch voices. Alice is, in fact, a kind of changeling whose various voices signify different representations of self. In general, her voice is what she calls "basic BBC correct" but she also has her revolutionary "'meeting voice,' for she had learned that this was necessary if she was to hold her own" (30, 9). Beckett's narrator appears to anticipate a character like Alice when he says: "I seem to speak, it is not I, about me, it is not about me.... What am I to do, what shall I do, what should I do, in my situation, how proceed? By aporia pure and simple?" (267). *The Good Terrorist* contains a multiplicity of projected voices or auditory images—all forms of kitsch—and Alice's reflect the warring sides of her personality. She seems to have an awareness (at least at certain points [30-34]) of the images she and others hide behind, but her insight is not great enough to enable her to resolve her inner conflict. As Hannah Arendt observed of Adolf Eichmann, "his conscience spoke with a 'respectable voice,' with the voice of respectable society around him" (Arendt 126).

The connection between Lessing the novelist and Arendt the political scientist is a significant one because both writers have extensively examined how individuals within totalitarian political movements are able to rationalize acts of atrocity. In this respect, *The Good Terrorist* performs an operation similar to the political and psychological analyses that Arendt took from Eichmann's trial. Alice, in fact, displays many of the characteristics of the "systematic mendacity" that Arendt delineated in her study of Eichmann's personality (52). As Arendt frequently points out, Eichmann's case is riddled with ironies and her own response to his self-deception—to the ridiculous disparity between appearance and reality—is often caustic. Eichmann, after all, was a salesman for the Vacuum Oil Company before he joined the ranks of the S.S. and became Hitler's expert on the Jewish question (Arendt 29).

Lessing's narrator can also be caustic, as Alice's partial awareness of her own duplicity merely makes her more adept at manipulating appearances in order to achieve her goals on behalf of the group. While she is fanatically dedicated to "[pulling] everything down" (406), she is equally committed to cleaning up the squat so that, as she tells Jim, "we will be just like everyone else in the street, and after a bit no one will notice us" (36). The group's subversive activities can, according to Alice's rationale, be more effectively carried out if the excrement and rubbish collected in and around the abandoned house are cleaned up. And she can, in fact, deftly manage her own appearance in order to deceive her new neighbors or the bureaucrats who want to tear the house down:

> She knew how she seemed: the pretty daughter of her mother, short curly fair hair nicely brushed, pink-and-white face lightly freckled, open blue-grey gaze. A middle-class girl with her assurance, her knowledge of the ropes, sat properly in the chair, and if she wore a heavy blue military jacket, under it was a flowered pink-and-white blouse. (25)

Similarly, Alice appears to her neighbors as "such a nice girl, standing on the green lawn with daffodils behind her," as she switches smoothly from the discourse of hate and subversion to that of "a nice street": "How do you do? I'm Alice Mellings. I've just moved into forty-three, and we're fixing the place up, and getting the rubbish out" (76-77).

Indeed, Alice can dispense with the killer inside whenever it seems necessary or convenient (65), and contrary to what she would like to believe—and have others believe—about herself, she is "full of the energy of hate" (5), and ready to steal from and use her friends and family. At her friend Theresa's expensive flat, she goes "to the bathroom, where she emptied herself.... She was hungry. She went to the kitchen and cut herself a lavish sandwich" (22). Even as Theresa agrees to lend her £50, Alice calls her a "rich shit" and later is tempted to "take one of those little netsukes and run out, they'll think it was the Spanish woman" (22, 40). She also loots her mother's house, stealing all the curtains and an expensive rug: "At the end of the street her mother was coming towards her.... Alice ran fast the other way, clutching the heavy rug" (57). Despising her father, Cedric, for "sucking up to shitty politicians on the make" (248), Alice has no qualms about stealing large sums of cash from both his house and his office (94, 231). To be sure, she empathizes with Philip and Monica, but, again, in order to be of help, particularly to Philip, she must set aside her violent instincts. As the narrator rather awkwardly puts it: "The murderess in Alice took herself off" (65). Although she can usually read others quickly and accurately, she does so to detect weaknesses that she can use to her own advantage. Even when she identifies with Monica, who desperately needs to find decent accommodations for her family (146), Alice's compassion constitutes the exception rather than the rule, and when her plan to send the destitute Monica to her mother's house backfires, Monica tells Alice, "You are all evil and mad in this house" (224). Philip also refers to the group as "parasites" (335).

Lessing's ironic narrative not only consistently portrays the gap between what Alice is and what she purports to be, it also demonstrates how Alice tries to conceal this disparity from herself. Her definition of "a thief, a real thief" excludes her own pilfering activities only by distorting reality:

> How could she describe herself as a revolutionary, a serious person, if she was a thief? ... No. Besides, she had always been honest, had never stolen anything, not even as a child. She had not gone through that period of nicking things out of her mother's handbag, her father's pockets, the way some small children did. Never. (228)

Alice even adds another twist to the lie by implying that a real thief is one who "[chooses] a likely house, watching for its inhabitants to be out," which constitutes "a step away from herself." By some sleight-of-hand, she excludes herself from this category (although "She felt confident that she could succeed") while simultaneously convincing herself that she had never stolen anything from "her father's pockets." This process of rationalization then leads to the decision to rob her father's firm (228). Thus, although Alice ostensibly is a terrorist who is "good"—although her middle-class rage for order seems to modify, if not contradict, her hatred of the status quo—she hardly fits the description of an "honest criminal." When she throws a rock through her father's window, "the speed and force of it, the skill, could never have been deduced from how Alice was, at any other time of the day or night, good girl Alice, her mother's daughter.... She heard the shattering glass, a scream, her father's shout" (160).

Moreover, just as Alice conceals her own dishonesty from herself, she also represses her middle-class upbringing, hiding from herself the fact that her maternal activities are the result of her need to please her mother:

> At home Alice was a good girl, a good daughter, as she had always enjoyed being. It was she who managed the kitchen.... Of course, her mother was pleased to have her do it. (There was an uneasy little thought tucked away somewhere here, but Alice chose to ignore it.) (54)

To be sure, both her yearnings for family life and her terrorist activities stem from the model provided by Dorothy's earlier matriarchal and left-wing pursuits. But when her mother renounces left-wing politics, sells her house for a dingy two-room flat, and calls Alice "an all-purpose female drudge" (406), Alice, her self-image still contingent on Dorothy, feels betrayed: "[Dorothy] laughed bitterly, demolishing all the lovely years Alice thought about so longingly, killing the old Dorothy Mellings" (406).

Like Winnie in Conrad's *The Secret Agent*, however, Alice prefers not to look into things. Deeply repressed and divided, and unable even to begin to re-define herself, she is subject to sudden eruptions of malicious fury: "a scene of suburban affluence and calm provoked in her a rush of violent derision, like a secret threat to everything she saw. At the same time, parallel to this emotion and in no way affecting it, ran another current, of want, of longing" (27). As I have outlined above, Alice's view of her backyard, where she and Jim have buried an eight-month accumulation of faeces, evokes her own repressed sensibility and preoccupation with surfaces. Because she secretly knows this about herself, Alice is threatened by any kind of access to knowledge. Universities are "the visible embodiment of evil" (290), and she avoids reading books:

> She used to wonder how it was that a comrade with a good, clear, and correct view of life could be prepared to endanger it by reading all that risky equivocal stuff that she might dip into, hastily, retreating as if scalded. She had even secretly read almost to the end of one novel recommended as a useful tool in the struggle, but felt as she had as a child: if she persevered, allowing one book to lead her on to another, she might find herself lost without maps. (73)

Finally, when other modes of denial and rationalization are inadequate or unsuitable, Alice simply blocks information from her memory: "For the thousandth time the situation was recurring where Alice said, 'I don't remember, no, you're wrong,' thinking that her mother maliciously made things up, while Dorothy sighed and pursued interesting thoughts about the pathology of lying" (401-02).

Perceiving herself as betrayed and abandoned by her mother, Alice clings to Jasper, "the meaning and purpose of her life," in order to continue to sustain her beliefs about herself and the world. Repeatedly throughout *The Good Terrorist*, Alice's wrist is described as "caught ... in his bony grip" (178), indicating her desire to be controlled and used by him. She is, in effect, willfully in his thrall so that she can continue to uphold both the middle-class virtues of caring for hearth and home and the leftwing political beliefs inscribed during her upbringing. (Indeed, Alice's situation is "ideal" during the four-year period when she and Jasper live with Dorothy, even though the latter two detest one another. The triangle nourishes Alice's beliefs until Dorothy breaks with her left-wing past, propelling Alice back into the world of squats.) Alice's self-image, moreover, vigorously qualifies her perception of Jasper, and thus proliferates the denial and self-deception.

To Alice, Jasper is "like an avenging angel" (238) whose dedication to social justice requires her unqualified admiration and support. In her mind, hatred is linked with purity, and Jasper becomes "good," so "good," in fact, that others are "Afraid of his truth" (23). Thus she interprets her first memories of him in terms of "something extraordinary.... The real thing" (271): "She remembered how she, too, when she had at first seen Jasper all those years ago, had felt some instinctive warning, or shrinking. And look how mistaken she had been" (120). Even when Jasper's ugliness and treachery are undeniable, Alice processes the information stupidly in order not to jeopardize her skewed sense of self: "He looked like a rat, she thought steadily, knowing that her love for him was not by an atom diminished" (184).

Again, although Alice and Jasper have no sexual contact with each other, although they actually do little together except spray-paint slogans on public property, Alice nevertheless imagines that this is "like a marriage: talking together before falling asleep" (100). In fact, the asexual nature of the relationship and the hooliganism both indicate Jasper and Alice's stunted development, and the narrator suggests at several points in *The Good Terrorist* that the pair are still children who are acting out rebellious fantasies. Jasper's homosexuality, what Alice calls "primly ... 'his emotional life'" (37), suits her own repressed desires, her "secret breathing body, which she ignored" (243), and the hooliganism clearly nourishes not only their infantile anger but also their need for immediate gratification: "The intoxication of it, the elation: *pleasure*. There was nothing like it!" (179). Jasper and Alice are married—grotesquely—in so far as they share a desire to destroy society, and Dorothy's scathing comment, "And then you are going to build it all up again in your own image," discloses a terrifying prospect (406). With striking similarities to what Arendt found in her analysis of Eichmann, Lessing portrays both Alice and Jasper as having built up a huge body of "self-deception, lies, and stupidity" (Arendt 52) in order to account for their failure to come to terms with their personal histories and with the world around them.

Dorothy Mellings is right when she tells Alice, "Against stupidity the gods themselves contend in vain" (64). As Lessing writes elsewhere of society in general, "Our left hand does not know—does not want to know—what our right hand does" (*Prisons* 13). Yet perhaps not all gods contend in vain. In a century in which terrorism has almost become banal, Lessing's irony makes for a lucid unveiling and examination of the psychology of kitsch. If Kundera is correct when he contends that kitsch conceals reality (or at least assumes that appearance *is* reality), then Lessing's irony makes it possible to understand more precisely how characters like Alice and Jasper can overwhelm others with their lies, twisted motives, and distorted communication.

NOTES

1. Regarding Swift's scatalogical poems, Ashraf H. A. Rushdy has recently stated: "Swift, more than any other English poet, has been the purveyor of the carnival consciousness; yet Swift, more than any other poet, has been the victim of a critical attention that attempts to deny the ramifications of the content of this consciousness" (2).

2. Specifically, Brown states: "Murry, like Strephon and the other unfortunate men in the poems [of Swift], loses his wits when he discovers

that Caelia—, and thus unconsciously bears witness to the truth of Swift's insight" (186); and, again, "The peculiar Swiftian twist to the theme that Caelia—is the notion that there is some absolute contradiction between the state of being in love and an awareness of the excremental function of the beloved" (186-87). In "The Protestant Era," Brown's second essay on *Studies in Anality*, he admits: "Other anal weapons employed by Luther in his fight with the Devil—my language is here more refined than Luther's—are injunctions to 'lick (or kiss) my posteriors' or to 'defecate in his pants and hang them round his neck,' and threats to 'defecate in his face' or to throw him into my anus, where he belongs'" (Brown 208). For all the praise and admiration he rightly bestows on Freud, Swift, and Luther for their blunt and unrelenting exposition of our culture's tendency to sublimate, Brown himself is strangely delicate at key points in his work.

3. In a latter and perhaps more crucial essay on anal erotism, Freud interchanges the terms *orderliness, parsimony*, and *obstinacy* with avarice, pedantry, and stubbornness, all of which are still easily seen in the character of Alice Mellings. See "Character and Anal Erotism" (1908) and "On the Transformation of Instincts with Special Reference to Anal Erotism" (1916).

4. There is, to be sure, reason to suppose at the end of the novel that if Alice isn't arrested by Peter Cecil, an intelligence officer, she will certainly be maimed or killed by Gordon O'Leary of the IRA for spiriting away his arms cache.

Works Cited

Arendt, Hannah. *Eichmann in Jerusalem: A Report on the Banality of Evil.* 1963. New York: Viking, 1965.

Beckett, Samuel. *The Unnamable. The Beckett Trilogy.* 1959. London: Picador, 1976.

Brown, Norman O. *Life Against Death: The Psychoanalytical Meaning of History.* Middletown, Conn.: Wesleyan UP, 1959.

Conrad, Joseph. *The Secret Agent: A Simple Tale.* 1907. London: Penguin, 1986.

Defoe, Daniel. *Robinson Crusoe.* Ed. Angus Ross. 1965. London: Penguin, 1985.

Eagleton, Terry. *Literary Theory: An Introduction.* 1983. Minneapolis: U of Minnesota P, 1989.

Flynn, Carol Houlihan. *The Body in Swift and Defoe.* New York: Cambridge UP, 1990.

Freud, Sigmund. "Character and Anal Erotism." *Collected Papers*. Vol. 2. Trans. Joan Riviere. New York: Basic Books, Inc., 1959. 45-51.

———. "On the Transformation of Instincts with Special Reference to Anal Erotism." *Collected Papers*. Vol. 2. 164-172.

Kundera, Milan. *The Unbearable Lightness of Being*. Trans. Michael Henry Heim. 1984. New York: Harper & Row, 1987.

Lessing, Doris. *The Good Terrorist*. 1985. New York: Random, 1986.

———. *Prisons We Choose To Live Inside*. 1986. Toronto: CBC Enterprises, 1988.

Rushdy, Ashraf H. A. "A New Emetics of Interpretation: Swift, His Critics and the Alimentary Canal." *Mosaic* 24.3-4 (1991): 1-32.

Swift, Jonathan. *Gulliver's Travels and Other Writings*. Ed. Louis Landa. Boston: Houghton Mifflin, 1960.

KAREN SCHNEIDER

A Different War Story:
Doris Lessing's Great Escape

Whom shall we blame for the folly of war?
Whom shall we tell these stories for?
Barbara Catherine Edwards, "Bomb Incident"[1]

The whole ghastly pathology [of war] brings us right back to the relations between women and men. For as long as we are unable to recognize the simple truth that men and women are above all brothers and sisters, and as long as we are unable to put an end to male supremacy ... and thus end the war between the sexes, then it is certain we will never be able to put an end to the wars between the nations, much less end the wars between people divided by race and class.
Anthony Wilden, *Men and Women, War and Peace*[2]

War, Doris Lessing once declared, has been the "most important thing" in her life.[3] Her fiction repeatedly affirms this observation, for war in its multiple guises insistently marches across the pages of Lessing's multiform texts. And appropriately so, for Lessing herself, like Martha Quest, is a quintessential child of violence: born out of the psychic ruins of the Great War, she was fated to become a keen observer of the grim and glaring

---

From *Journal of Modern Literature* 19, 2 (Fall 1995). © 1995 by Temple University.

holocaust of World War II and, afterward, an intervening prophet of imminent secular "Armageddon."[4] Ruing the on-going violence of the twentieth century, Lessing has remarked, "[T]he human imagination rejects the implications of our situation. War scars humanity in ways we refuse to recognize."[5] Her self-appointed task as a writer has been to scrutinize those scars, to reveal us to ourselves through the stories that we tell, and to teach us that we can—must—"force ourselves into the effort of imagination necessary" to realize our full humanity and to disinherit our legacy of violence.[6]

Lessing's history as a paradigmatic child of violence and her consequent assessment that since World War II we have been living on the edge of oblivion has contributed to, and been tempered by, her equally strong and somewhat paradoxical conviction that "We are living at one of the great turning points of history" ("Voice," p. 7). "We all have extraordinary, non-rational capacities," Lessing believes[7]; more, she foresees a crucial epistemic shift: "We're just on the verge of a complete revolution in how we make sense of things."[8] Thus, although she believes some violent apocalypse inevitable, she refuses to abandon her vision of new life arising out of the ashes: "Some terrible new thing is happening. Maybe it'll be marvelous.... Maybe out of destruction there will be born some new creature.... What interests me more than anything is how our minds are changing, how our ways of perceiving reality are changing."[9]

As it did for Virginia Woolf, then, World War II crystallized Lessing's conviction that "something new was demanding conception," something which would enable us to "live differently," something almost incommunicable because straining the limits of language.[10] Nevertheless, Lessing has been determined not only to articulate this "something new," but to model it by means of her persistent re-telling of war stories. For she has astutely identified storytelling as a key site for both the validation and subversion of dominant ideologies and conceptual paradigms—as a "resource ... for ... acquiescence," certainly, but also for "revolt."[11] We tell stories, Lessing has said, because "it is the way we structure reality."[12] She seems always to have understood that, as Alan Sinfield explains:

> stories are *lived*. They are not just outside ourselves, something we hear or read about. They make sense for us—of us—because we have been and are in them. They are already proceeding when we arrive in the world, and we come to consciousness in their terms.... They become common sense.[13]

In Lessing's view, the traditional stories with which we have structured and made sense of our lives have doomed us to the "nightmare *repetition*" which we must escape if we are to survive (*Marriage*, p. 77)—a narrative and conceptual feedback loop, or a hall of mirrors in which our grotesque images reflect and refract infinitely through a series of epistemological/ontological "prisons called race, class, male and female."[14] Plots of racial, national, and gender difference, heterosexual romance, cultural imperialism, and war constitute interlocking strands of history's "master" narratives. Accordingly, these very plots comprise the multiple storylines of Lessing's epic *roman à clef*, the aptly titled *Children of Violence* series (1952–69). Like her creator, the series' heroine Martha Quest feels locked into the meaning—making narratives that emplot and constrain not only her life's stories but the whole history of humankind. As a writer, Lessing must additionally contend with the integrally related constraints of method and form, which at this stage of her career were defined not only by a personal preference for nineteenth-century realism, but by the ideological pressures of the Marxist con-demnation of literary Modernism's experimental abandon.[15] These two story-telling limitations (in short, content and form) implicitly collide at the very heart of *Children of Violence*, creating a narrative tautology that eventually led Lessing to seek a digressive and experimental—although by no means final—resolution to her authorial dilemma.

* * *

The *Children of Violence* sequence opens with the adolescent Martha doggedly trying to resist the normative stories that she was born to, stories effortlessly perpetuated and perpetually figured by adults. She counters their stories by flaunting Havelock Ellis, whose story of sexuality she imagines has some revelatory power to free her from the preceding (white, British, middle-class) generation's repression, homogeneity, and conventionality. Martha looks to this purportedly shocking (and thus potentially disruptive) text, rather than elsewhere, because she images "herself ... in the only way she was equipped to" (*Martha*, p. 7)—through the beguiling lens of the "literature that was her tradition" (*Martha*, p. 2). She does not yet fully understand that the stories which have most indelibly and insidiously shaped her consciousness, while (re)inscribed between the covers of books, are those lived and told (relived) with mesmerizing repetition by everyone around her.

As *Martha Quest* opens, Mrs. Quest and her Afrikaaner neighbor Mrs. Van Rensberg chat about their children, their African servants, their homes—the "dull staple of their lives" (*Martha*, p. 2). Their husbands,

resolutely sitting "[a]t the other end of the verandah" with "their backs ...
turned on the women," similarly discuss their daily concerns—work, the
government, and the "native problem." Playing her expected role of "'young
girl' against [the adults'] own familiar roles," Martha seems merely an
observer caught between these two discursive positions. She responds with
irritation and bitter resentment that "they should have been saying the same
things ever since she could remember." The women's stories of domesticity
and the men's of public affairs are equally familiar to Martha, who has
"listened to such talk for a large part of her life" until "the two currents ran
sleepily on inside her"; she is an unwilling and helpless participant in life as
they tell it, with its overdetermined but seemingly natural, unbridgeable
divisions by gender, class, and race.

But Lessing throws into question all the stories Martha has grown up
with by foregrounding the nature of storytelling itself—inevitably a process
of censorship and reconstruction that, when scrutinized, reveals not only the
disparity between lived experience and its representation, but also the
common reliance on story—telling patterns deeply etched into cultural and
individual consciousness through frequent repetition, and the function of
such stories in the incessant process of cultural (re)production. As Mrs.
Quest and Mrs. Van Rensberg nostalgically recall their lost girlhoods,
defined by episodes of courtship and romance, they share "not the memories
of their behaviour, but the phrases of their respective traditions" (*Martha*, p.
5). Their stories are "heavily, though unconsciously censored," for
"[t]radition demanded ... a cautionary moral" (*Martha*, p. 6), especially in the
presence of the malleable young. In this way stories of romance, the family,
state politics, and the past—all filtered through an unquestioned assumption
of essential divisions between male and female, black and white, rich and
poor—interlock and cohere into the narrative structure that ultimately will
afford Martha—and Lessing—the "resources for both acquiescence and
revolt."[16]

Children of Violence painstakingly records Martha's struggle to refuse
acquiescence and thus to escape her apparently pre(in)scribed fate. As she
slowly discovers, however, she cannot make her great escape until she accepts
the "ambiguities of [her own] complicity" with this culturally reproductive
process, develops new modes of consciousness, and imagines less violent and
coercive alternatives to history's grand narratives.[17] As a writer, Lessing feels
an imperative to expose, demythologize, and rescript these ancient plots, all
of which seem to merge with compelling urgency in the "clarifying moment"
of the Second World War.[18] Accordingly, the five volumes of *Children of
Violence*—which begins with the staid realism of *Martha Quest* and ends with

the futuristic fantasy of *The Four-Gated City*—ultimately constitute a recursive series of literary revisions, a linked chain of familiar history, stories, and myths refashioned and retold. Carrying the burden of the tenacious past and assuming responsibility for the imperiled future, *Children of Violence* models a paradoxical process by which Lessing suggests the possibility of insuring that future by revisioning reality with the stories that we tell. But the key to the ultimate shape and completion of Lessing's project to reconfigure war and its plots cannot be located in *Children of Violence* itself; rather, it may be found in an apparently discrete and tangentially related fictional project. *The Golden Notebook* (1962), Lessing's most formally experimental novel, tells the story behind the altogether different story of war which *Children of Violence* finally inscribes—a story that discursively and epistemologically challenges the inevitably of history as lethally redundant narratives of mastery and multiform war.

* * *

World War II (and, by extension, war in general), Lessing tells us, was the result of a dysfunctional habit of mind she often calls, simply, a "failure of imagination ... of sympathy."[19] Her healing prescription entails a shift in focus, a widening of our perceptual gaze to include the kinds of (suspect) knowledge shunted to the periphery of human understanding—or, to put it another way, the kinds of knowledge associated with the "negative" ("female") side of the "[h]ierarchical dualisms [that] ... lie at the foundations of western epistemology and moral thought."[20] As philosopher and myth critic Donna Wilshire has pointed out, "knowledge (accepted wisdom)" and "ignorance (the occult and taboo)" head up a long list of supposed oppositions which, going beyond the mind/body, reason/emotion, individual/social splits, also includes "order/chaos," "objective/subjective," "literal truth, fact/poetic truth, metaphor, art," "goals/process," "seeing/ listening," and "permanence, ideal (fixed) forms/change, fluctuations."[21]

Lessing repeatedly demonstrates that these contradistinctions express and reinforce (in Wilshire's words) "value judgments that have unnecessarily brought about human alienation from self, other, and planet" because "they have disastrously limited what we think is desirable and worth knowing." Like Wilshire, Jane Flax, and other contemporary feminist thinkers concerned with metaphysics, Lessing dissents from Cartesian rationalism, positing instead the idea that knowledge "comes from many kinds of knowing working together or taking turns," that "no one manner of knowing—not disinterested cognition [if there were such a phenomenon], intuition, inspiration, sensuous awareness, nor any other—is sufficient unto itself to satisfy our need to know ourselves and the world."[22] Accordingly, in a proto-Derridean enterprise, Lessing envisions an epistemological/ontological process by which one can elude the "metaphysical logic of dichotomous" thought.[23] She thereby hopes both to encourage and to provide appropriate tools for the re-examination of history and its lifeless plots, for release from history's self-sustaining cycle of absolute difference, antipathy, and discord, and, finally, for consequent self--and cultural transformation.

In a 1984 interview, Lessing reproves her correspondent for presenting her with preclusive alternatives: "Why do you make it 'or, or, or?' It could be 'and, and, and.' You don't have to have an either/or...."[24] Appositely, Martha's fundamental quest is realization of her youthful revelation on the veld when she ephemerally achieves that "difficult knowledge" which emerges from an experience of "slow integration," when everything "became one, shuddering together in a dissolution of dancing atoms" (*Martha*, pp. 53, 52). In the lifelong struggle against the "sickness of dissolution" that follows, Martha slowly accretes understanding and strategies that equip her to overcome the formidable obstacles which she faces. First, she must conquer the "fear" that resists "a new sort of understanding."[25] She has to unlearn the "rigid formulas" that distort her perceptions and limit her inquiry (*City*, p. 359). She must learn to refocus, to reconsider the mundane, for it is "through banalities" that the "most interesting discoveries" are made (*City*, p. 37). So-called "normality," she discovers, is a "condition of disparateness," for the "compartmented, pigeonholed" human mind compulsively "separated, and divided" (*City*, pp. 61, 33, 79). With this knowledge, Martha finally "understood *really* (but in a new way ...), how human beings could be separated so absolutely by a slight difference ... that they could not talk to each other, must be wary, or enemies" (*City*, p. 79).

But Martha comes to this understanding behind the scenes, as it were. Until well into *The Four-Gated City*, there remains an enormous disparity between what the narrator acknowledges and Martha's profoundly felt but incompletely formulated understanding of the interlocking cultural patterns repeatedly inscribed in the preceeding texts. Indeed, Lessing temporarily displaces Martha's full understanding of the gender-race-war matrix onto a surrogate in a different novel, Anna Wulf, another manifestation of Martha Quest and their creator. Apparently having reached, in *Ripple from the Storm*, a literary and philosophical impasse, before continuing *Children of Violence* Lessing wrote *The Golden Notebook*. In this intensely introspective novel, she confronts the many questions which *Children of Violence* had so far raised about the inter-connected, fluid nature of reality, the necessity of additional ways of knowing, the nature and function of story-telling, and, finally, her consequent doubts about realism (yet another "rigid formula") as her chosen vehicle for social commitment—in short, her increasingly prohibitive suspicion that in telling Martha's life story she was somehow at odds with her own enterprise.

What Lessing consequently viewed as the shortcomings of the "conventional novel" (which she touches on in the Preface to *The Golden Notebook*) can be more broadly defined as realism's implicit assertion of the oppositional, hierarchical condition of the *status quo*, the transparency of language, and the logic of rationalism—in general, the meaning—making systems that falsely render our over-determined sense of reality natural and inevitable. As Catherine Belsey has observed, classic realism is "intelligible as 'realistic' precisely because it reproduces what we already seem to know."[26] Or, as Shoshana Felman explains, realist texts and their commensurate reading strategies are

> designed as a stimulus not for knowledge and cognition, but for acknowledgement and *re-cognition*, not for the *production* of a question, but for the *reproduction* of a foreknown answer— delimited within a pre-existing, pre-defined horizon, where the "truth" to be discovered is reduced to the natural status of a simple *given*.[27]

Conventional (realistic) novels, Lessing has thus justifiably (if paradoxically) complained, "always ... lie."[28]

Gayle Greene accurately identifies Lessing's problem as how to create a self-consciously subversive discourse out of signifying systems unavoidably "inscribed within the culture she would oppose."[29] This presents a more than awkward dilemma for a writer committed to realism, who must then wrestle with questions that anticipate poststructuralist notions of the interdependence of language, fictional form, mechanisms of power, and social reality. In *The Golden Notebook*, Lessing steps off stage in order to reconsider and to clarify her assumptions before raising the curtain on *Children of Violence* once again. Inasmuch as it interrogates realist storytelling and its relation to philosophical systems fundamental to war, *The Golden Notebook* is a metafictional comment on and an integral part of the Martha Quest series. Sprague and Tiger have observed that between *Ripple* and the last two volumes of the series "falls the great shadow of *The Golden*

Notebook."[30] Rather than demarcating an obscurance or a gap, however, it functions both as a bridge and as an illumination of the whole.

During *The Golden Notebook* interval, as Lessing has explained, she realized that her "philosophy ... was absolutely inadequate"—that is, that her thinking about thinking and about art had been divorced from her own experience and what she was to discover she was really "thinking and feeling."[31] Writing *The Golden Notebook* was the pivotal "crystallizing process" out of which "[a]ll sorts of ideas and experiences I didn't recognize as mine emerged." "I was learning as I wrote," she continues. "The actual ... writing ... was really traumatic: it changed me."[32] By way of Anna's creation and the telling of her story—that of a writer in search of "subjugated knowledges," a reality not over-determined by a metaphysics of conflict and appropriate forms of representation—Lessing meticulously enacts her frustration with the ideological/epistemological prison of traditional story-telling.[33] She then forges that trauma into a healing vision of shape-changing inter-connection. Her developing adherence to both/and thinking is manifest in the narrative alterity that structures *The Golden Notebook*.

In Anna Wulf's only novel, a story of gender and race antagonism on the African homefront during World War II (aptly entitled *The Frontiers of War*), the seemingly discrete elements of race and romance, whose edges blur but only fleetingly merge for Martha, pointedly coalesce against the larger canvas of global war, thus providing a miniature reprisal of *Children of Violence* up to this point. As Anna's novel concludes, romantic jealousy, racial difference, and the war seemingly conspire to doom the lovers to their separate and gender-encoded fates. Unable to bear her loss, Anna's heroine sacrifices her body to men and to commodification, ironically choosing prostitution to express her independence, an act that simultaneously embodies self-punishment and despoliation. The "Ace pilot," in contrast, immediately turns his eye to a greater purpose, the mythically glorious "death that awaits him" in war.[34] Both are victims of this familiar love/war story, but the black woman's fate conventionally signifies an ignominious, self-immolating defeat, and the white male's a praiseworthy and meaningful assertion of the heroic self. In this way, Anna's novel does indeed reproduce a definitive male/female opposition valorized in stories of both war and miscegenation.

Doing their part to censor the stories which we hear (see) and to obscure the mutually informative nature of the novel's intertwined themes, film promoters edit out the all-important racial plot, play up the "melodramatic sexual relationships" (*Notebook*, p. 60), and rename their clichéd and white-washed product *Forbidden Love*. Their misappropriation proves ironically fitting, however, in light of the novel's tacit assertions of war-intensified differences (gender, race, class), which poison love—and human relations in general—at the root. But while manipulators of popular culture attempt to erase the racial component from the cultural matrix, Anna refuses their silencing gesture, explaining, "This war was presented to us as a crusade against the evil doctrines of Hitler, against racialism, etc., yet the whole of ... [colonized] Africa ... was conducted on precisely Hitler's assumption—that some human beings are better than others because of their race" (p. 65).

The popular perception of her novel only confirms Anna's notion that the "novel has become a function of the fragmented society, the fragmented consciousness" (p. 61). More, it feeds her fears that because she is utterly self-divided, barred by "education, sex, politics, [and] class" from "completion," she lacks the "qualities necessary" to form a "new sensibility ... a new imaginative comprehension (p. 61). Despite her best intentions, *The Frontiers of War*, she concludes, fails to tell the truth about war or race or anything else. As a conventionally tragic interracial/wartime romance, it merely repeats ancient lies, not only promoting "racist voyeurism," but, worse, invoking a "dangerous delicious intoxication ... the secret ugly frightening pulse of war itself ... the death that we all wanted, for each other and for ourselves" (p. 153).[35] Inspired and informed by "the unhealthy, feverish illicit excitement of wartime ... [a] terrible lying nostalgia lights every sentence" (p. 63). To her mind, then, the novel is "immoral," for nostalgia—the insistent recollection of self-destructive, self-deluding fictions—represents a powerful form of "nihilism, an angry readiness to throw everything overboard.... This emotion," Anna contends,

> is one of the strongest reasons why wars continue. And the people who read *Frontiers of War* will have had fed in them this emotion, even though they were not conscious of it. That is why I am ashamed, and why I feel continually as if I had committed a crime. (p. 64)

But Anna's guilt over the culturally reproductive function of her novel does not by itself account for her writer's block. The war behind her, tragic love stories reappear to the point of obsession in Anna's own life and in the fictional free-writing with which she tries to distance and come to terms with the plot of heterosexual romance. In the Yellow Notebook, the one devoted to fiction, Anna jots down brief plot synopses for numerous projects that she will never complete. With one parodic exception, all depict variations of the wounded woman in love theme, starkly illuminate her own dysfunctional relationships with men, and imply the most muted of protests against gender-based asymmetries that invariably leave the woman "diminished" or "destroyed" (*Notebook*, p. 534). Anna's artistic crisis is not merely a block but a stutter—the inability to tell any story except that of women victimized by their love for men and by their own romantic notions. Not until Anna can reject the role of victim, accept the ambiguities of her own complicity, and imagine other plots does Lessing choose to return to Martha's story, ready to take it in the direction of an effectively oppositional discourse. As will Martha, Anna finds that madness, dreams, and intuitive epiphanies—marginalized or discredited ways of knowing—combine with (not replace) rational analysis to form new ways of "making sense" of her life as a woman and of her writing. Anna's epistemological breakthrough dramatically illustrates Donna Wilshire's representative claim that "no one manner of knowing" can suffice, that adequate knowledge "comes from many kinds of knowing working together or taking turns."

As Martha's more intellectual surrogate, Anna too seeks liberation from the nightmare repetition: "I want to be able to separate in myself what is old and cyclic, the recurring history, the myth, from what is new, what I feel or think that might be new" (*Notebook*, pp. 472–73). She envisions the latent potential in similarly receptive individuals as "a gap in a dam" through which "the future might pour in a different shape—terrible perhaps, or marvellous, but something new" (p. 473). But Anna herself remains ill-prepared and unaware of how to breach the dam, the wall of consciousness behind which forgotten or undiscovered truths glimmer dimly, because she remains epistemologically enslaved by seemingly timeless, overlapping fictions of men, women, and war.

As Saul Green, in an uncensored eruption of masculine egotism, harangues Anna about how to raise a girl to be a "real woman," Anna comes to see his repeated assertion of privileged knowing and human (male) being in opposition to femaleness as an act of male violence, indeed, an act of war: "I, I, I, I, I—I began to feel as if the word *I* was being shot at me like bullets from a machine gun. For a moment I fancied that his mouth ... was a gun of some kind" (p. 556). Anna's figures suggest that she perceives Saul's insistence—by means of which he conspicuously reiterates language that splits the I from the Other—as an assault, more, as the source of a war-like violence with which men bully and subject women, the reified Other. The next time Saul's "I, I, I, like a machine-gun ejaculating regularly ... spew[s] out hot aggressive language, words like bullets" (p. 628), Anna not only recognizes his "I, the naked ego" (p. 629) as "I against women" (p. 630), but she conflates it with a nightmare in which she "knew, but really knew, how war waited" (p. 629).[36]

But this notion proves too one-sided, as Anna discovers during a crisis sparked by a seemingly random coincidence of love and war stories. As she anticipates the inevitably unhappy conclusion to her love affair with Saul (who sneaks off "like a prisoner escaping" [p. 586]), she similarly despairs of the newspaper's predictable reports of "a war here, a dispute there" (p. 588). Contemplating these seemingly disparate events in tandem, Anna is suddenly

> invaded by ... the fear of war ... of the real movement of the world towards dark, hardening power. I *knew* ... that whatever already is has its logic and its force, that the great armouries of the world have their inner force, and that my terror ... was part of the force .... And I know that the cruelty and the spite and the I, I, I, I of Saul and of Anna were part of the logic of war, and I knew ... these emotions were ... part of how I saw the world. (pp. 588–89)[37]

Moreover, Anna knows "finally, that the truth for our time was war, the immanence of war" and, most importantly, that "war was working in us all, towards fruition" (pp. 591, 594). Anna's new knowledge forms the crux of a fresh understanding that Martha finally shares but never quite articulates.

Rather than a surrender to fear or despair, this awareness indicates a "kind of shifting of the balances of [her] brain ... [a] realignment" that enables her (at least for the moment) to dispel the man as warmonger/woman as victim dichotomy and to reintegrate the "principle of joy—in destruction" that she had been projecting onto men (p. 588). In a dream, she accordingly becomes the

> malicious male-female ... figure, the principle of joy—in destruc-tion: and Saul was my counterpart, male-female, my brother and my sister .... We came together and kissed, in love. It was terrible .... Because I recognised ... the caress of two half-human creatures, celebrating destruction. (pp. 594–95)

For the first time, she sees through male and female role-playing to the life-denying "gender symbiosis" that prevents their full humanity and creates instead miscreants, who, as in the mermaid and minotaur metaphor employed by Dorothy Dinnerstein, together seem determined and destined to "meet death half-way."[38] Years prior to publication of Dinnerstein's provocative argument, Lessing attributes the institutionalization of war, humanity's "drift ... toward despotism in societal authority," and our precarious existence "at the edge" of nuclear and/or environmental apocalypse to a "male-female collaboration to keep history mad."[39] That the collaboration is unconscious neither palliates its consequences nor lessens our responsibility for its eradication.

This "new knowledge," partial and periodic as it proves to be, leads Anna through a series of waking and sleeping dreams in which she at first identifies with the victims of ideological coercion: "an Algerian soldier stretched on a torture bed ... the British conscript ... killed for futility ... a student in Budapest ... a peasant" (*Notebook*, p. 596). But her shifting consciousness insistently illuminates the shadowy underside of her self-righteous revolutionary zeal:

> I was not Anna, but a soldier. I could feel the uniform on me....
> But I didn't know who the enemy was, what my cause was.... Yet
> Anna's brain was working in this man's head, and she was
> thinking: Yes I shall kill, I shall even torture because I have to, but
> without belief. Because it is no longer possible to organise and to
> fight and to kill without knowing that new tyranny arises from it.
> Yet one has to fight.... (pp. 600–601)

Anna's cross-dressing and assumption of a male body not only reaffirm her earlier vision of shared responsibility for war, but also image the integration of both male/female and victim/victimizer (thus portending Martha's vision in *The Four-Gated City* of herself as both Nazi and concentration camp fatality).

But for Anna the writer, as for Lessing, this merging of the Self and the Other, this Escheresque way of thinking about being, has expressive repercussions. Significantly, this dream scene begins with Anna's abortive attempt to record the supposedly nostalgia-free facts of her life in the Blue notebook, in order to hold chaos and fragmentation at bay. Instead of a pen, however, Anna finds that she grasps a gun in her hand. She cannot know truth, heal her psychic fracture, accept the Woolfian paradox of "unity out of multiplicity,"[40] and rewrite her life until she comes to grips with that gun, at once the phallic apparatus of death, the polyvalent symbol of her own involvement, and an instrument of scripts.

Appropriately, her recurring dream of soldiering is succeeded by a dream of romance, still defined, however, in terms of strict opposition. She watches herself "playing roles, one after another, against Saul, who was playing roles. It was like being in a play, whose words kept changing, as if a playwright had written the same play again and again, but slightly different each time" (*Notebook*, p. 603–04).[41] A paradigmatic couple, Anna and Saul "played against each other every man-woman role imaginable." Her dream captures the essence of the stuttering Yellow Notebook, evidence of her "failure of imagination." Faced with such sterile redundancy, Anna admits to her writer's block and at last begins to locate its source in her frustration with the maddening repetition of the stories with which she has ordered (determined) the material of her life.

Anna eventually succeeds in reconceiving her life because the real and the imagined, the rational and the emotional, the conscious and the unconscious at last work in concert. This life-saving process emerges from that tantalizing landscape in which all these supposedly antithetical modes of knowing and being kaleidoscopically flow into protean patterns—her dreams. Anna watches her life unfold as if it were a film. Alternately speeding up and slowing down, the images are "rough, crude ... [and] rather jerky," for they lack the polish of a consciously manipulated, edited narrative. When the film slows down, she "watched, absorbed, details" previously unnoticed. When it speeds up, those things "to which the pattern of [her] life had given emphasis, were now slipping past, fast and unimportant." All the seemingly noteworthy events—the designated major moments of her life story—"had given place to what was really important," what happened between the lines, so to speak (*Notebook*, p. 634). Calling into question the ways in which lives are shaped into stories, Lessing enacts a self-conscious shuffling of "plot" elements, a radicalized "cognitive estrangement," that enables one to perceive and narrate reality anew.[42] This perpetually shifting, reassessing orientation exceeds a mere reversal of the central and the marginal, the important and the trivial (an immediately self-defeating gesture) to call into question the epistemological rigidity that engenders and fixes such notions.

Finally, the film re-vision of Anna's life moves "beyond [her] experience ... beyond the [dividing, channeling] notebooks, because there was a fusion; and instead of seeing separate scenes, people, faces, movements ... they were all together." As the film slows for the last time, it offers a series of seemingly unrelated images—a hand dropping a seed into the earth, a rock slowly worn away by dripping water, a man standing on a moonlit hillside, "eternally, his rifle ready on his arm," and a woman choosing life rather than suicide (*Notebook*, p. 635). In this closing comment on the form/content of Anna's life, time, implicitly synchronic and diachronic at once, becomes timeless. The two images which conventionally connote death or decay are held within the embrace of two acts of life, the first setting new life into motion, the latter refusing to cut the life process short. Thus does the story of Anna's life, including the events depicted in *The Frontiers of War*, become a paradoxical but ultimately life-affirming vision of vitality and dissolution together, of awaiting death and deferring it—all part of the inclusionary whole.

Anna makes a gift of her dream's single image of war—the man on the hillside, rifle in hand—to Saul, whose task is to turn it into a re-vision of his own, a rescription of the conventional war story. A similar task will fall to Lessing when *Children of Violence* resumes. In *The Golden Notebook*, however, Anna/Lessing accepts the challenge which Saul presents with his opening line for the story that signals and enacts the cure of her writer's stutter. "The two women were alone in the London flat" portends a tale of insulated domesticity, but in the skillful hands of a transformed writer it becomes instead *The Golden Notebook* itself, which not only subsumes Saul's story of war, but endlessly denies the limitations implicit in the content and structure of the opening/reopening sentence that he provides for her (pp. 639, 3). *The Golden Notebook*, then, is a novel about war—geopolitical war, racial conflict, war between the sexes, and, finally, the struggle to salvage life and redirect the future by revising our maladaptive stories. It exemplifies the "self-consuming artifact" described by Stanley Fish, the literary text that turns back on itself, thus (as Jeanette King similarly argues) denying *telos* and origin, having no center and no margin, no hierarchy of discourse.[43] Moreover, in this war story, Lessing's *tour de force*, one cannot definitely differentiate among the novel's subject, author, and narrator, who become one another and yet remain themselves. Wholeness ultimately consists of interfused, reciprocally informing fragments that encourage the reader to take nothing for granted, to reconsider radically what has come before, and to develop a shifting, inclusionary perspective capable of seeing both the parts and the whole while at the same time appreciating the futilty of seeing them as separate. Finally, with its interleaving of the classically realist (and ironically titled) "Free Women" sections and the disruptive "notebooks" sections, *The Golden Notebook* demonstrates the would-be-subversive storyteller's dilemma: how to speak intelligibly both within and against known discourse, how to weaken and expand the borders of a discursive "reality" from which one can never be altogether free. Paradoxically, Lessing escapes this dilemma by embracing it, relying on and exploiting realist methods while destabilizing them, thus once again proving the efficacy of both/and over either/or.

In this way, Lessing frustrates the premises of literary realism and paves the way for the necessarily less formal break with realism and more subtle revision of time-worn stories that she executes in the last two volumes of

Children of Violence. Having worked through and demonstrated that all of her transformative strategies (admitting to the ambiguities of complicity, dilating one's consciousness, revising stories) overlap and merge, she has taught herself how to escape the epistemological prison of traditional war stories and how to transform her own (life) stories into a "resource ... for ... revolt." And in her flight, she has journeyed into the elusive territory of truly oppositional discourse.

Like Thomas Stern's enigmatic notebook (in *Landlocked*), the varied and exceedingly iconoclastic stories spun out in *The Golden Notebook* inscribe "a different story or, at least, made of the original a different story" (*Landlocked*, p. 269). Lessing's meta-fiction not only constitutes her own epistemological and narrative breakthrough, but bespeaks the possibility of a profound transformation of reality that perhaps one day will give material expression to her phoenix-like sense of life emerging from the ashes of lifeless stories. Along with Anna, Lessing wants to believe that "If people can imagine something, there'll come a time when they'll achieve it" (*Notebook*, p. 276). But the phoenix allusion does injustice to Lessing's hopeful revisionary fictions, for this mythic bird, endlessly reborn only to perish again and again, never breaks free of the circularity that constitutes the crux of its tale. This myth thus presents still another counter-productive story in need of revision, one that purports to offer hope and compensation, but actually reflects and reinscribes an inescapable cycle of conflict and violent immolation—in short, the "nightmare repetition" that Lessing would leave behind.

NOTES

1. *Chaos in the Night: Women's Poetry and Verse of the Second World War*, ed. Catherine Reilly (Virago, 1984), p. 38.

2. Routledge and Kegan Paul, 1987, p. 228.

3. Quoted in *Doris Lessing: Life, Work and Criticism*, Katherine Fishburn (York Press, 1987), p. 5.

4. See Nissa Torrents' interview, "Doris Lessing: Testimony to Mysticism," *Doris Lessing Newsletter*, IV (1980), pp. 1, 12–13; p. 13.

5. Jonah Raskin, "Doris Lessing at Stony Brook: An Interview," *A Small Personal Voice: Essays, Reviews, Interviews*, ed. Paul Schlueter (Knopf, 1974), pp. 61–76; p. 76.

6. Lessing, "A Small Personal Voice," in Schlueter, *A Small Personal*

Voice, pp. 3–22; p. 9. All subsequent references will be cited parenthetically as "Voice" in the text.

7. Torrents, p. 12.

8. C.J. Driver, "Profile: Doris Lessing," *The New Review* [London] (November 1974), pp. 17–23; p. 22.

9. Raskin, p. 66.

10. Lessing, *Martha Quest* (1952), repr. (Plume, 1970), p. 53; and *A Proper Marriage* (1952), repr. (Plume, 1970), p. 320. All subsequent references will be cited parenthetically as *Martha* and *Marriage*, respectively, in the text.

11. Alan Sinfield, *Literature, Politics, and Culture in Postwar Britain* (University of California Press, 1989), p. 31.

12. Heidi Ziegler and Christopher Bigsby, *The Radical Imagination and the Liberal Tradition: Interviews with English and American Novelists* (Junction, 1982), p. 206.

13. Sinfield, pp. 24–5.

14. Ziegler and Bigsby, p. 199.

15. Lessing discusses her commitment to realism at length in "A Small Personal Voice."

16. Sinfield, p. 31.

17. The "ambiguities of complicity" is the phrase which Lessing uses to describe the theme of Kurt Vonnegut's *Mother Night* in "Vonnegut's Responsibility," Schlueter, *A Small Personal Voice*, pp. 139–142; p. 140.

18. In the introduction to *Behind the Lines: Gender and the Two World Wars*, eds. Margaret R. Higonnet, Jane Jenson, Sonya Michel, and Margaret Collins Weitz (Yale University Press, 1987), the editors argue that war has generally "acted as a clarifying moment, one that has revealed systems of gender in flux and thus highlighted their workings" (p. 5). The premise of my argument is that war as a moment of illumination goes well beyond the issue of gender and race relations to include a pervasive metaphysics of conflictual opposition.

19. Lessing, *Landlocked* (1965); repr. (Plume, 1970), p. 187. All subsequent references will be cited parenthetically in the text.

20. Donna Wilshire, "The Uses of Myth, Image, and the Female Body in Revisions of Knowledge," *Gender/Body/Knowledge/: Feminist Reconstructions of Being and Knowing*, eds. Alison M. Jaggar and Susan R. Bordo (Rutgers University Press, 1989), p. 92.

21. Wilshire, pp. 95–6.

22. Wilshire, p. 92. For additional discussion of the limitations of, and

alternatives to, Cartesian (Western) philosophy, see Jaggar and Bordo in general and Jane Flax, "Political Philosophy and the Patriarchal Unconscious: A Psychoanalytic Perspective on Epistemology and Metaphysics," *Discovering Reality*, eds. Sandra Harding and Merrill B. Hintikka (Reidel, 1983), pp. 245–81.

23. Shoshana Felman, "Women and Madness: The Critical Phallacy," *Diacritics*, V (1974), p. 3.

24. Susan Stamberg, "An Interview with Doris Lessing," *Doris Lessing Newsletter*, VIII (1984), p. 4.

25. Lessing, *The Four-Gated City* (1969); repr. (Plume, 1976), pp. 489, 357. All subsequent references will be cited parenthetically as *City* in the text.

26. Belsey, *Critical Practice* (Methuen, 1980), p. 47.

27. Felman, p. 10.

28. *Doris Lessing: Critical Studies*, eds. Annis Pratt and L.S. Dembo (University of Wisconsin Press, 1974), p. 11.

29. Greene, "Doris Lessing's *Landlocked*: A New Kind of Knowledge," *Contemporary Literature*, XXVIII (1987), p. 82. This is a dilemma with which certain feminist theorists are centrally concerned. According to Lacan, the difficulty is insurmountable since all signification arises from an inevitably male symbolic order—the "Law of the Father." Lacan's revision of Freud leaves no meaningful, positive space in which women can name or even conceptualize their being and experience. This ex-communicating double-bind has prompted feminist respondents to Lacanian psychoanalysis such as Julia Kristeva and Luce Irigaray to theorize alternative "feminine" modes of thought and representation. Indeed, Kristeva's notion of the pre-Oedipal semiotic and Irigaray's theory of the repressed feminine, external to the male symbolic order, both seem relevant to Lessing's own explorations (tentative and nebulous as they are) of the possibility and efficacy of periodic other-than-Symbolic thought.

30. *Critical Essays on Doris Lessing*; eds. Claire Sprague and Virginia Tiger (G.K. Hall, 1986), p. 8.

31. Ziegler and Bigsby, p. 200.

32. "Preface to *The Golden Notebook*," in Schlueter, p. 27.

33. The term "subjugated knowledges" is Foucault's and has two meanings: "historical contents that have been buried and disguised in a functionalist coherence or formal systemisation" and "a whole set of knowledges that have been disqualified as inadequate to their task or insufficiently elaborated: naive knowledges, located low down on the hierarchy, beneath the required level of cognition or scientificity." See *Power/Knowledge: Selected Interviews and Other Writings*, ed. Colin Gordon

(Pantheon, 1980), pp. 81–2. The excavation of both kinds of "subjugated knowledges" antedates Foucault's "archeology of knowledge" techniques in women's writing and developed more or less coetaneously with feminist criticism and theory.

34. Lessing, *The Golden Notebook* (1962); repr. (Bantam, 1979), p. 59. All subsequent references will be cited parenthetically as *Notebook* in the text.

35. The phrase "racist voyeurism" is Jenny Taylor's, from "The Deconstruction of a Colonial Radical," quoted in Sprague and Tiger, p. 4.

36. Saul's aggressive "I, the naked ego," which is also "I against women," would seem the identical twin of "the straight dark bar," the insistent "I" noted by Virginia Woolf, that lies "across the page" of a certain representative Mr. A's writing. See *A Room of One's Own* (Harcourt Brace Jovanovich, 1929), p. 103. For Woolf, the "dominance" of this "I," whose arid and lifeless shadow obscures all else, betrays Mr. A's "self-conscious ... virility," which in his fiction has taken the intrusive and artless form of "protesting against the equality of the other sex by asserting his own superiority" (pp. 104, 105). As she makes clear in *Three Guineas*, Woolf associates such irruptions of self-conscious virility with fascism.

37. In "Her Story of War: Demilitarizing Literature and Literary Studies," *Radical America*, XX (1986), Lynne Hanley also points to this passage in *The Golden Notebook*, but she attributes the "convergence" of love and war to war's having "invaded and shaped [Anna's] emotions" (p. 22). That is, rather than seeing gender relations and war as twin manifestations of particular ways of seeing and being, she argues that "the combat zone invades the protected zone of intimate relations between men and women, forcing those relations to conform to the law of the battlefield." However, Hanley later calls this dichotomy into question, arguing that

> The prevention of war would seem to require ... the reconstruction of the prevalent form of the relation between the sexes in western culture, so as to erode the boundaries between male and female, white and black, the abstract and the concrete, the professional and the personal. (p. 23)

Hanley goes on to discuss Lessing's *The Marriage Between Zones Three, Four, and Five* as a "blueprint ... for altering the prevalent construction of manhood and womanhood in western culture, a construction that breeds combat between nations and lovers alike" (p. 23). Thus, although I find *Zones* more problematic in this regard than Hanley admits, this part of her argument is finally quite similar to mine.

38. See *The Mermaid and the Minotaur: Sexual Arrangements and Human Malaise* (Harper Colophon, 1976), pp. xii, 149.

39. Dinnerstein, pp. 163, 276.

40. Virginia Woolf, *Three Guineas* (Harcourt Brace Jonovovich, 1938), p. 143).

41. In this sense (and many others), Lessing's World War II fiction bears comparison with Woolf's *Between the Acts*.

42. Darko Suvin uses the term "cognitive estrangement" to describe certain distancing techniques (such as displacement into the future or creation of an alternative reality) commonly used in science fiction. See *Metamorphoses of Science Fiction: On the Poetics and History of a Literary Genre* (Yale University Press, 1979), pp. 4–11.

43. See Fish, *Self-Consuming Artifacts: The Experience of Seventeenth-Century Literature* (University of California Press, 1972). In *Doris Lessing* (Edward Arnold, 1989), Jeanette King similarly argues that there is "no 'conclusion' to *The Golden Notebook* because the end of the novel directs us immediately back to its beginning, making us feel that we need to re-read the whole novel differently in order to grasp its meaning" (p. 53). King also notes that the novel "succeeds in resisting the hierarchization of discourse which determines the relationship of centre to margin," adding that "there is no single originator of meaning" (pp. 52, 53).

SHEILA ROBERTS

Sites of Paranoia and Taboo: Lessing's The Grass is Singing and Gordimer's July's People

Although *July's People* (1981) appeared thirty-one years after *The Grass is Singing* (1950), and while the plot-lines and their stylistic and structural treatments are dissimilar, the novels exhibit remarkable congruities. Both encode indictments of racism and yet both, in my opinion, reinforce colonial fantasies of racial and sexual otherness. In this essay I should like to explore the power of this reinforcement as well as how both, by their use of gothic devices, transform fairly ordinary female protagonists into "the image of woman-plus-habitation" (Holland and Sherman 279). That is, the dwellings the protagonists are forced to inhabit become extensions of themselves and thereby configurations of the uncanny. I hope to conclude by demonstrating how both novels, while couched in the realistic mode, incorporate aspects of fabulation.

Mary Turner of *The Grass is Singing* and Maureen Smales of *July's People* are white South African women in their late-thirties when a time of life-threatening crisis emerges. The causes of the crises are different, yet both unsettling moments are compounded by the disadvantages the women share: they are trapped in colonial preconceptions; they inadequately understand the cultural underpinnings of the rural communities in which they find themselves, and they are married to men who cannot maintain a normative male-spousal strength. As married women they have both come to

From *Research in African Literatures* 24, 3 (1993). © 1993 by Indiana University Press.

rely on what they perceive as a special relationship with a black man. In this regard, both venture onto sites of the colonial forbidden and taboo—Mary more so than Maureen.

The black men the women rely on are their servants. Clearly both Lessing and Gordimer wished to explore through their protagonists not only the realm of the taboo but also the conflictual economy of gender-difference. In her essay "Madam and Boy: A Relationship of Shame in Gordimer's *July's People*," Barbara Temple Thurston points to the fact that in South Africa the vast majority of domestic workers are women (51). Thus the authors' choice of male domestics as antagonists was motivated by the desire to imbricate the already uneasy master/servant cathexis with the dissonance of gender. Moreover, the male servants are neither physically small nor mentally subservient. Mary's servant, Moses, is a huge man with a proud bearing and a missionary-school education. Maureen's "boy," July, is the headman of his own rural village.

Mary Turner is on the surface a simpler woman than Maureen Smales. She is less educated, less sophisticated, and has never taken the trouble to interrogate South African racism and arrive at a position of political liberalism, as Maureen has done. Whereas Maureen, until her moment of situational crisis, has enjoyed a successful marriage (successful so long as its dynamic was reinforced by middle-class trappings and rituals), Mary is a woman who through childhood trauma has been incapacitated for marriage. When she does marry because of perceived social pressures, she is almost immediately unhappy. The importance of Mary's childhood trauma will be taken up again later in this essay. However, both women arrive at points of total estrangement from their husbands and both venture willingly toward the locus of destruction.

Mary Turner, the child of unhappy parents (the father a drunkard and the mother rendered frustrated and bitter through poverty), succeeds in creating a comfortable modus vivendi for herself by doing secretarial work and living in a "girls" club. She is "a good pal" to her men and women friends and is content to remain unmarried. At age thirty she still wears "her hair little-girl fashion on her shoulders, and ... little-girl frocks in pastel colors, and [keeps] her shy, naive manner" (37). Her smooth routine and her peace-of-mind are destroyed one evening when she overhears gossip about herself. She hears herself accused of having "something missing somewhere" because she shows very little romantic interest in men (39).

Mary alters her appearance and tries altering her behavior toward men, but is "revolted" when they try making love to her. At this time, interestingly enough, she goes more frequently to the movies, but comes out of the cinema

> feverish and unsettled. There seemed no connection between the distorted mirror of the screen and her own life; it was impossible to fit together what she wanted for herself, and what she was offered. (44)

Mary's predicament here arises from her situation as a female spectator of presumably Hollywood movies (the time-frame of the novel is the late-thirties to early-forties), movies for which, as Mary Ann Doane points out, "the woman is deprived of a gaze, deprived of subjectivity and repeatedly transformed into the object of a masculine scopophiliac desire" (*The Desire to Desire* 2). Mary Turner, trying to align herself with the male gaze, can neither identify herself with nor learn from the cinematic male object of desire how to comport herself. If she ever was the naive spectator, a role "assigned to women in relation to systems of signification," where there is "a tendency to deny the processes of representation, to collapse the opposition between the sign (the image) and the real" (Doane 1), Mary can no longer inhabit such a role. That she has always wished to avert the male gaze from herself is probable from her retention of a childlike image into her thirties, and her desire to continue living in a girls' club, and is early evidence of her fear of being observed—of which more later. In a ghastly reversal of her chosen mode of comportment during happier times, toward the end of her life when she is enshrouded in paranoia, she greets a visitor to the farm in this way:

> "Why, good evening!" she said girlishly. "Why, Mr. Slatter, we haven't had the pleasure of seeing you for a long time." She laughed, twisting her shoulders in a horrible parody of coquetry. (206)

At which her husband, Dick, averts his eyes.

To return to the aforementioned moment in the cinema: soon after Lessing has described Mary's experience, she offers the reader a tableau of the male gaze in operation. Dick Turner (not yet known to Mary) visits the cinema with a friend. He is, however, not interested in the film, "The long-limbed, smooth-faced women bored him; the story seemed meaningless." Distracted, he looks around him and then notices along his row of seats "a shaft of light [falling] from somewhere above, showing the curve of a cheek and a sheaf of fairish glinting hair. The face seemed to float, yearning upward" (46). Dick's gaze leads him to infatuation with its object—Mary's face transformed by the light. He seeks her out, only to be disappointed in her actual lack of beauty. But he marries her because he is lonely and she is very willing. She marries him, literally to *save face* among her friends.

The suggestions we have already noticed, that the novel incorporates the iconology of female paranoia, are reinforced when Mary is brought as a bride to Dick's farm, her paranoia now exhibiting the classical symptom of an irrational fear of being menaced (as Freud discusses in "A Case of Paranoia Running Counter to the Psychoanalytical Theory of the Disease"). At the moment of arrival,

> Mary, who was half asleep roused herself to look at his farm, and saw the dim shapes of low trees, like great soft birds, flying past; and beyond it a hazy sky that was cracked and seamed with stars. (52)

When the car stops, the trees become "vague dark presences," and when Mary climbs out of the car, "a cold breath blew out of them, and down in the vlei beyond them hung a cold white vapor" (33). Nervously, she ventures to the stones bordering the house, but when a strange bird calls, "a wild nocturnal sound," she turns and runs back, suddenly terrified (54).

That the "gothic"—the fictional mode exploring the uncanny—is being inscribed in a so-far realistic novel is evident from Mary's response to the house itself. When she enters "there was a strong musty smell, almost animal-like," the smell arising from the skins of animals thrown on the floor. She sits down and forces herself to smile, "though she felt weak with foreboding" (54-55). After Dick tells her the story of how he built the house,

> she got to her feet with an awkward scrambling movement, unable to bear it: possessed with the thought that her father, from his grave, had sent out his will and forced her back into the kind of life he had made her mother lead. (56)

The reader's mind turns to all the uncanny houses of gothic literature, perhaps even to Poe's House of Usher where the narrator says, "With the first glimpse of the building, a sense of insufferable gloom pervaded my spirit" and that "There was an iciness, a sinking, a sickening of the heart—an unredeemed dreariness of thought which no goading of the imagination could torture into aught of the sublime" (231).

Dick's house is a very ordinary, simple construction on an ordinary farm, yet these disquieting and uncanny emanations arising from it and its surroundings presage the breakdown of the barrier between the internal and external in Mary's psyche, a state also symptomatic of the paranoid. What will in time emerge through the breakdown of this barrier will be "a hidden familiar thing that has undergone repression," as Freud explains in "The Uncanny" (247). The traumatic Oedipal experiences of Mary's childhood are about to return to torment her and make it impossible for her to cope rationally with the vicissitudes of her life.

Until her marriage, Mary has had very little to do with black people. As a child she was forbidden to speak to her mother's servants and she was encouraged to fear blacks in general. Very soon she becomes impatient with the "boys" Dick engages to work in the house. Her impatience grows into intolerance, and she falls into a pattern of dismissing the men one after the other for trifling offenses. Her initial annoyed indifference turns to hatred:

> She hated them all, every one of them, from the headboy whose subservience irritated her, to the smallest child.... She hated their half-naked, thick-muscled black bodies stooping in the mindless rhythm of their work. (130)

And although she has only temporary dealings with black women when Dick tries running a general-store on the farm, she loathes them, "the exposed fleshiness of them, their soft brown bodies." She hates "the way they suckled their babies, with their breasts hanging down for everyone to see," and "their calm satisfied maternity" makes her "blood boil" (105). It seems that the perpetual evidence of uninhibited physicality among the Africans is like an insistent beating on the doors of Mary's repression, an intolerable situation that becomes maddening when she is forced into dependence on a black man.

By the time Dick takes on Moses to work in the house (insisting that this servant is not to be dismissed by Mary), their poverty has worsened and Mary's health, physical and mental, is breaking down. She suffers particularly from the oven-like heat of the house, which has no ceilings under a corrugated iron roof. If on the night of her arrival as a bride she had been infused with the thought of her dead father condemning her to a life such as her mother lived, as the years pass her sense of taking on the identity of her mother increases. Her voice copies the harsh tones of her mother, and as Dick's farming ventures repeatedly fail, she finds "the memory of her own mother recurring more and more frequently, like an older, sardonic double

of herself walking beside her" (99). I am reminded here of Tania Modleski's
work on the gothic novel, particularly where she cites from William
Meissner's *The Paranoid Process* in elucidating women's fears of becoming as
passive as their mothers; becoming their mothers, in fact, and deserving of
punishment. Meissner states that

> The paranoid usually comes from a family whose power structure
> is greatly skewed: one of the parents is perceived as omnipotent
> and domineering, while the other is perceived as submissive to
> and victimized by the stronger partner ... the paranoid patient
> tends to introject these images of his/her parents and, even more
> importantly, internalizes the dynamics of the parental interaction.
> (66)

Thus, the menace within the gothic novel is the fictional embodiment of
women's fears of victimization because of their femaleness. As Modleski
points out, because of the patriarchal structure of the ideal family in our
culture "the female is more likely than the male to retain the (feminine)
"victim" introject and to deny (project) feelings of aggression and anger"
(99). It makes sense, therefore, that the gothic heroine and the reader will
want to be saved from victimization, which can only happen if they are *not*
their mothers, not passive. Modleski goes on to describe the gothic heroine's

> sensation of actually being possessed, the feeling that past and
> present are not merely similar but are "intertwined," etc. In each
> case the heroine feels suffocated—as well as desperate and panic
> stricken in her inability to break free of the past. (*Loving with a
> Vengeance* 70-71)

The above discussion of the paranoid, Meissner's from 1978 and Modleski's
from 1988, could hardly apply more closely to Mary Turner's situation, and
Doris Lessing's seemingly intuitive understanding of this form of neurosis is
penetrating and astute.

While Mary fears that she will transform into her mother, she is also
plagued by dreams of her father, particularly one based on a game where

> [h]er father caught her head and held it in his lap with his small
> hairy hands, to cover up her eyes, laughing and joking loudly
> about her mother hiding. She smelled the sickly odor of beer and
> through it she smelled too—her head held down in the thick stuff

of his trousers—the unwashed masculine smell she always associated with him. She struggled to get her head free, for she was half suffocating, and her father held it down, laughing at her panic. (190)

From this dream she wakes up screaming, "fighting off the weight of sleep on her eyes, filled with terror" (190). The word "suffocated" appearing in this excerpt and in the quotation from Modleski's work is highly significant, clarifying the quality of Mary's interwoven fears of being the double of her mother and of being forced into a kind of sexual partnership with her father. Oneiric memories of this game, a moment of Oedipal trauma in which Mary is plunged into incest dread (to use Freud's phrase), and which Kristeva explains as a phobia of non-differentiation, of uncertain and unstable identity (*Powers of Horror* 58), reappear with intensity during the term of Moses's employment in Mary's house. In other words, her various fears—of being confined in the hot boxlike house; of being non-differentiated from her mother; of the presence of the patriarchal black "other"—become sutured to form a suffocating psychic pall from which Mary cannot escape.

I should clarify at this point that I am not trying to suggest that *The Grass is Singing* is a generic gothic novel, merely that it incorporates elements we have come to associate with that form of fiction. Yet an examination of Modleski's definition of the typical gothic novel reveals the influence of the form on Lessing's work. "In the typical Gothic plot," Modleski's writes, "the heroine comes to a mysterious house, perhaps as a bride, perhaps in another capacity, and either starts to mistrust her husband or else finds herself in love with a mysterious man who appears to be some kind of criminal" (59). The mysterious man in the case of *The Grass is Singing* is Moses, the African. Soon after Dick brings him to work in the house, Mary observes Moses washing himself, a Lawrentian scene that jerks Mary "clean out of her apathy" (166), and goads her into an hysterical assertion of herself against the black man. Mary grows hysterical as she tries subconsciously to deny her attraction for Moses and the fact that when their eyes met, "the formal pattern of black-and-white, mistress-and-servant, had been broken" (167). Moreover, Mary cannot treat Moses with her usual intolerance because he will not accept her behavior: he threatens to leave and Mary has to back down, being fearful of Dick's anger if yet another servant decamps. This coerced dependence on her part becomes complicated by the unavoidable human interaction and contiguity when Moses helps her nurse Dick through an illness and then begins ministering to Mary herself as her disorientation and lassitude increase.

If the popularity of gothic novels arises from their focus on the understandable fears of women in cultures where the feminine is undervalued and women frequently abused, and if the gothic's ultimate appeal lies in its happy ending where the coldness of the powerful male (whether husband or lover) metamorphoses into love, then the disturbing power of Lessing's manipulation of the form becomes clearer to the reader. For, in proportion to Moses's parental care-giving, Mary's paranoia (and not any sense of reassurance) strengthens. Her response forms a multiplex of repulsion and attraction, anger and gratitude, passivity and fear—fear being the strongest affect. On one occasion when, emboldened by the extent of her weakness and misery, he hands her a glass of water and then tries to propel her to the bedroom to rest, Mary experiences the event

> like a nightmare when one is powerless against horror: the touch
> of this black man's hand on her shoulder filled her with nausea;
> she had never, not once in her whole life, touched the flesh of a
> native. (275)

Even within the strictures of racial division in South Africa, Mary's reaction here is an extreme one, encouraging the reader to connect her "nausea" with her sickened panic at having her face thrust into her father's lap. To restate the obvious, by transforming her confused Oedipal feelings for her father into a fear of all physical intimacy, and yet by gradually assuming the identity of her mother, Mary cannot help but project onto Moses the sexual power of the father. Moreover, Moses is huge and black, the embodiment of colonial fears of African sexual prowess. Commenting on Mary's dream-memory of the sexual game her father played with her, Eva Hunter remarks:

> The dreams ... reveal that she is unable to protect herself against
> pain and punishment because she has been taught that resistance
> is useless—to be a woman is to be powerless, at least in relation
> to a man. (148)

Mary's perceived powerlessness within patriarchy, and within the rigid patriarchal norms of colonialism, is of course exacerbated by her worsening ill-health. Toward the end of her life she has become a "strange, silent, dried-out woman who seemed as if she had forgotten how to speak" (216), and a "poor twisted woman, who was clearly in the last stages of breakdown" (220). In allowing Moses to minister to her, touch her, and even help her dress, Mary has given herself into his keeping like a child. She has also committed the colonial unthinkable and ventured into the realm of the taboo, though, as her disintegration progresses she seems hardly aware of this trespass.

Lessing does not make it clear whether Mary has a sexual relationship with Moses. The young Tony Marsden, recently out from England and assigned to help Dick Turner, at first believes this is the case but then discards his suspicions. The fact that Moses decides to kill her when she finally rejects him strongly suggests a relationship deeper than a merely compassionate and color-blind one (on his part). But what this deeper relationship might be from his perspective is never explored in the text; and Lessing, who all this time has been recording Mary's inner life, is strangely remiss in describing Mary's thoughts in this regard.

Hunter posits that in the work of Lessing "the house often represents the body itself" in the language of dream and metaphor (156). It follows then that Mary's body and the dilapidated cottage that imprisons her function as two images in a metaphoric exchange. Like the houses of whites in other Lessing novels, in *Going Home* and in the "Children of Violence" series, and like the House of Usher, the cottage will collapse after Mary's death and Dick's departure. In other words, the house and Mary's disintegrating body become "the horrible and fascinating abomination which is connoted in all cultures by the feminine" (Kristeva, "Psychoanalysis and the Polis" 90). Because Mary has represented in herself an acceptance of the return of the repressed (or the uncanny) no possibility of rescue could be available to her or the dwelling that housed her.

From a different perspective, both the house and Mary's body may be interpreted as representatives of colonialism, both to be destroyed by "Africa." However, I do not believe the thematic of the novel can be so neatly drawn to conclusion. The thin dry tormented figure of Mary can scarcely support symbolization as colonialism in action. Lessing contrives to destroy her protagonist in an almost ritualistic murder to be committed by the one person in her life who has achieved an emotional connection with her, however neurotic or "diseased." Mary foresees her killing and does not try to save herself from it: in fact, she goes walking out into the night as if to greet it. Eva Hunter sees Lessing's punishment of Mary as upholding "the widespread cultural notion attaching to women as daughters of Eve" (154) and therefore culpable, and she offers an interesting analysis of the highly-charged language used to describe the killing, asserting that "The woman, sterile, unnatural, guilty, is sacrificed by the author, as well as by Moses—who represents the natural, the whole, the fertile, and the innocent—to a new 'dawn.'" And "in *The Grass is Singing*, masculine ascendancy acquires transcendental significance" (154-57). The valorization of the masculine hardly constitutes a critique of colonialism or a prophecy of its demise. Mary's death does not usher in any changes to the farming community which hated her. While the novel is clearly an indictment of racism, racist conditioning is only a part of Mary's complex nature and not the part that leads to her breakdown.

I would assert that Mary's death not only does not change anything in the community, a community that is merely confirmed in its conviction that white and black should remain separate, but that its ultimate meaninglessness for a reader who is unconvinced by Lessing's mythic coloration of the event reflects negatively onto the figure of Moses. Even before it becomes obvious that Moses plans to kill Mary, the reader has perforce empathized with Mary's nervousness in his presence. His largeness, blackness, and silent appearances are repeatedly emphasized. There is also an earlier event which I have not mentioned so far, an occasion when Mary, directing Dick's "boys" in the fields, strikes Moses in the face with a whip. The possibility that he might be nurturing revenge lurks in the reader's mind for a time until Moses's kindness dissipates it. But because the narrative voice (until the last few pages) is directed from Mary's cognition, her confused sense of Moses as a menace becomes the reader's. The sense of menace maintains itself, moreover, because Moses's motives in behaving compassionately, even parentally, toward Mary remain hidden. To interpret him as a humane person, able to put aside any resentment he feels at the rigid racism of South African society, is a simplistic reaction in view of the murder, committed ostensibly out of pique and jealousy. Lessing's appending a diction that foregrounds ideas of purging, cleansing, and rebirth seems mere obfuscation as she tries in some discomfort to conclude a text whose loose ends have already escaped her grasp. As a result, the book seems to me to undermine its own message of the horrors of racism and the moribundity of colonialism. A "skewed" childhood, marriage, and Moses kill Mary; not "Africa."

Unlike Mary who assumes a radical difference between white people and black, Maureen Smales in *July's People* nurtures a humane creed and a belief in "equality of need" (65). She is presented as an employer of unusual kindness and courtesy (in South African context). Her servant, July, is provided with a reasonably comfortable room and a bathroom with hot-and-cold running water, a rarity in domestic quarters. He receives two weeks' paid vacation a year, and is allowed to entertain a woman-friend in his room: again, an indulgence most South African employers would not condone. Although Maureen does not intrude on his privacy, on the rare occasion when July is ill, she brings him a "tray of light food she had prepared for him herself" (66). Such consideration would have been unthinkable for Mary

Turner, who would have been sickened at the thought of entering a "boy's" room, or so we can surmise. Maureen's kindly behavior arises not only out of a desire not to lose July but also out of her "belief in the absolute nature of intimate relationships between human beings" (64). Of course, what she fails to realize is that her relationship with July can never be absolute or intimate, for it is the studiedly constructed master-servant cathexis dependent on understood verbal and gestural niceties.

Because Maureen's relationship with July is natural-seeming to her, having the smooth appearance of an intersection between courteous service and generous reward, she believes that she and July understand each other. When July saves her and her family from the violence of the revolution and brings them to his village, she comes to assume that their loss of white urban status will lead to a greater equality of interaction between her family and July's. In this respect she is even more seriously mistaken than in her assumption of a normal intimacy and understanding between herself and July in her suburban home.

While the inscription of the *unheimlich* or uncanny is very much stronger in *The Grass is Singing* than in *July's People*, there are, however, suggestions of its presence in the later novel that increase the atmosphere of foreboding created on the first page by the short paragraph:

> The knock on the door
> no door, an aperture in thick mud walls, and the Sack that hung
> over it looped back for air, sometime during the short night. *Bam,
> I'm stifling; her voice raising him from the dead, he staggering up from
> his exhausted sleep.* (1, Gordimer's emphases)

The Smales family, having driven through the bush for three days and nights, have spent the night in a rondavel in July's village. While the rondavel is a familiar African dwelling, and while this one is "the prototype from which all the others had come" (2), yet the details of its interior are certainly unhomely:

> a stamped mud and dung floor, above her, cobwebs stringy with
> dirt dangling from the rough whattle steeple that supported the
> frayed grey thatch. Stalks of light poked through. A rim of shady
> light where the mud walls did not meet the eaves; nests glued
> there, of a brighter-coloured mud—wasps or bats. A thick lip of
> light round the doorway. (2)

This uncomfortable one-room structure into which chickens and large insects wander, where there is the rustling of rats and mice at night, and into which rain-water leaks takes on a more disturbing ambience when, within its constricting space, the ordinary, satisfying, white middle-class marriage of the Smaleses' begins to destabilize. The first intimation of change is Maureen's disorientation in time. On the second day after their arrival in the village, she is taken by July to his wife's hut to meet his wife and his mother. There, she "was aware, among them in the hut, of not knowing where she was, in time, in the order of a day as she had always known it" (17). Her disorientation is similar to that of Mary Turner's, as well as her growing sense of aimlessness, although it overtakes her more rapidly and, because of the shorter time-frame of *July's People*, does not become as disabling as Mary's.

Both Maureen and her husband, Bam, deprived of their master-bedroom (their mastery, privacy, and routinized sexuality, the reader assumes) and the objects of their suburban home, experience a mutual defamiliarization. Within a matter of weeks, her ungroomed and ungroomable female body—unshaven legs and armpits, broken nails, hair "like the tail of a dirty sheep" (17), skinny chest without a bra—will cause him to mutter "Oh my god" at the sight of her removing her filthy T-shirt, "His lips turned out in disgust, distaste, on her behalf" (89). Although Maureen is a woman of the eighties, one with self-confidence and accustomed to decision-making, like Mary and like women everywhere, she is judged on her appearance. Bam, too, will deteriorate, more in manner than in physical appearance, so that on an occasion when he tries to get their radio to work, Maureen will see him as having "the baffled obstinacy of a sad intelligent primate fingering the lock on his bars" (50).

That the hut itself begins to have transformatory powers over its occupants is emphasized when, after the Smales family has enjoyed a rare dinner of roasted pig, and after Maureen and Bam make love, he wakes to see menstrual blood on his penis. He experiences a momentary but horrifying hallucination that he has the dead pig's blood on him. This detail of the bloody penis, an image of castration, suggests in part the return of the repressed to Bam's consciousness, the site of the return being, predictably, the unhomely hut in which he has recently "entered" his wife. Doane points out that "for both Freud and Weber, the uncanny is the return of the repressed, and what is repressed is a certain vision of the female body as the signifier of castration and hence disunity" (140). Thus, for both sexes the repressed is incest-dread, the woman's fear being of transformation into her mother and thereby becoming partner to the father, and the man's knowledge of the castrated body of the mother. Bam's disgust at Maureen's unkempt female presence and unfamiliarity, the sight of her menstrual blood, weaves into his growing sense of emasculation and confinement and expresses itself in a nightmare of castration. While Bam has actual cause to fear the future and reason to be immobilized by his own helplessness, one might also say that for him the image of woman-plus-habitation; i.e., Maureen growing physically repulsive in the confines of the dirty hut, helps reduce him to a state of paralysis, toward the end of the novel, he lies on the mattress in the hut, face downwards, "as the father had never done before his sons" (145).

As I pointed out at the beginning of this essay, the situational similarities between Mary Turner and Maureen Smales are fairly close. However, as *July's People* progresses, Maureen's behavior becomes more self-preserving than Mary's. As with Mary, Maureen loses her ability to negotiate the world of everyday existence: her "hodological map" (Sartre 78) has become useless to her and she can't maneuver her way in this new life according to its chart. She does not fully understand the gender-dynamics of July's village; she is frustrated in her attempts to be part of the life of the women there; her husband becomes unrecognizable to her; and her perceived relationship with July is dismantled suddenly and completely in a scene where, angry with and contemptuous of her, he berates her in his own language, which she does not understand. His outburst conveys that there was no authenticity in their former interaction of Madam and "boy"; that her interpretation of reality in her former life was as without foundation as is her current status as wife, mother, and Madam. Deprived of her hodological or cognitive map (as Mary was), Maureen, however, does not sink into a benumbed passivity as Mary did and as Bam is in danger of doing. When rescue appears to present itself in a helicopter hovering over the area, she is able to throw off instantly all her former (eroded) selves as wife, mother, employer, transforming into "a solitary animal at the season when animals neither seek a mate nor take care of young, existing only for their lone survival, the enemy of all that would make claims of responsibility" (159). Throughout the text animal imagery has inscribed Maureen's inner and outer selves. In the last pages, as she runs for the helicopter, the feral kinesis of the images increases in power. She first "walks" then "stalks." She "jolts down the incline, leaps stones, breaks into another rhythm." Then she runs and jumps, balances, and clambers, then runs again, "trusting herself with all the suppressed trust of a lifetime" (159). Thus we observe the swift movement down the incline and over the river and through the underbrush, not of a suburbanite but of a creature of the wild.

The way Gordimer ends *July's People* has encouraged much speculation about its meaning, as Nicholas Visser expounds in "Beyond the Interregnum: A Note on the Ending of *July's People*," one positive reading being that she is running "toward her revolutionary destiny" (62). To return to the unstudied animality of her action, it makes a certain sense that she would act spontaneously and without the conditioned rationality of her former life— given how many of the trappings of her former life she has lost. But I find it unimaginable that the pilot and crew of the helicopter (and we never learn to which side it belongs) will have the time and inclination to assure Maureen's safety or induct her into a life of activism. Where, the reader asks, will that place of safety be? In the war-torn cities? In a prison-camp? In any event, this speculation goes beyond the text and leads nowhere. My own reading of the ending interprets it as Gordimer's desire to punish Maureen. She is the major consciousness of the narrative and the most interesting character, but she is nonetheless a white female liberal, as limited as all liberals are in Gordimer's view. Gordimer's break with liberalism has been well-documented and I will not go into it here. Even more reprehensible, Maureen has generated swiftly into a physical repulsiveness beyond mere lack of grooming, and any follower of Gordimer's career will know that she has no respect for female unattractiveness. Early on Maureen discovers that "she smelled bad between her legs" (9). Later she is forced to use old rags during menstruation, and she has a "cold-cat smell" when she sweats (151). At the penultimate climactic moment in the novel, when she realizes that July is rejecting totally her and their relationship of so-called understanding, she "lurch[s] over and pose[s] herself, a grotesque, against the vehicle's hood, her shrunken jeans poked at the knees, sweat-coarsened forehead touched by the moonlight, neglected hair standing out whispy and rough" (153). Maureen's obviously hideous appearance and her placing herself in this provocative pose for her one-time servant reduce her to the same object of pity and disgust that Mary presents to Slatter, the visitor to the farm, while also conveying Maureen's complete abandonment of her role as Madam to July. Also, in adopting the stance of seductress, Maureen ventures onto the site of the taboo, seeming to assert, however mockingly, that there is no relationship available between the polarities of employer and concubine for her with July.

Maureen's final fording of the river in pursuit of the helicopter has been interpreted mythologically as some sort of crossing of the Rubicon, or as a trope of rebirth. But I would posit that the moment of her posing sexually for July is also Rubiconal. Even if circumstances should change, she can never again revert to her old stable self as July's employer.

> A. Tudor defines a genre as a relatively fixed culture pattern. It
> defines a moral and social world, as well as a physical and
> historical environment. By its nature, its very familiarity, it
> inclines toward reassurance. (180)

In so far as *The Grass is Singing* and *July's People* incorporate elements of the
gothic genre, they reinforce the social world of South African racism to a
certain extent. In spite of the admirable intentions of their politically
dissident authors, the books contextualize colonial fears of the
unpredictability and unreliability of black Africans, *The Grass is Singing* in the
mysterious figure of Moses, and *July's People* in July, Daniel, and the Chief.
Also, both books, in their foregrounding of female physical ugliness,
perpetuate values of gender inequality and the necessary punishment of
women.

I must emphasize, however, that this encoding of colonial and
masculine fears does not completely undermine the thematic of the novels,
which is an indictment of the South African apartheid system and, in the case
of *July's People*, a critique of the inadequacies of liberalism.

I mentioned in my introduction that these novels tend toward
fabulation. I base my assertion on unexplained unrealistic elements in both
texts. The dramas of both novels are played out in peculiar situations of
isolation. Conveniently (for Lessing), Mary Turner had lost her siblings and
her parents by the time she reached her twenties, and Dick is an orphan.
Likewise, while the Smaleses are only in their thirties when they escape to
July's village, no mention is ever made of the fate of their parents or extended
families back in the cities. They are all strictly on their own in this moment
of crisis. Moreover, within the already reduced settings of their narratives,
both authors stage-manage a limited number of objects, chosen, it would
seem, to facilitate the breakdown of the female protagonists. For instance,
when the Smaleses pack (granted, hastily), they bring a box with money, a
bag of oranges, a radio, some tinned food, a toy racing-track, Manzoni's
novel *I Promessi Sposi*, a supply of toilet paper, and some malaria tablets.
While most of these objects are useful, the reader has to accept them at face
value, i.e., evidence of panic; or else follow a futile line of questioning why
an experienced housewife and mother of three packed no clothes, blankets,
pillows, soap and towels, nor the contents of the medicine cabinet. In fact,
there is an almost bizarre quality to the diversity within strict limits of the
objects Gordimer permits the Smaleses to have with them in the bush.

Before her marriage, Mary Turner is a private secretary, "earning good
money" we are told and capable if she wanted to take "a flat and [live] the

smart sort of life" (34). Yet at the time of her marriage, she has only enough money to buy "flowered materials" for curtains and cushions, and "a little linen, crockery, and some dress lengths" (64). Even at this early stage of the novel, Lessing is making sure that Mary has few creature comforts to soften the initial strangeness of marriage.

What contributes greatly to Mary's worsening health is the lack of ceilings in Dick's house, a house with an iron roof in a tropical climate. For something like ten years, until Mary's death, Dick steadily refuses to put in ceilings, pleading poverty. Yet he spends money on other farming ventures. Lessing never offers a convincing explanation for Dick's cruel stubbornness, nor does she ever mention that Dick might also find the oven-like house hot. The reader could interpret Dick's lack of action as a desire to torment Mary, but the text does not support such a reading. Dick remains solicitous of Mary to the end. Also, if he had wanted to drive Mary to collapse, why then does he go mad when she dies? His sudden madness, moreover, is a turn of events with insufficient foreshadowing and is introduced, I would argue, to reinforce the image of Mary as a harmful presence to the men, black and white, who care for her.

What I am suggesting is that in order to foreground the horrific nature of these South African racial situations, situations presented predominantly in realistic modes, the authors avail themselves of a mysterious and unsettling ambience similar to that recognizable in gothic fiction, as well as the limited stage-properties of the fable. By means of this blend of the real and the unreal, they aim to interrogate racism and liberal shortsightedness, and they do so. But these devices are finally too effective for this reader. The physical discomfort the women find themselves in is so unsettling that I can only wish Mary Turner had never married and that the Smaleses had left South Africa in time, wishes that work against the political agenda of the novels.

In conclusion, I should like to reiterate that in traditional gothic novels (for example, *The Castle of Otranto, Jane Eyre, The Woman in White* and, more recently, *Dragonwyck and Rebecca*), the threatened female protagonist discovers that her fears were groundless. Either by her own courageous good sense, or the intervention of a good man, she is rescued and re-empowered. Whatever the means toward it, the ending is happy. In the protagonist's re-empowerment, she is reassured, consciously or unconsciously, that she is not her mother, that poor creature of passivity and victimization. The happy ending reassures the reader as well that she may act boldly on her own behalf. In *The Grass is Singing*, however, Mary Turner has no will or strength remaining to her to save herself, nor can her ineffectual husband help her. Her half-naked corpse lying on the stoop and being licked by dogs is a shocking and disgusting final image for the reader. The female reader, particularly, may be left not only unenlightened but conflicted. Does Lessing punish her protagonist because she turned into her mother vis à vis Moses, the father? There is no answer. White male authority, however, remains unchallenged.

The final image of *July's People* is not that of a witch-like woman's corpse but of a dirty barefoot woman fording a river, leaping over stones and running for her "life." She is not like her mother, a housewife who called her servant "our Jim" to distinguish him from her husband who was also named Jim (dupling the implications of possession in the book's title). Maureen has sloughed off all her selves as she runs away from the known to the unknown. But the reader is left with a vision of a woman running toward her death, and without any sense that the longed-for South African revolution has brought anyone any joy or encouragement. The text incorporates no projections of a better life to come, not even a hint. If such atavistic regression is what will happen in the so-called interregnum of the epigraph, then, the reader might suggest, shouldn't we all try to postpone it?

Both novels are important texts in the ongoing literary challenge to the master narratives of colonialism, and the substance of both has the power to haunt the reader long after the final page has been turned. Yet both, as I hope I have shown, are discomforting texts because of their barely submerged contradictions. However, perhaps at the interregnal stage of South Africa's democratic trajectory, no fully uncontradictory text can be written, and certainly not by whites.

WORKS CITED

Doane, Mary Ann. *The Desire to Desire*. Bloomington: Indiana UP, 1987.

Freud, Sigmund. "A Case of Paranoia Running Counter to the Psychoanalytical Theory of the Disease." *Sexuality and the Psychology of Love*. New York: Macmillan, 1963.

——. "The Uncanny." *The Standard Edition of the Complete Psychological Works of Sigmund Freud*. London: Hogarth, 1968. 17: 218-52.

Gordimer, Nadine. *July's People*. London: Penguin, 1982.

Holland, Norman N. and Sherman, Leona F. "Gothic Possibilities." *New Literary History* 8.2 (1977): 279-94.

Hunter, Eva. "Marriage as Death: A Reading of Doris Lessing's *The Grass is Singing*." *Women and Writing in South Africa*. Ed. Cherry Clayton.

Marshalltown: Heinemann Southern Africa, 1989. 139-61.

Kristeva, Julia. *Powers of Horror: An Essay on Abjection*. Trans. Leon S. Roudiez. New York: Columbia UP, 1982.

——. "Psychoanalysis and the Polis." *Critical Inquiry* 9 (1982): 77-92.

Lessing, Doris, *The Grass is Singing*. New York: Granada, 1980.

Modleski, Tania, *Loving with a Vengeance*. New York: Routledge, 1988.

Poe, Edgar Allan. *The Complete Tales and Poems*. New York: Modern Library, 1938.

Sartre, Jean-Paul. *Sketch for a Theory of the Emotions*. London: Methuen, 1971.

Temple-Thurston, Barbara. "Madam and Boy: A Relationship of Shame in Gordimer's *July's People*." *World Literature Written in English* 28.1 (1988): 51-57.

Tudor, A. *Image and Influence: Studies in the Sociology of Film*. London: Allen and Unwin, 1974.

Visser, Nicholas, "Beyond the Interregnum: A Note on *July's People*." *Rendering Things Visible*. Ed. Martin Trump. Johannesburg: Ravan Press, 1990. 61-67.

BETSEY DRAINE

The Four-Gated City:
The Pressure of Evolution

W hile the critics are aware that Lessing has called her series a *Bildungsroman*, a number have quarreled with the label. Dagmar Barnouw, for instance, explains that it is necessary for a *Bildungsheld* to move toward a meaningful choice, and in the world of *Children of Violence* such a choice does not seem to be available. "The first four volumes of the *Children of Violence* are not *Bildungsromane* in the strict sense of the concept," Barnouw writes. "Matty is neither moving toward a choice, a determining decision she will make at one time or the other, nor is the fact that she is incapable of such a choice integrated into the substance and structure of her development."[1]

On the contrary, both the plot and the system of tropes which structures the five-novel series show Martha moving through a series of stages, each climaxed by either a willed decision or an acquiescence to destiny. Indeed, the question of whether active choice or passive acceptance is the appropriate response to life is the chief issue on which the whole series is based. In the early books, especially, Martha is continually choosing the wrong things—marriage to Douglas, abandonment of her child, marriage to Anton—while fate delivers to her door every good she is later to cherish— the birth of her child, the affair with Thomas Stern, her friendships with Maisie and Athen, and the association with the Coldridge household, her ultimate means of salvation. Through images of entrapment, of change

From *Substance Under Pressure: Artistic Coherence* and *Evolving Form in the Novels of Doris Lessing*. © 1983 by The University of Wisconsin Press.

without change, and finally of growth, conversion, and evolution, Lessing develops a metaphoric apologia for her concept of self-development. Although Goethe emphasized the necessity for organic rather than willed self-development, most writers in the *Bildungsroman* tradition have sanctioned the active striving and romantic rebellion of their heroes. Lessing retreats from this late-romantic idea of *Bildung*, returning to Goethe's original insight that the hero must develop naturally out of what he is and that, to that end, receptivity is fully as important a trait as assertiveness. Martha thus finally learns that growth cannot be willed but can be nurtured, enhanced, and protected from impediments.

Lessing's depiction of Martha's organic self-development comes as a shock to readers schooled to admire and relish the dramatic revolts of Stephen Dedalus and Julien Sorel. Patricia Spacks, for example, finds Martha lacking in heroic stature precisely because she holds back from full rebellion: "If Martha Quest, then, figures as a heroine, she must be a heroine of a very peculiar sort. She stands for nothing, defies nothing successfully, cannot endure her condition without self-defeating gestures of escape. She is passive when she should be active, obtuse when she should be perceptive. Her heroism consists merely in her suffering and her rage, not in any hope or promise of effect."[2] In contrast to Spacks's view, I contend that by holding back from decisive action, personal or political, the young Martha keeps herself open to the wisdom that Thomas Stern and others bring to her, while at the same time she gives herself time to feel the stirrings of the desires and intuitions that require development if she is to come to true maturity.

D. J. Enright, for his part, does not quarrel with Martha Quest's seeming passivity, but he complains that "there is no true—no artistically true—connection between the Martha Quest whom we first met as a fifteen-year-old in the novel named after her and the old woman whose death on a contaminated island somewhere off Scotland is casually mentioned in the 'Appendix' to *The Four-Gated City*."[3] That the *Bildungsheld* could change, even markedly, should not be surprising to Enright. It is common that the *Bildungsheld* undergoes a conversion experience and sheds the callow skin of youth. As Count Jarno explains to Wilhelm Meister, there is bound to be a marked appearance of difference between a man's youthful character and his mature self.

> "It is right that a man, when he first enters upon life, should think highly of himself, should determine to attain many eminent distinctions, should endeavor to make all things possible; but when his education has proceeded to a certain pitch, it is

advantageous for him, that he learn to live for the sake of others, and to forget himself in an activity prescribed by duty. It is then that he first becomes acquainted with himself, for it is conduct alone that compares us with others."[4]

According to this model, Martha Quest gives up youthful rebellion, self-assertion, and idealism—all of which *seemed* the defining traits of her selfhood—only to find herself more truly in "an activity prescribed by duty." Upon joining the Coldridge household, Martha gives up her self-absorption, extending herself outward to tend the needs of the writer Mark Coldridge, his disturbed wife Lynda, and the two emotionally battered children, Francis and Paul. It is in the course of living for the sake of these others that she comes to know and develop her defining talents, her clairvoyance and her capacity to save others from coming disaster. These talents are an outgrowth of the capacities shown by the very young Martha Quest. Mark revives in Martha her youthful vision of the four-gated city and helps her to see that this city can be, indeed must be, a reality in the time of world catastrophe. Lynda restores to Martha her youthful capacity to see things outside the frame of "normal" vision; the perceptions that Martha becomes attuned to give Martha the knowledge necessary to her role as savior of the special children. Similarly, the young people, Francis and Paul, force Martha to recall both her youthful fury against the blindness and stubbornness of authority and her willingness, in youth, to take terrible personal risks in order to live outside the net of that authority; such recollections prepare Martha to defy governmental authorities and risk her life in an attempt, at the time of the Catastrophe, to establish a counter-society on Faris Island.

There is, it seems, a great deal more continuity in the presentation of Martha Quest than Enright gives Lessing credit for. This continuity, moreover, is established largely through metaphor—a device that one hopes Enright would admit as "artistically true." Through the imagery of growth and evolution that pervades *Children of Violence*, Lessing prepares the reader to follow Martha and her society through stages of growth that lead finally to a virtual metamorphosis. Failing to see the continuity in Martha's development, Enright misses too the continuity in the parallel development of Martha's society. He complains, for example, that the apocalyptic events chronicled in the Appendix to *The Four-Gated City* are "not in accordance with the rest of 'Children of Violence.'"[5] Enright can be refuted by an examination of the imagery that threads through the series, prefiguring and expressing the gradual evolution of both individual and collective.

The best image to start with is the image of the growing tree,[6] an image that Lessing seems to have borrowed, from Goethe, as the central running motif of her series. Expounding to his fellow actors in *Hamlet*, Wilhelm declares: "To me it is clear that Shakespeare meant, in the present case, to represent the effects of a great action laid upon a soul unfit for the performance of it. In this view the whole play seems to me to be composed. There is an oak-tree planted in a costly jar, which should have borne only pleasant flowers in its bosom: the roots expand, the jar is shivered."[7] For Wilhelm, the image of the tree expanding beyond the capacity of its container is a warning against his tendency to embark on projects for which he has no natural, but only a romantic, inclination. At each step of his self-development, he must ask if he is fitted for the task before him, if it suits his soul and gives room for the development of his genius. He makes mistakes—trying to fit himself into the role of actor, which is beyond his talent, and trying to create happiness for Mignon and the Harper, a task that is beyond human skill. His self-development comes to fruition when he has fitted the roots of his soul to a suitable vessel—a society of friends who will give spiritual support, a wife who will temper his romantic impulses, and, most importantly, an ambition that is matched to his talents and his opportunities.

Doris Lessing has also used the symbol of the growing tree as a standard by which to measure the development of her *Bildungsheldin*, Martha Quest. In every novel of the series there is a tree or a group of them that is emblematic of a particular stage in the opening of her consciousness. The young Martha has a tree that she calls her own and that she later visits as if it were a shrine. This tree, "hard under her back, like a second spine," has roots sunk deep into the African soil, and it is the solid post against which she leans as she reads *The Decay of the British Empire*, Engels's *Origin of the Family*, and other books aimed against the social milieu in which she finds herself placed. The firm-rootedness of the tree, in tension with the uprooting impulse of the revolutionary literature she reads, reassures the rebellious but frightened girl. The tree is a locus for her unconscious knowledge that the African landscape, along with her experience of natural rhythms there, is the root and support for everything good that will grow within her in later years. When she confronts threats to her identity, it is important to have that past to lean back on, as the young Martha leaned back on the tree.

As Martha pursues an independent life in the city, she is caught by impulses that flow not from her inner nature but from the social rhythms of a corrupt society—the impulse to marry as a solace in the time of war-making, the desire for material luxury as a substitute for spiritual health, even the falsely romantic urge to create a political utopia (especially false in Martha's case, since it involves the rejection of her daughter and of her own nurturing capacity). While Martha is far from her inner self, pursuing these inappropriate goals, the image of the tree is held at a distance. Her world is far from nature now; she is shut up in stuffy offices or enclosed in the boxes of a middle-class suburb. Nonetheless, at moments of pain, when Martha fleetingly feels the distance between her innermost urgings and her daily reality, she often glimpses a tree outside a window or beyond a gate.[8] Or, as she stands under the shelter of a tree, she momentarily opens herself to a fresh vision of things. For example, in a scene from *A Ripple from the Storm*, Lessing uses the image of dust to indicate the aridity of Martha's life as wife and comrade to Anton, the Communist group leader, along with the image of the tree to express the continuing presence of her inner urge toward growth, threatened as it has been by lack of tending:

> The smell of dry dust filled her nostrils; an odour of dry sun-harshened leaves descended from the darkening gum trees above. She thought—and it was a moment of illumination, a flash of light: I don't know anything about anything yet. I must try to keep myself free and open, and try to think more, try not to drift into things. (*RS*, pp. 171–172)

At last, through her relationship with Thomas Stern, Martha learns to live from the roots of her being. Thomas is, literally, a tree-nursery man, and the hut where he makes a shelter for his lovemaking with Martha is the city base for his nursery: "From this centre she now lived—a loft of aromatic wood from whose crooked window could be seen only sky and the boughs of trees, above a brick floor hissing sweetly from the slow drippings and wellings from a hundred growing plants" (*L*, p. 98). As Martha relearns the rhythms of her own body and of nature, she luxuriates in natural sensations. The descriptions of setting thus proliferate, as Lessing reflects Martha's consciousness of life around her, and references to trees abound—jacarandas, trees festooned with golden shower creeper, on the veld or in town, luxuriant or dusty.

Finally, the maturing Martha, having abandoned Africa and her political connections, sits in a small bedroom in Bloomsbury and watches "the structure of the sycamore tree disappear in spring green" (*FGC*, p. 199). Day and night she charts its quiet, hidden growth. In the Coldridge household Martha has been transformed from a self-centered girl to a generous woman nurturing a family of sad children and emotionally disturbed adults. Her bedroom is her only privacy in this house where she owns nothing and no one. So the tree outside her window becomes her mandala, the symbol of her potential growth:

> There she was, in her room, empty, at peace. She watched other people developing their lives. And she? In every life there is a curve of growth, or a falling away from it; there is a central pressure, like sap forcing up a trunk, along a branch, into last year's wood, and there, from a dead-looking eye, or knot, it bursts again in a new branch, in a shape that is inevitable but known only to itself until it becomes visible. (*FGC*, p. 201)

This is a freer image than Wilhelm's oak in a jar. He had to find the proper form to contain his growth; there is a conservative, curbing impulse in his metaphor. (One may imagine Wilhelm having to be pruned now and again to fit his chosen container, the Society of the Tower.) Martha's metaphor, in contrast, is organic and progressive. She must follow the impulse of her own growth, when it comes. In the meantime, she must watch and wait, not force or prune. Whereas for Wilhelm the shattering of the jar would be the moment of defeat, for Martha such a moment is a triumph.

Children of Violence is a series of episodes in which Martha Quest comes to recognize that she is enclosed by a containing structure (metaphorically, a cage, a net, a shell, or a room) in which she will be stifled and out of which she must break. The net is different in each volume, but the struggle and the metaphors for it remain the same. Martha escapes the family web, only to fall under the net of the Sports Club and its expectations. In *A Proper Marriage*, two forces threaten to trap her—the claims of the utopian vision she had fostered as a girl, now exerting pressure on her in the form of the Contemporary Politics Discussion Circle, and the opposing claims of her marriage and maternity. In her first exposure to the socialist group, which will absorb nearly all her energy for the next decade, Martha feels "the old fear as if nets were closing around her" (*PM*, p. 194). As she will later learn, every social group has its net—a set of beliefs, expectations, and vocabulary in terms of which life must be experienced—and in committing oneself to the group, however tacitly, one agrees to live under the net. What Martha seems to intuit is that no group with a dogma can foster the free and organic development of personal or social potential. Thus, although in *The Four-Gated City* Martha finally works with others to foster the developing psychic abilities of the race, she performs her service outside the nets of any dogmatic group. When confronted with the demands of the Contemporary Politics

Discussion Circle, then, the young Martha acts instinctively for her survival when she tries to shake "herself free of this mesh of bonds before she had entered them; she thought that at the end of ten years these people would still be here, self-satisfied in their unconformity, talking endlessly" (*PM*, p. 194). The irony is that for a long time she will be with them.

While Martha is on one front resisting her political destiny, her biological destiny (as she sees it) simultaneously threatens to overwhelm her. Suddenly, Lessing's prose is full of images of entrapment, as Martha's pregnancy calls up her old fear of inevitability. When Martha thinks of her child growing in the womb, she does not link this process with the free growth of trees or plants. Rather, she mourns for the "doomed" child "bubbling continuously in its cage of ribs" (*PM*, p. 131) and continually refers to her womb as a prison. Birth, however, is no release. If "the web was tight around her" (*PM*, p. 99) while she was pregnant, afterwards "there was this band of tension, felt deeply as a web of tight anxiety, between her and the child" (*PM*, p. 201). But even the fact that "she would be bound for months and months of servitude, without any escape from it," is nothing to the "bored thought that this was a baby like any other, of no interest to anybody, not even herself" (*PM*, p. 152).

The underlying anxiety, for which pregnancy becomes almost a symbol, is the still unresolved dilemma of determinism. What could be more determined, more repetitious, than the cycle of generations?

> And now Martha was returned ... into her private nightmare. She could not meet a young man or woman without looking around anxiously for the father and mother: that was how they would end, there was no escape for them. She could not meet an elderly person without wondering what the unalterable influences had been that had created them just so. She could take no step, perform no action, no matter how apparently new and unforeseen, without the secret fear that in fact this new and arbitrary thing would turn out to be part of the inevitable process she was doomed to. She was, in short, in the grip of the great bourgeois monster, the nightmare *repetition*. (*PM*, p. 77)

The ferris wheel outside her window is, then, negatively an emblem of fate's cyclic repetitions; but, when feeling trapped by marriage, she "looked at the wheel steadily, finding in its turnings the beginnings of peace. Slowly she quietened, and it seemed possible that she might recover a sense of herself as a person she might, if only potentially, respect" (*PM*, p. 24). Critics have focused on the ferris wheel as a negative symbol, representing the mindlessness of a bad marriage and the endless circles of procreation and family life—"like a damned wedding ring," as Martha herself thinks crossly (*PM*, p. 29).[9] However, even in *A Proper Marriage*, Lessing foreshadows through this image a positive theme that she will develop fully in *The Four-Gated City*. Lessing believes that one cannot find freedom by jumping off the wheel of fate; rather, one must "hold on" (a frequent phrase in Martha's mouth) and live each moment through. Therefore a pregnant Martha is affirming an instinct for life, rather than denying it, as several critics suggest, when she revolves "on the great wheel as if her whole future depended on her power to stick it out" (*PM*, p. 92).

When Martha rebels against the idea of repetition, the uses of which she will discover in *The Four-Gated City*, she commits the one irrevocably wrong act of her youth, the repudiation first of her pregnancy, then of the child she has borne. Through this repudiation Martha intensifies her self-division.

> She was essentially divided. One part of herself was sunk in the development of the creature, appallingly slow, frighteningly inevitable, a process which she could not alter or hasten, and which dragged her back into the impersonal blind urges of creation; with the other part she watched it; her mind was like a lighthouse, anxious and watchful that she, the free spirit, should not be implicated; and engaged in daydreams of the exciting activities that could begin when she was liberated. (*PM*, p. 127)

This split between the rational watcher and the irrational, impersonal experiencer widens as the years go by, until in *The Four-Gated City* Martha seeks out a psychiatrist to help her come to terms with the division.

In the meantime, the youthful Martha is almost proud of her ability to maintain a distance from her feeling self. Her compartmentalizing of experience is expressed in images of shells, rooms, walls, and houses. In her political work, for example, Martha becomes aware of how her double self operates:

> She was engaged in examining and repairing those intellectual's *bastions* of defence behind which she sheltered, that *building* whose shape had first been sketched so far back in her childhood she could no longer remember how it then looked. With every year it had become more complicated, more ramified; it was as if

she, Martha, were a variety of soft, *shell*-less creature whose survival lay in the strength of those *walls*. (*PM*, p. 94, my italics.)

While Martha remains aware of the need to keep a lighthouse keeper's vigilance over her separate selves (*L*, p. 14) she is warmed by the presence of her friend Maisie, who "always understood by instinct what was going on underneath everybody's false shells" (*L*, p. 14). Nevertheless she admonishes herself that "she must keep things separate" (*L*, p. 14). This need is figured in her dreams and fantasies of being a housekeeper who attends a large house filled with people who must not leave their own rooms or be suffered to "meet each other or understand each other and Martha must not expect them to. She must not try to explain, or build bridges" (*L*, p. 15). Lessing suggests that this separating of though ultimately life-denying, is nevertheless a temporary necessity for Martha. In fact, as is the case often in *Landlocked*, Lessing is rather too obvious in her use of dream symbolism and in her directions to the reader as to how to evaluate the dream.

Martha's dreams, always a faithful watchdog, or record, of what was going on, obligingly provided her with an image of her position. Her dream at this time, the one which recurred, like a thermometer, or gauge, from which she could check herself, was of a large house, a bungalow, with half a dozen different rooms in it, and she, Martha (the person who held herself together, who watched, who must preserve wholeness through a time of dryness and disintegration) moved from one room to the next, on guard. These rooms, each furnished differently, had to be kept separate—*had* to be, it was Martha's task for this time. For if she did not—well, her dreams told her what she might expect. The house crumbled drily under her eyes into a pile of dust. (*L*, p. 14)

Before her exodus from Africa, Martha could not integrate the separate rooms of her experience except through the unifying power that belonged to Thomas Stern. Precisely as a result of his tutelage, however, Martha learns to feel dissatisfied with a divided existence, so that in London she no longer feels content to live the sterile and divided life that seems typical of her generation. At the beginning of *The Four-Gated City*, Martha arrives in London and goes to the house of an old pal, Jack. She feels simultaneously attracted and repelled by his neat little box of a room: "People like her, for some reason, in this time, made rooms that were clean and bare and white: in them they felt at home, were safe and unchallenged. *But she did not want to feel like this"* (*FGC*, p. 49). Later, she realizes that, for her, rooms become containers for discrete emotions and that her life is unbalanced because she is unable to hold together various emotions and insights. At one time her room in the Coldridge house is filled with an atmosphere of death tempting her to suicide. Weeks later it is "all sexual fantasy, anger, hatred" (*FGC*, p. 201). The basement flat, where the supposedly mad woman, Lynda, lives, is at one time a refuge and days later a threat: "The basement flat, its occupants, were isolating themselves in her mind, as if it was a territory full of alien people from whom she had to protect herself, with whom she could have no connection" (*FGC*, p. 221).

Martha finally comes to realize that the walls of these rooms must be broken down. While tending Lynda through a period of madness, Martha has a moment of revelation.

> Now she understood very well what it was Lynda was doing. When she pressed, assessed, gauged those walls, it was the walls of her own mind that she was exploring. She was asking: Why can't I get out? What is this thing that holds me in? Why is it so strong *when I can imagine, and indeed half remember, what is outside?* Why is it that inside this room I am half asleep, doped, poisoned, and like a person in a nightmare screaming for help but no sounds come out of a straining throat? (*FGC*, p. 494)

If the walls that block out a clear perception of unified experience could be broken down, there would be no need for Lynda's bizarre pantomime.

The message that cries out from Martha's stream of thought for her own recognition is Forster's dictum, "Only connect!" As Selma Burkom shows with special reference to *The Golden Notebook*, this need for integration is always one of Lessing's central themes.[11] One begins to see the relevance of the dervish teaching story used as the dedication to *The Four-Gated City*:

> Once upon a time there was a fool who was sent to buy flour and salt. He took a dish to carry his purchases.
>
> "Make sure," said the man who sent him, "not to mix the two things—I want them separate."
>
> When the shopkeeper had filled the dish with flour and was measuring out the salt, the fool said: "Do not mix it with the flour; here, I will show you where to put it."
>
> And he inverted the dish, to provide, from its upturned bottom, a surface upon which the salt could be laid.

The flour, of course, fell to the floor.

But the salt was safe.

When the fool got back to the man who had sent him, he said: "Here is the salt."

"Very well," said the other man, "but where is the flour?"

"It should be here," said the fool, turning the dish over.

As soon as he did that, the salt fell to the ground, and the flour, of course, was seen to be gone.

The story expresses the paradoxical difficulties that Martha faces in the Coldridge household. Practicality would seem to dictate that opposites—for example, the insane Lynda and her sane family—be kept apart. However, when one fixates on the task of separating one aspect of the world from another, both aspects—the salt and the flour—may be lost to you, as both Lynda and her son are almost lost to each other, to life, and to the larger Coldridge household. In coming to this insight, Martha is beginning to recover the mystic experience of her youth—the "slow integration, during which she" and all her environment "became one, shuddering together in a dissolution of dancing atoms" (*MQ*, p. 52). She is beginning to accept the challenge to see life whole—the challenge which she has not been able to accept up to this time.

With Thomas Stern she finds herself living from one center for a brief time, but she loses the ability when he goes away. Again, when she first reaches London, in a delirium of hunger and fatigue, she remembers the Arnoldian wisdom that "it is a question of trying to see things steadily all the time" (*FGC*, p. 35). In this heightened state she enters an intense sexual experience with Jack and discovers that the "normality" that others accept is a condition of disparateness, both within the parts of the self and between the self and others. For Martha and Jack, the condition of normality is one to be outgrown by those who are capable of reaching a higher state. Sex is the vehicle that Jack recommends. Through his tutelage Martha discovers that "when the real high place of sex is reached, everything moves together" and disparateness is overcome (*FGC*, p. 64). Finally, after exploring madness with Lynda, Martha realizes:

There is something in the human mind which makes it possible for one compartment to hold Fact A which matches with Fact B in another compartment; but the two facts can exist side by side for years, decades, centuries, without coming together. It is at least possible that the most fruitful way of describing the human brain is this: "It is a machine which works in division; it is composed of parts which function in compartments locked off from each other." Or: "Your right hand does not know what your left hand is doing." (*FGC*, p. 523)

The machine has its revenge, however, when it begins to switch from Fact A to Fact B without warning. Marion Vlastos points out that here, as throughout her work since *The Golden Notebook*, Lessing echoes or perhaps borrows the concepts of R. D. Laing, the radical British psychiatrist who believes that schizophrenia is an extreme protest by sensitive individuals against the society's demand that they constantly divide off approved perceptions from disapproved ones.[12] Vlastos quotes Laing in a statement that could act as a gloss for *The Four-Gated City*:

It has always been recognized that if you split Being down the middle, if you insist on grabbing *this* without *that*, if you cling to the good without the bad, denying the one for the other, what happens is that the dissociated evil impulse, now evil in a double sense, returns to permeate and possess the good and turn it into itself.[13]

In *The Four-Gated City*, images of conversion between negative and positive electrical states express the wonder and the danger of this phenomenon. Part Three begins with a selection of "Various Remarks about the Weather from School Textbooks." These are statements about the composition of air, which according to Lessing is shocked by the action of lightning into losing its nitrogen to the soil: "A lightning flash is only a spark which bridges cloud and earth or cloud and cloud. But in order for this spark to happen, one place must be negatively charged and the other positively charged" (*FGC*, p. 290). Out of the conflict of negative and positive impulses, lightning fire is born. This image is a figure for psychological processes that operate by means of conversion or dialectic. In the Coldridge household a number of people undergo "conversions" from one "pole, or opposition point" to another—in political or personal terms. Mark "switches" (note the vocabulary of electricity) from an aristocratic liberalism to Communism and finally through both to a cynical idealism. Martha feels herself flipping from love to hate, from left to right, and wonders what the "pressure" or the "switch" is that causes the change. Moreover, she begins to think that this phenomenon is not purely personal. Just as she had noted that the impulse to separate things off into neat little rooms was characteristic of her generation, she now notices that the time when she is susceptible to conversion is a time when a great many people are breaking out of past patterns. "It was a year of protest and activity and lively disagreement— ... change, breaking up, clearing away, movement" (*FGC*, p. 292). But Martha realizes that this change may not be progressive. It represents a conversion of energy but not necessarily a push in the right direction.

Jack is the first person through whom Martha becomes aware of an impersonal energy that operates like electricity. Her love-making with him is described at first in terms of currents and pulses of the sea (the metaphor for her affair with Thomas Stern) but these terms are simultaneously the terms of electrical energy. Martha begins to see Jack as an "instrument" that focuses a "high alert tension" and acts as a dynamo to wash the lovers "through and through by currents of energy" (*FGC*, pp. 61, 62, 64). However, while Jack positively acts as the instrument that makes both lovers "conductors or conduits for the force which moved them and lifted them" (*FGC*, p. 495), he at the same time hints to the uncomprehending Martha about the negative potential of this energy He mentions that it is necessary to maintain firm control of these processes, for there "is a sort of wavelength you can tune into" and it is a apt to be the wavelength of hate as the place of love:

> "If you can get beyond *I hate*—then you find, *there is hatred, always there.* You can say, I am going into hatred now, it's just a force. That's all, it's not anything, not good or bad, you go into it. But man!—you have to come out again fast, it's too strong, it's too dangerous. But it's like a thousand volts of electricity." (*FGC*, p. 60)

When Martha consciously tries to recover the state of receptivity that she had accidentally entered as a girl on the veld and with Jack in London, she finds herself victimized by the "pairs of opposites," which continually switch on and off in her mind. She finds herself gripped by sadistic impulses, then suddenly by masochistic fantasies. She finds herself using the language of anti-Semitism and as suddenly repudiating her own statements. Gradually she comes to see that these are "what all those books call 'the pairs of opposites.' ... Every attitude, emotion, thought, has its opposite held in balance out of sight but there all the time. Push any one of them to an extreme, and boomps-a-daisy, over you go into its opposite.... A body is a machine for the conversion of one kind of energy into another" (*FGC*, pp. 539, 550).

Especially through the second and third sections of the novel, when she is trying to share the energy of madness with Lynda, images of vibration, wires, dynamos, volts, currents, tension, and fields or grounds fill Martha's narrated monologue. When she becomes aware that it is possible for individuals to share the same "wavelength" or to tap into each other's stream of thought, these electrical images mix with images of electronic communication.[14] The brain is likened to a radio and the various pools of universal emotion are called stations, bands, or wavelengths. Thoughts or emotions may be "in the air" for sensitive individuals to "pick up" or "tune in to." At best, these metaphors point to a sort of Jungian pan-psychism. Martha understands at one point, for instance, that Jack brings to her a timeless range of sexual responses, and that she can connect these with a pool of universal sexual energies that she shares with others:

> There was woman coming to man for sex, and her reactions, which were expected, known, understood. There was woman experiencing this new thing, sadism, masochism—succumbing to it then holding it off, refusing it, looking at it. And different from either, an impersonal current which she brought from Mark, who had it from Lynda, who had it from ... the impersonal sea. (*FGC*, p. 496)

Negatively, these metaphors can be used to account for madness. Lessing, influenced by R. D. Laing, reflects here his notion that the so-called mentally ill are those who are particularly receptive to reality and able to hear the thoughts of other people by simply tuning in to their wavelengths. Operating at the threshold of human capabilities, these special individuals are sometimes unable to control their experiences:

> There were people whose machinery had gone wrong, and they were like radio sets which, instead of being tuned in to one programme, were tuned in to a dozen simultaneously. *And they didn't know how to switch them off.* Even to imagine the hell of it was enough to make one want to run, to cover one's ears. (*FGC*, p. 518)

Even if the sensitive "receivers" are not overloaded by being attuned to too many wavelengths at once, they may still be destroyed if they become stuck on a channel that transmits only negative messages. This is Martha's metaphor for Lynda's state. As a girl Lynda had been too aware of the hatred that adults directed against her, and she learned to hear too exclusively the self-hater, the inner voice that echoes and amplifies the criticisms that come from outside the self. Moreover, everyone conspired to deny her the knowledge her specially developed senses gave her. Since no one wanted to hear that Lynda's stepmother hated her, everyone denied that she did—and particularly denied that Lynda could possibly sense such a fact, even if it were true.

It is suggested that the alarming number of people who have nervous breakdowns in the novel do so because like Lynda they are being worn down by the tension between society's pressure to repress a body of knowledge that lies within them and the opposite pressure of the knowledge, which wants to force itself out into the open. In earlier volumes of *Children of Violence*, Lessing repeatedly expressed this tension, in the image of a well that is filled with an emotion ready to overflow at any moment, threatening to pour through the "cracked surface" of a social facade.[15] In *The Four-Gated City*, Lessing abandons that image in order to express the conviction that there was once access to the insight or emotion in question and that it has been deliberately suppressed. Martha therefore speaks of putting experiences into cold storage and of burying evidence, and later of conducting a salvage operation to recover lost perceptions, of opening locked doors and rediscovering once-known territories.

These metaphors become so vivid that the reader almost comes to believe in the existence of a literal "tempting, dangerous, glamorous territory lying just behind or interfused with this world of ... landscapes, shores, countries forbidden and countries marked Open, each with its distinctive airs and climates and inhabitants living and dead, with its gardens and its forests and seas and lakes" (*FGC*, p. 462). Martha lives this fantasy—and the one about an empty, lit space to be found at the center of her consciousness—so intensely that the fantasy becomes as real for the reader as the Coldridge house itself, which in turn becomes a bit fantastic, a symbol of Martha's divided self. In depicting the reality of her character Martha, Lessing adheres to her statement of belief in "The Small Personal Voice": "I define realism as art which springs so vigorously and naturally from a strongly-held, though not necessarily intellectually-defined, view of life that it absorbs symbolism."[16]

It is important to keep this perspective on Martha's metaphors, if we are not to reject as simply insane her conviction of having developed a special ability to hear the thoughts of others. For example, Martha describes a time when she begins to hear Paul's thoughts. She says that she seems to have switched on to a radio channel that carries Paul's fantasies. She begins wondering whether she is picking up Paul's words in their original form or whether some mechanism might be translating his feelings into words. She speaks, too, of the law by which "one did not hear something, pick up something that one didn't know, or was prepared to accept, already" (*FGC*, p. 371). While Martha is thinking in terms of the radio metaphor, her speculations may seem bizarre. But she finally states the case in pedestrian prose: "Perhaps it was more a question of remembering—that was a more accurate word, or idea" (*FGC*, p. 371). All the metaphors of cold storage, salvage operations, hidden territories, and radios express one psychological fact—that society and our own instincts for self-protection cause us to repress the great bulk of what we perceive, but that through great effort we may remember these perceptions and achieve extraordinary insights into reality. If we were to be conscious of all we already know, reality would be so much more than we now know that it would be as if whole new countries had suddenly appeared next to the one we have consciously lived in.

Now perhaps we can understand the relevance of the epigraph to part one, a passage from Rachel Carson's *The Edge of the Sea*:

> In its being and its meaning, this coast represents not merely an uneasy equilibrium of land and water masses; it is eloquent of a continuing change now actually in progress, a change being brought about by the life processes of living things. Perhaps the sense of this comes most clearly to one standing on a bridge between the Keys, looking out over miles of water, dotted with mangrove-covered islands to the horizon. This may seem a dreamy land, steeped in its past. But under the bridge a green mangrove seedling floats, long and slender, one end already beginning to show the development of roots, beginning to reach down through the water, ready to grasp and to root firmly in any muddy shoal that may lie across its path. Over the years the mangroves bridge the water gaps between the islands; they extend the mainland; they create new islands. And the currents that stream under the bridge, carrying the mangrove seedling, are one with the currents that carry plankton to the coral animals building the offshore reef, creating a wall of rocklike solidity, a wall that one day may be added to the mainland. So this coast is built. (*FGC*, p. 2)

As the mangrove root connects shoal to shoal, extending the mainland, so Martha's salvage operations recover territory and add it to her personal "landscapes, shores, countries" (*FGC*, p. 462). And as with the mangroves, this change is "being brought about by the life processes of living things."

A whole series of metaphors links Martha's development with the natural evolution of living things growing beyond the previous limits of their nature. These images begin in the first volume, *Martha Quest*, when in her moment of difficult knowledge, Martha "felt the rivers under the ground forcing themselves painfully along her veins, swelling them out in an unbearable pressure; her flesh was the earth, and suffered growth like a ferment.... It was as if something new was demanding conception, with her flesh as host" (*MQ*, pp. 52–53).

The tension in this experience, the image of fluid straining against a swelling vessel, and the suggestion of rebirth are repeated toward the end of the volume, when Martha remembers a scene from the farm. In a passage that fittingly retains the pastoral simplicity of an idyll, while it moves toward a distasteful over-ripeness, Martha encounters an image that exhilarates her, though at this point she cannot understand what it signifies.

> She saw, as if the deep-green substance of the leafage had taken on another form, two enormous green caterpillars, about seven inches long, the thickness of a wrist; pale green they were, a sickly intense green, smooth as skin, and their silky-paper surfaces were stretched to bursting, as if the violence of this pulsating month was growing in them so fast (Martha could see the almost liquid substance swimming inside the frail tight skin) that they might burst asunder with the pressure of their growth before they could turn themselves, as was right and proper, into dry cases, like bits of stick, and so into butterflies or moths. They were loathsome, disgusting; Martha felt sick as she looked at these fat and seething creatures rolling clumsily on their light frond of leaves, blind, silent, their heads indicated only by two small horns, mere bumpish projections of the greenish skin, like pimples—they were repulsive, but she was exhilarated. She went home singing. (*MQ*, p. 199)

These creatures are participating in their proper cycle of development: yet, repulsively, they push their development beyond its former bounds, stretching their skins to the limit. This image becomes a model not only for Martha's unorthodox process of self-development but also for the evolution of the human race. In *Landlocked*, Martha's teacher Thomas Stern suggests that the pains of her life are simply her straining against a "frail tight skin" like the caterpillar. Perhaps, he proposes, there may come one day a mutation that will allow a transformation in the human race such as the caterpillar's metamorphosis from crawling insect to butterfly. "Perhaps that's why we are all so sick. Something new is trying to get born through our thick skins" (*L*, p. 116). The loathsomeness of the "fat and seething creatures" is analogous to the seeming madness of the many persons who compose the vanguard in a process of psychic evolution. "I tell you, Martha," he says, "if I see a sane person, then I know he's mad. You know, the householders. It's we who are nearest to being—what's needed" (*L*, p. 116).

These caterpillars with overexpanded skins are about to become butterflies. Lynda, Martha, and Thomas Stern are "in the main line of evolution," yet society rejects them because of their highly developed psychic capacities.

> In spite of ... society's never having been more shrilly self-conscious than it is now, it is an organism which above all is unable to think, whose essential characteristic is the inability to diagnose its own condition. It is like one of those sea creatures who have tentacles or arms equipped with numbing poisons: anything new, whether hostile or helpful, must be stunned into immobility or at least wrapped around with poison or a cloud of distorting colour. (*FGC*, p. 451)

Thus poisons, drugs, and hypnosis become images of all those processes by which society prevents the natural course of human evolution. Martha observes this poisoning process at work in her first meeting with a member of the British upper class. The first thing she notices about Henry Matheson is his complacency. To his discomfort, she reproaches him: "You're drugged, you're hypnotised, you don't seem to be able to see facts when they're in front of you. You're the victim of a lot of slogans" (*FGC*, p. 30). This encounter leads her to the conviction that she must "live in such a way that I don't just—turn into a hypnotised animal" (*FGC*, p. 98).

Like everyone else, Martha does allow herself to be hypnotised, but through Lynda's tutelage she learns to waken herself. Awakening means remembering all that society has required she forget; even harder, it means seeing at every moment all of an experience, not just the part that society requires one to focus on. There is a long passage of intense, almost surreal description, in which Martha goes out for a walk, having awakened her sensibilities. The prose alternates between the raptures of full perception and the tortures of seeing other people who are blinded and poisoned, uncomprehending. At the sight of the sky and the foliage she exclaims:

> Let me keep this, let me not lose it, oh, how could I have borne it all these years, all this life, being dead and asleep and not seeing, seeing nothing; for now everything was so much there, present, existing in an effulgence of delight, offering themselves to her, till she felt they were extensions of her and she of them, or at least, their joy and hers sang together, so that she felt they might almost cry out, Martha! Martha! for happiness, because she was seeing them, feeling them again after so long an absence from them. (*FGC*, pp. 505–506)

On the other hand, she is repelled by the humans, because they are such a perversion of what they naturally should be. A long Swiftian passage depicts the sluggish creatures in all their vileness. Finally Martha identifies the worst horror about these "defectively evolved animals":

> The eyes had a look which contradicted their function, which was to see, to observe, for as she passed pair after pair of eyes, they all looked half drugged, or half asleep, dull, as if the creatures had been hypnotised or poisoned, for these people walked in their fouled and disgusting streets full of ordure and bits of refuse and paper as if they were not conscious of their existence here, were somewhere else: and they were somewhere else, for only one in a hundred of these semi-animals could have said, "I am here, now, and conscious that I am here, now, noticing what is around me." (*FGC*, p. 506)

A bit more prosaically, Martha had seen the same vision when she ate dinner with Henry Matheson, her would-be benefactor: "It was like talking to—well, the blind, people blinkered from birth" (*FGC*, p. 33). Nonetheless, blindness and stupor are not confined to the upper class; they are human afflictions wherever society has had its effect on the individual.

Martha herself battles continually to waken herself from lethargy and impercipience. At the very brink of her final moment of vision, Martha feels "herself as a heavy impervious insensitive lump that, like a planet doomed always to be dark on one side, had vision in front only, a myopic searchlight blind except for the tiny three-dimensional path open immediately before her eyes in which the outline of a tree, a rose, emerged, then submerged in dark" (*FGC*, p. 591). How far she is, at this point, from the children of the coming apocalypse, who will not only luxuriate in the sun, sea, and flowers that presently surround them but also sense the sounds and sights of distant places. Indeed, these survivors of the apocalypse will awaken to heights of perception heretofore unknown. From her station on Faris Island, after the disaster, Martha will report:

> It is a place with a rare fine air, a "high" air, if I can use that word. Sometimes it seems that inside ordinary light shimmers another kind of brilliance, but very subtle and delicate. And the texture of our lives, eating, sleeping, being together, has a note in it that can't be quite caught, as if we were all of us a half-tone or a bridging chord in some symphony being played out of earshot with icebergs and forests and mountains for instruments. There is a transparency, a crystalline gleam.
>   It is the children who have it, who are sensitive to it—being with them means we have to be quick and sensitive ourselves, as far as we can be. (*FGC*, pp. 645–646)

These children are Martha's butterflies, born out of the straining of their thick caterpillar skins (*MQ*, 199; *L*, p. 116). They are the mutants by way of radiation who were predicted by the students on the Aldermaston March (*FGC*, p. 414). They are the response to a necessity that man acquire new organs of perception, as the Sufi prophet Idries Shah says in the passage used as epigraph to part four of *The Four-Gated City*. Shah states in flat prose the belief that Lessing has been expressing metaphorically:

> Humanity is evolving towards a certain destiny. We are all taking part in that evolution. Organs come into being as a result of a need for specific organs. The human being's organism is producing a new complex of organs in response to such a need. In this age of the transcending of time and space, the complex of organs is concerned with the transcending of time and space. What ordinary people regard as sporadic and occasional bursts of telepathic and prophetic power are seen by the Sufi as nothing less than the first stirrings of these same organs. The difference between all evolution up to date and the present need for evolution is that for the past ten thousand years or so we have been given the possibility of a conscious evolution. So essential is this more rarified evolution that our future depends on it. (*FGC*, p. 448)

Martha, with her intermittent access to heights of perception, is, as one of the new children reports, "a sort of experimental model" of which nature has had enough now that the clairvoyant children have been born. She has done her duty as part of the evolutionary line. Like the sycamore tree, Martha waited for her "curve of growth" to develop, until "from a dead-looking eye, or knot, it bursts again in a new branch, in a shape that is inevitable but known only to itself" (*FGC*, p. 201). She was admirably persistent in nurturing the growth of her extrasensory skills—surrounded as she was by a society hostile to such growth. After all, "how long did roots live under a crust of air-excluding tarmac?" (*FGC*, p. 8). The condition of her growth has been a willingness to move in response to the rhythms of life, a fluid sort of patience. "She had learned that one thing, that most important thing, which was that one simply had to go on, take one step after another: this process in itself held the keys" (*FGC*, p. 588). The steps may seem to take one in repetitious circles, but when all the working-through is done "you start growing on your own account" (*FGC*, p. 454). In the meantime, repetition, the turning of the ferris wheel, affords the finest wisdom that one may achieve. Martha's final wisdom comes through a voice that has repeated in her brain since the first vision of her girlhood. It says that beauty, transcendence—whatever she is seeking—is "here, where else, you fool, you poor fool, where else has it been, ever ... " (*FGC*, p. 591).

If the novel proper ends with a vision of beauty in the present moment, the Appendix takes the reader over to an apocalyptic future time in which prophecy is fulfilled. The metaphors of poisoning that have appeared in the whole series intensify throughout *The Four-Gated City*, culminating in Lynda's vision of a contaminated England, looking like "a poisoned mouse lying dead in a corner" (*FGC*, p. 566). She also sees a "kind of frozen dew" that covers everything with "a faintly phosphorescent or begemmed stillness" (*FGC*, p. 566). In the Appendix these images are fulfilled in accounts of England's contamination by radiation after a nuclear accident. In fact, the exiled Martha speculates that before the catastrophe everyone had an unconscious foreknowledge of coming disaster. The accuracy of these prophecies, along with the appearance of the predicted special race of children, seems to point toward the existence of the "certain destiny" of which Idries Shah spoke. Thus Martha was right when she suspected that life was inexorably determined by forces beyond her control, but she was wrong to fear these forces and to believe that inevitability was inimical to the human race. Martha had thought that inevitability implied the worthlessness of human will and consciousness. But now she learns that it is possible for her to live with dignity in harmony with the will of evolution.

There is a difference between fatalistic resignation and a fruitful receptivity. One may, Martha discovers, accept the demand that the future be conceived in one's own flesh (*MQ*, p. 52). One may be one's own midwife and assist the future in its birth. One may, like the mangrove, throw off seeds that will ultimately join the mainland (the dominant society) to the islands (groups of innovators, such as the children on Martha's island). Or one may refuse, like Mark Coldridge.

Thus, inevitability is Janus-faced. While it destroyed the will of some, others "it quietened and sobered; made them grow fast, developed them" (*FGC*, p. 601). The attitude of fatalism that plagued the young Martha Quest, causing her to lie down and let fate march over her, also victimizes Mark Coldridge, author of the utopian novel, *A City in the Desert*. Affected by the "fatalism, the determinism, which is so oddly rooted in [Communism] that revolutionary party" (*FGC*, p. 148), he falls from idealism into nihilism and loses his will. He, like Martha and Thomas Stern before him, imitates Nasrudin of the Sufi fable: When a chill runs through him, he becomes convinced that he is dead and just lies on the grass while wolves eat his donkey (*L*, p. 213). It may seem illogical to retain one's sense of free will in the face of determinism, but that is what the wisdom of the tale and of *Children of Violence* counsels. If one gives up believing that one's decisions and acts matter, one ends a cynic like Mark, moaning, "What point has there ever been?" (*FGC*, p. 653). On the other hand, if one follows continually the drift of events, using intelligence and imagination to chart a survival course, one may, at last, like Martha arrive at an island where even "the face of the world's horror could be turned around to show the smile of an angel" (*FGC*, p. 643).

While the jaded Mark only dreams mawkishly of the ideal city about which he had once written a prophetic novel, Martha actually labors to bring it about. As a girl she had envisioned "a noble city, set foursquare and colonnaded along its falling, flower-bordered terraces," a fabulous and ancient city where children of all races play together among white pillars and tall trees (*MQ*, p. 11). As an adult she is haunted by the image of the ideal city, the purity of which contrasts so painfully with the actual, rotten capitals of Zambesia and England. This double vision is incorporated in Mark's novel *A City in the Desert*, vaguely reminiscent of Borges's "Tlön, Uqbar, Orbius Tertius." As a "shadow city of poverty and beastliness" threatens to overwhelm the ideal city, it is protected by its gardeners, the hidden keepers of an ideal order:

> A great number of the inhabitants spent their lives in the gardens,
> and the fountains and parks. Even the trees and plants were

known for their properties and qualities and grown exactly in a relation to other plants, and to people and buildings; and it was among the gardeners, so the stories went, that could be found, if only one could recognize them, most of the hidden people who protected and fed the city. (*FGC*, p. 140)

Through the metaphor of the gardeners, the dilemma of Martha's private *Bildung*—and that of the collective as well—is resolved. She learns to come to terms with the inner order of experience and thus is able to save a number of people from destruction. It is on account of her intuition of the coming apocalypse that a small number of people are sequestered on an island, where the gifted children of a new age are born. These children she refers to as "our guardians." The prophecy of Mark's novel seems due for fulfillment when Martha sends the most gifted of these children, Joseph, to become a gardener in Nairobi, the city in the desert where Francis heads a colony of refugees from the holocaust. And with these gardens we return to the guiding metaphor of organic growth. The order of the garden is natural, but human gardeners must learn the principles behind that order and tend it continually.

In accepting the natural order of life, Martha Quest has not simply given up choice, as Barnouw suggests; rather, she has given up egocentric willfulness in order to exercise choice wisely in the service of a collective *Bildung*. She is not passive to the point of despair, as Spacks asserts, but rather she waits until the time for action is ripe—she knows the value of latency. Moreover, far from there being "little positive meaning" in Martha's attempts to free herself from the horrors of her past, the movement of her life is positively redemptive. Finally, through the metaphors that thread through the five-novel sequence, Lessing supplies what critic Enright did not see: an "artistically true ... connection between the Martha Quest whom we first met as a fifteen-year-old in the novel named after her and the old woman" who nurtures the children of violence.

In an interview given just after the publication of *The Four-Gated City*, Lessing expressed a strong faith in the future of mankind, even though that future may be born out of violence. "Maybe out of destruction there will be born some new creature. I don't mean physically. What interests me more than anything is how our minds are changing, how our ways of perceiving reality are changing. The substance of life receives shocks all the time, every place, from bombs, from the all-pervasive violence. Inevitably, the mind changes."[17] Images of growth, evolution, and energy conversion present her hope, while images of enclosure, constriction, blindness, poisoning, and stupor present the obstacles to that hope, which is finally embodied in the image of the four-gated city and its hidden gardeners. In the struggle between the human desire for good and all within us that holds us back from attaining it, the good will prevail. That vision is nowhere more vivid than in Martha Quest's report of a year on her island:

> During that year we hit the depths of our fear, a lowering depression which made it hard for us not to simply walk into that deadly sea and let ourselves drown there. But it was also during that year when we became aware of a sweet high loveliness somewhere, like a flute played only just within hearing. We all felt it. We talked about it, thinking it was a sign that we must be dying. It was as if all the air was washed with a bright promise. Of what? Love? Joy? It was as if the face of the world's horror could be turned around to show the smile of an angel. It was during this year that many of us walking alone or in groups along the cliffs or beside the inland streams met and talked to people who were not of our company, nor like any people we had known—though some of us had dreamed of them. It was as if the veil between this world and another had worn so thin that people from the sun could walk together and be companions. When this time which was so terrible and so marvellous had gone by some of us began to wonder if we had suffered from a mass hallucination. But we knew we had not. It was from that time, because of what we were told, that we took heart and held on to our belief in a future for our race. (*FGC*, p. 643)

Notes

Chapter Three: *The Four-Gated City*

1. Dagmar Barnouw, "Disorderly Company: From *The Golden Notebook* to *The Four-Gated City*," in *Doris Lessing: Critical Studies*, ed. Annis Pratt and L. S. Dembo (Madison: Univ. of Wisconsin Press, 1974), pp. 83f.

2. Patricia Meyer Spacks, *The Female Imagination*, p. 157.

3. D.J. Enright, "Shivery Games," *The New York Review of Books*, July 31, 1969, p. 22.

4. Johann Wolfgang von Goethe, *Wilhelm Meister's Apprenticeship*, Bk. VII, Ch. 9, p. 461.

5. D.J. Enright, "Shivery Games," p. 22.

6. As is evident in the title *The Tree Outside the Window*, the image of the tree is central to Ellen Cronan Rose's analysis of *The Four-Gated City*. In

that analysis, she regards Lessing as setting up an analogy: just as a tree gains its nutrients from the soil and returns nutrients to it, so a person gains life from a social context and returns life to it, so a person gains life from a social context and returns life to it. Rose tests *The Four-Gated City* against this model and finds it wanting. "The image of the tree," she says," makes its generic statement by a willful superimposition of meaning which turns Martha from the particular into the exemplary 'individual conscience in its relations with the collective.' While Lessing's use of the metaphor makes it clear that she does not intend her protagonist's achievement of identity to be an exercise in solipsism, it does not succeed in defining precisely the manner of Martha's final relation to society" (p. 57). Rose ends her discussion of *The Four-Gated City* by declaring that "the collective, as Lessing describes it in *Children of Violence*, is hostile to the individual. The logical conclusion to the conflict between the two occurs at the end of Part Four of *The Four-Gated City*. It is a bleak and pessimistic acceptance of the irreconcilability of the self and society" (p. 68).

One can agree with Rose that Martha's Quest's "society" is much more hostile to her perceptions than Wilhelm Meister's was to his—that is, if one defines Martha's "society" as the group of persons in power in the British government at the time of the Catastrophe. It seems equally valid, however, to define Martha's "society" as the subgroup of persons (analogous to Wilhelm's Society of the Tower) who share her values and her vision of a better world. Since I tend to the later view, I consider the analogy that Rose has pointed out to be both a valid and a consistently *successful* one, as it operates in the novel: Martha takes life and learning from her various societies—her parents, Solly and Josh, her political allies, the Coldridge family—and returns life and wisdom to the refined society of post-Catastrophy Europe.

Here in chapter three, written before my reading of Rose's monograph, I examine another side of the image of the tree—its function as a remainder of the organic quality of Martha's development from child of the veld to sage of Faris Island.

7. Johann Wolfgang von Goethe, *Wilhelm Meister's Apprenticeship*, Bk. XIII, Ch. 14, p. 234.

8. See A Proper Marriage, pp. 63, 98, 247. In notes and text, the following abbreviations will be used for the volumes of *Children of Violence*:

MQ: *Martha Quest* (1952; rpt. New York: New American Library, 1970).

PM: *A Proper Marriage* (1954; rpt. New York: New American Library, 1970).

RS: *A Ripple from the Storm* (1958; rpt. New York: New American Library, 1970).

L: *Landlocked* (1965; rpt. New York: New American Library, 1970). *FGC: The Four-Gated City* (1969; rpt. New York: Bantam Books, 1970).

9. Frederick P.W. McDowell is the most perceptive of these critics when he says that "the fluctuating image of the great wheel at the town carnival emphasizes Martha's own restlessness and futility" ("The Fiction of Doris Lessing: An Interim View," p. 333). It is Martha's reaction to the idea of repetition that is futile, not the cycle itself. In my opinion, Robert Morris, Nancy Porter, and Lloyd Brown arrive at unnecessarily limited interpretations because they ignore the suggestion that there is saving power in the cycle of repetition. For them, the ferris wheel is simply an image of futile repetition without change. See Robert Morris, *Continuance and Change: The Contemporary British Novel Sequence*, p. 17; Nancy Porter, "Silenced History—*Children of Violence* and *The Golden Notebook*," *World Literature Written in English*, 12, no. 2 (November 1973): 165; and Lloyd Brown, "The Shape of Things: Sexual Images and the Sense of Form in Doris Lessing's Fiction," World Literature Written in English 14, no. 1 (April 1965): 179.

10. Several critics have noted Lessing's use of rooms, walls, and houses as symbols, most notably: Frederick Karl, "Doris Lessing in the Sixties"; Ellen Cronan Rose, *The Tree Outside the Window*, esp. pp. 49-56, 59-60, 64-65; and Claire Sprague, "Without Contraries is no Progression': Lessing's *The Four-Gated City*," *Modern Fiction Studies* 26 (Spring 1980): 96-116.

11. Selma R. Burkom, "'Only Connect': Form and Content in the Works of Doris Lessing," p. 53.

12. Marion Vlastos, "Doris Lessing and R. D. Laing: Psychopolitics and Prophecy," *PMLA* 91, no. 2 (March 1976: 245-258. This is a beautifully crafted article explaining clearly the connections between Laing's and Lessing's theories about madness.

13. Ibid., p. 247, quoting R.D. Laing, The Politics of Experience (1967; rpt. New York: Ballantine Books, 1970), p.75.

14. Sydney Janet Kaplan notes the imagery of electronics and radios and says, "It is, of course, all in keeping with the struggle to connect individual and communal consciousness—a process of communication" ("The Limits of Consciousness in the Novels of Doris Lessing," in Doris Lessing: Critical Studies, p. 127).

15. See PM, 220, 255, 324; *RS*, 122, 230.

16. Doris Lessing, "The Small Personal Voice," p.4.

17. "Doris Lessing at Stony Brook: An Interview by Jonah Raskin," p. 66.

CLAIRE SPRAGUE

Mothers and Daughters/ Aging and Dying

A faint warning voice from the well of fatality did remark that a girl child was in the direct line of matriarchy she so feared.

—Doris Lessing, *A Proper Marriage*

"Imagine being old. Imagine when no one will turn to look at me. I'll be like that old woman there—an old grey sheep in a hair-net. It must be like being a ghost, moving among other people, and no one noticing you at all. Perhaps there's no one to care when she comes in and goes out. She lives in a room by herself, and if she died, no one would even notice it. Perhaps she doesn't know herself that she is alive?"

—Doris Lessing, *Retreat to Innocence*

The loss of the daughter to the mother, the mother to the daughter, is the essential female tragedy.

—Adrienne Rich, *Of Woman Born*

J ulia Barr, the spoiled upper-class innocent of *Retreat to Innocence*, will not fare well in old age. We are meant to dislike her shallowness and her stereotypically female commitment to appearance. At age twenty-one she cannot imagine not being noticed by others. Old women are invisible. Julia's

From *Rereading Doris Lessing: Narrative Patterns of Doubling and Repetition.* © 1987 by Claire Sprague.

fear of invisibility and isolation are vividly captured in her unexpectedly original image of the old woman as "an old grey sheep in a hair-net."

Presumably other Doris Lessing characters will prove to have a finer, fuller appreciation of aging and aged women. In fact, Julia's fear of old age is duplicated in characters we are meant to judge positively. It initiates a fear of the aging process in Lessing protagonists that culminates in *The Diaries of Jane Somers*, published nearly thirty years after *Retreat to Innocence*, and that includes her five-volume *Canopus in Argos* series as well as her earlier five-volume *Children of Violence* series. It includes the unnamed narrator (she can be called the survivor) of *The Memoirs of a Survivor*, as well as Kate Brown of *The Summer before the Dark*. It should include Susan Rawlings of the short story "To Room Nineteen," for no discussion of Lessing's thinking about aging women can ignore her analysis of the mid-life crisis, one Lessing tends to fix in the early or mid-forties. Susan does not survive her crisis, but Kate Brown does. Kate Brown can, in fact, be described as Susan Rawlings positively reimagined. In Kate Brown's survival is writ the postulate that old age cannot be reached or successfully negotiated without a resolution of the mid-life crisis. But the problems of aging and dying, as Lessing addresses them, cannot be neatly placed within the simpler contemporary confines of the phrase "mid-life crisis."

There are many examples of women who nearly or actually break down or commit suicide in Lessing's fiction (e.g., Mary Turner in *Grass*; Susan Rawlings; Kate Brown; Anna Wulf in *The Golden Notebook*; Martha Quest, Lynda Coldridge, Dorothy Quentin, and Sarah/Sally Coldridge in *The Four-Gated City*). There are also examples of survival. Lynda Coldridge and Martha Quest are the most powerful. (Emily and her surrogate mother are also high on the survivor list.) Lynda Coldridge does more than survive a lifetime of bizarre treatment as a mental patient. In *Shikasta*, she collaborates with a doctor in training a new generation in the techniques of telepathy. Martha's life is conducive to our imagining a chapter called "Martha Quest: Sage and Survivor." But a little reflection shows how partial such an approach and such a chapter would finally be, how falsely upbeat in the face of Lessing's fundamental insistence on uncertainty and skepticism. Yes, Martha does become a sage, even a telepath, but her old age is more imagined than felt, more an afterthought in the appendix section to *The Four-Gated City* than a reality in the novel proper. Above all, to acclaim Martha and to ignore the most powerful portrait of the aging woman in all of Lessing's work until *The Diaries of Jane Somers* would be scandalous, especially when it occurs in the same novel. We cannot talk about Martha Quest in old age without talking about May Quest in old age.

Once May is mentioned the issue of the aging process in women becomes enormously complicated. We discover that it is impossible to talk about aging in women without talking about the mother-daughter relationship. In May and Martha the mother-daughter fulcrum is at its most intense and most negative. From Mary Turner's memories of her defeated, supposedly feminist, mother in *The Grass Is Singing* or Julia Barr's rivalry with her feminist and political mother, Jane Barr, to Jane (Janna) Somers's relationship with her surrogate mother, Maudie, or Alice Mellings's exploitation of her mother, Dorothy, in *The Good Terrorist*, Lessing restlessly works and reworks her vision of the mother-daughter relationship. That relationship is never resolved, unless we wish to call it resolution when mothers or daughters develop temporary working relationships with surrogate, nonbiological daughters or mothers, as the survivor and Emily Mary do in *Memoirs*, or as Kate and Maureen in *Summer* or Janna and Maudie in *Jane Somers* do. The mother-daughter tie is never dissociated from the process of growing and aging. Mothers—surrogate or otherwise—forever function as mirrors for their daughters. The complex circularity of daughters fighting mothers and then becoming mothers themselves both repeats and advances Lessing's themes and patterns.

I have not mentioned Anna Wulf in this connection. She is obviously exceptional in at least two ways. Her biological mother is absent (yet briefly present through the given name, May, she shares with Martha's mother). Instead she has the surrogate Mother Sugar whose role would be significantly diffused and defused if Anna's natural mother were also present. Anna is given a father and a unique single and professional life-style. She does have a daughter, Janet, who chooses boarding school, with its uniform dress code, in deliberate opposition to her mother's "free" style. Janet, who does not want to be like Anna, recalls Martha, who does not want to be like May. Janet's bourgeois longings are exaggerated in Janna Somers's glossy life-style. Janna Somers may also remind Lessing aficionados of the motherless Anna, as Maudie may remind them of Molly, Anna's other self. The echoic elements of Anna/Janet and Anna/Molly in Janna/Maudie do not destroy the integrity of the fictional characters in their respective works. The reverse is true. Their recurrence with variation opens small slits of light into authorial compulsions; the repetitions that lightly link novel to novel create special layers of meaning for the reader. The two women Anna is, to use the phrasing of *The Golden Notebook*, seem indeed to have resurfaced in the figures of Janna and Maudie.

The media and Lessing herself were delighted with the deceptive game that presented Jane Somers instead of Doris Lessing to the public as the author of *The Diaries* (see Sprague and Tiger, introduction). Lessing claimed as her motive for the pseudonym her desire to expose the difficulties that face an unknown writer. Her altruism is suspect. Artistic deception is never that simple. The Jane Somers caper involved more profound personal and artistic needs. Through Jane/Janna Somers Lessing confronts more directly than she could in earlier novels or in the Canopus novels her own guilt and her own fears about aging and dying.

Thus problems of aging and dying in Lessing's work are unexpectedly localized in the always painful and always inescapable mother-daughter relationship. They are understandably located in women rather than in men both because Lessing is a woman and because women are on the whole more enslaved to physical appearance than men are. These problems are addressed fully and directly in *The Diaries of Jane Somers*, and less fully or directly in earlier works.

The Canopus novels consider the anguish of mortality from an indirect and species point of view. Here the problems of aging and dying seem to disappear, for Canopeans, Sirians, and Shammatans live for millennia. Yet the Canopean archives are an extremely painful record of the rise and fall of peoples and empires, of the collective suffering of inferior peoples like ourselves—inferior because they/we are so ridiculously short-lived and myopic, so impossibly greedy, corrupt, and victimized by hunger, poverty, disease, and racism. Finally and paradoxically, the world of the Canopean novels, its galactic stage and immortal foreground figures notwithstanding, is claustrophobic and filled with fatality.

There is a more pointed relationship between the fourth volume, *The Making of the Representative for Planet 8*, and Lessing's recent return to realism in *The Diaries of Jane Somers* and *The Good Terrorist*. *The Making of the Representative*, fabular and haunting as *Jane Somers* is not, can nonetheless be described as a dress rehearsal for the later novel. In *Making*, Lessing confronts species annihilation as a form of transcendence. Perhaps criticism of her space fiction adventures coalesced with her own need to return to earth and its smaller but more vivid problems of time and aging and dying. However we interpret the *Diaries*, their obverse relationship to *Making* is striking. Both works are concerned with coming to terms with mortality. But in the *Diaries* the universe is no longer abstract or galactic or remote. Ambien II's sexless androgyny disappears; the long millennial view is discarded. In the *Diaries* Lessing turns to the malodorous and incontinent world of ill and aged women, to their invisibility and isolation, to their imprisonment in state care in the form of Good Neighbours and Meals on Wheels, to the world that so terrified Julia Barr.

Making and *Diaries* form a paradoxical dialectical encounter with issues of aging and dying that reimagines the characteristic location of these problems in earlier mother-daughter dyads: May and Martha, Kate and Maureen, the survivor and Emily. The most recent dyad, Dorothy and Alice Mellings of *The Good Terrorist*, both reverses and sustains Lessing's earliest interpretation of the mother-daughter configuration. The rebellious, dependent daughter and the powerful mother are still there, but their psychic organization has undergone an ironic revolution. The daughter cannot escape her dependence, but the mother can. Dorothy abandons Alice instead of vice-versa. Furthermore, the mother figure is wholly sympathetic and the daughter figure wholly unsympathetic.

The temporal angst located in the mother-daughter relationship seems especially acute in the figures of Martha and May Quest in *The Four-Gated City* and in Jane Somers and Maudie Fowler in *The Diary of a Good Neighbour*. The angst in *The Making of the Representative for Planet 8* is related to the apparently unrelated earlier texts. The kinship between these temporal and transcendent novels asserts itself in unexpected ways.

MARTHA AND MAY

Martha and May—the sounds of their names are close enough to suggest sisterhood and equality rather than the authority-dependency roles of the child-parent relationship. Both daughter and mother dread yet feel compelled to accomplish their final reunion in London. The novel is *The Four-Gated City*, the year approximately 1954; May is about sixty-four, Martha, thirty-five. May postpones her trip from Africa twice; Martha, terrified at the prospect of her mother's visit, turns in desperation to the medical establishment in the person of Dr. Lamb. Martha ironically perceives May's projected visit as an interruption of the excavation of her past that is her consuming project. That special excavation—Martha calls it "work"—is the indispensable precondition to mastery of the self. Martha makes no conscious connection between her interior analysis of the past and her mother's visit. The reader must make that connection and recognize a colossal irony: theoretical confrontation with the past is one thing, its materialization in the person of May Quest quite another. If the impending visit of mother to daughter can threaten breakdown and flight to the psychoanalyst, then Martha is still enslaved to her past and very far from the wholeness she so covets.

The central consciousness in *The Four-Gated City* and in its four predecessors is Martha Quest. There are times when that center shifts (as it does to Jimmy or to Mrs. Van in *A Ripple from the Storm*) or is diffused within a group of characters (as it is in the Aldermaston chapter of *The Four-Gated City*). But there is no shift so disruptive—even so violent, although the words and the scene are very quiet—in any of the novels as the one that transfers the point of view to May Quest in Cape Town in chapter 4, part 2, of *The Four-Gated City*. The omniscient opening line is a shock: "An old lady sat in a flower-crammed balcony high above the breathing sea" (247). The extraordinary narrative shift and the empathy displayed toward the lonely, limited, psychically imprisoned Mrs. Quest belong to the authorial voice, not to Martha Quest. It is a point of view brought in from outside as though the authorial voice were making up for what Martha cannot do. Its intrusion is so emphatic and disruptive that it proclaims an unresolved artistic problem and suggests an unresolved personal one.

May thinks more about her own girlhood than she does about Martha on her voyage to England. Her most haunting memory is of her first menses. Fittingly, that memory is triggered by a daughter figure aboard ship who bends over and dislodges and then tosses overboard "a little bloody swab." The generational contrast is painful. May remembers "a long story of humiliation and furtiveness, great soaking bloody clouts that rubbed and smelled, and which one was always secretly washing, or concealing, or trying to burn; headaches and backaches and all kinds of necessary tact with obtuse brothers and fathers; and then her breasts, her first sprouting breasts, about which the family had made jokes and she had blushed—but of course, had been a good sort" (268). May had earlier admired the athletic, healthy young woman of the 1950s, but her furtive act, occurring as if May were not present, and her casual remark, "'Plenty of room in the sea'" (267), make May seethe, rage, suffer.

This episode and recall (probably a pastiche of her mother's stories and her own experiences) are typical of Lessing's immense sympathy with the older woman out of step with the mores of the younger generation. May Quest may not understand her subjections and her humiliations, but Lessing makes the reader understand them in ways that Martha cannot. Martha has typically taunted her mother with her sexuality and her intellect and will do so again both wittingly and unwittingly, affronting her with capacities traditionally denied to women, capacities May rejects in her daughter and in other women. Instead of criticizing Mrs. Quest for her obvious failures, as Martha has always done, Lessing makes the reader understand May's rage at having been cheated and her transference of that rage to the young woman and to Martha.

May's London visit is doomed to failure. Her racism, her anti-communism, her inability to understand Martha's sexual life with the man who is Lynda's husband in name only, make her do everything wrong. She cannot stop herself. Her reflex response of a lifetime—compulsive housecleaning—could not be more wrong. Martha's bottled rage and inability to act for herself sends her in turn to Dr. Lamb to act for her. He does Martha's dirty work. May returns home to wait for death, having been, in her last years, able to relate only to children—to white ones in England, black ones in Africa. Mrs. Quest does, in fact, as we later offhandedly learn, die less than a year later, an exemplar of Adrienne Rich's judgment that "the mother stands for the victim in ourselves, the unfree woman, the martyr" (*Of Woman Born*, 238). Mother and daughter are indeed, to use Rich's language, tragically lost to one another (240), unable to break the patterns of their shared past.

In 1958, when Martha is almost thirty-nine, she describes herself as a middle-aged woman, "a kind of special instrument sensitised to [the] mood and need and state" of each member of the family (352), "being the person who ran and managed and kept going" (354). She has become "her old antagonist, the competent middle-aged woman" (219), whom "she hated and feared more than any other" (360). Like Susan Rawlings of "To Room Nineteen," she looks forward to time alone; unlike Susan, she doesn't have to leave home to begin to understand her quest. (She discovers it through Lynda Coldridge in the basement rooms of the Coldridge house.) Later Martha graduates to her own room in the house of one of her nonbiological sons. Martha's relationship with her large, non-kin brood—one more like a commune than family—makes her movement in and out of the family more possible and less filled with anger and resentment than in her earlier kinship families. These, the one she is born into and the ones she makes by her own two marriages, are failures. They crack under strain. They lack the organic quality of the Coldridge house and brood, which are like the tree outside Martha's window in their ability to grow and change.

The double ending of *The Four-Gated City* needs to be insisted upon. The appendix should be kept separate from the novel proper. Martha's old age and death are reported in the appendix indirectly and fitfully in part of a letter written to Francis Coldridge in 1997. In it Martha says without anxiety or regret that she will die next winter. Her abilities as a "seer" and "hearer" enable her to know how and when she will die. The psychological meaning of her special knowledge has a sharp ironic edge, for ordinary humans have no foreknowledge of the time of their death. Such foreknowledge signifies exceptional power; it is a form of control denied to the rest of us. This element of control can be described as the underside of the calm readiness that defines Martha's acceptance of death. May Quest could not have gone quietly to her death. She had no knowledge and no power.

Martha's new community of all ages and colors is quite different from the communities Francis and Mark Coldridge manage. Their communities are, in essential ways, clones of our own, replete with corruption, mistrust, rigidities. Only racism seems significantly reduced in the post-Catastrophe world. The painful point is that there is no utopia after this catastrophe or any other catastrophe. The four-gated city belongs to the future. Martha's pastoral island community is exceptional and temporary, for after her death the outside world finds Faris and disperses its members.

Martha dies on an island community poor in material things but rich in survival and communal skills. In retrospect, the Coldridge household seems a fit preparation for Martha's post-holocaust collective. The little community on the island of Faris, north of Scotland, is the closest candidate for the ideal community—it is pointedly and significantly not a city—in all of Lessing's fiction until Lessing constructs her Canopean cities, which are, like her four-gated cities, mythic rather than actual. No one on Faris is marginal or nonfunctional. Martha shares her learning, her accumulated wisdom, with her peers and the younger members of her collective. The Faris community functions much like Francis's earliest commune, without rules yet with unstated understanding of communal roles and values. In a community brought together by the right shared ideology, aging seems to present no dangers. On Faris Martha escapes "the tyranny of the family" and the obsolescence of the elderly. In her old age, the time of her life that should be, as the clichés of our youth culture would have it, arid, imprisoned, and isolated, Martha is paradoxically freer than she has ever been, although she continues to perform typically female caretaker roles.

Janna and Maudie

Martha's idealized aging rewrites the kind of aging her mother experienced. It occurs in another world. The aging women in *The Diary of a Good Neighbour*, the first of the two novels in *The Diaries of Jane Somers*, belong to the Euroamerican world of today. (The second novel, *If the Old Could* ..., belongs to the genre of self-parody.) They enter our consciousness through the remove of the newspaper headline and the television newscast. We see them, but we do not see them. Still, they are a presence. They are there, aggressively asserting their kinship to the Martha we knew before the appendix to *The Four-Gated City* shot her into the future. They share the twentieth-century world of war, poverty, racism, and madness that marks the *Children of Violence* series, although they come to fictional life later in time, directly after the five Canopus novels. Lessing's move from the world of Canopus to the world of Meals on Wheels represents a shocking reversal of gears. It's as though Lessing were saying to critics of the Canopus series: "You wanted me to go back to the 'real' world; well, here I am. Can you take it?"

The specific private failures that haunt Janna may well have haunted Lessing. Janna was unable to give solace to her dying mother and her dying husband. Martha Quest knows that sending her mother back to Africa will significantly shorten her life. She chooses to save herself rather than be kind to her mother. Martha never looks at her guilt; Janna, so to speak, does it for her. It seems reasonable to postulate that the death of Lessing's second husband deepened her already deepening concern with aging and death. (Peter Lessing, their son, was still living with his mother.) Furthermore, the manner of his death must have been a shock, for in 1979 Gottfried Anton Lessing, then ambassador for the German Democratic Republic, was murdered by Tanzanian troops in Uganda "while supporting, in accordance with official policy, Idi Amin."[1] It is reasonable to think that Janna's need to come to terms with her guilt about her failures of feeling and behavior toward her mother and her husband represents in part a distancing of Lessing's response to the deaths of her own mother and husband. These biographical parallels are in the background, as participants in the genesis of *Diaries* and Canopus.

Jane Somers, familiarly known as Janna, is a woman in need. Her perfectly groomed exterior hides an existential emptiness and guilt whose exorcism is the subject of the novel. The editor of a woman's magazine called *Lilith* (compare the name with *Home and Hearth*, the magazine Ella writes for in the Yellow Notebook—these names simultaneously suggest and parody the homebound 1950s woman and the feminist 1980s woman), Janna is also a successful romantic novelist and serious sociologist. She cannot manage life without daily baths and elegant clothing. Her glossy life-style jostles violently against the realities of Maudie Fowler's life. Maudie, over ninety, poor, alone, incontinent, dirty, is wholly dependent on the bureaucracy that has created Home Help, Meals on Wheels, and Good Neighbours. This Maudie, whose bodily deterioration is a constant affront, becomes Janna's living hairshirt.

The Janna-Maudie relationship revises earlier mother-daughter relationships. In this version of that key relationship the daughter has all the power. Janna wants independence if not control even before she chooses Maudie. This is pointedly asserted when Janna rejects a relationship with her seventy-year-old neighbor, Mrs. Penny, because "she would take over my life" (11). Liking what she sees of Maudie at the chemist's shop, Janna follows her home; she decides when to visit and when not to visit, when to shop for Maudie, when to clean her body, her rooms, her clothing. She decides the terms of their conversations, asking Maudie to retrieve her past, to recollect and relive it—"For all the time I am trying to get her life mapped, dated" (101)—treating Maudie as a living artifact who can reveal and preserve a vanished way of life. Like other writers, Janna will use this material; Maudie's life as a milliner becomes part of Janna's novel, *The Milliners of Marylebone*. (Could this title be a deliberate and ironic recall of George Eliot's "mind and millinery species"?) Maudie is Janna's responsibility, not the reverse. Janna functions as Maudie's mother.

The popular description of old age as a second childhood accords with this description of role reversal. Maudie even physically resembles a young girl in some ways, most vividly in "her crotch like a little girl's, no hair" (127). Maudie also acts out. In her dependency and her histrionic flair she does seem more like Molly of *The Golden Notebook*, whereas Janna, who manages everything so well, seems more like Anna. Despite the age difference between them, Janna and Maudie do share qualities with these names and characters that go back over twenty years.

These aspects of their characters may make Lessing's prefatory remarks about the genesis of Janna more understandable. She does not say the obvious, that Maudie derives from Lessing's mother, Emily Maude McVeagh. She says instead that thinking "about what my mother would be like if she lived now: that practical, efficient, energetic woman," went into the making of Janna Somers (viii). Her silence about what went into the making and the naming of Maudie Fowler is conspicuous. Maudie, described as "a fierce angry old woman," has something in common with May Quest and Emily Maude McVeagh Tayler.

At least one other woman went into the character of Maudie, although Lessing credits her with affecting the making of *Making* and perversely leaves her out of the picture in her preface to *The Diaries*. This ninety-two-year-old friend took "a long cold time to die, and she was hungry too, for she was refusing to eat and drink, so as to hurry things along" (144). This friend is, therefore, a source for two very different kinds of novels.

In a 1985 talk in San Francisco Lessing was more open and more detailed about the sources of her Jane and Maudie figures than she is in her preface. Maudie comes from Lessing's experiences with the old and their social services. Jane has at least three sources. She is in part based on a friend insulated from suffering and poverty who "joined the human race" after the death of her husband; this woman "changed completely" after two or three years. Another source for Jane is an "extremely beautiful" woman friend obsessed with the need to present a perfectly groomed self. Another source is a friend who writes for a magazine. These three women (Lessing's mother is not mentioned) or "these ideas went to form Jane Somers, who is efficient, practical, obsessively tidy, orderly, rather conservative, and to whom the darker sides of life come as a continual surprise" ("Doris Lessing Talks about Jane Somers," 5).[2]

Janna, functioning as both mother and daughter to Maudie, also has two sister selves, Joyce, her other self at *Lilith*, and Georgie, her biological sister. When yet another J figure is introduced in the person of Janna's niece Jill, the effect is almost comical. (The J's proliferate as Janna's family name turns out to be James, and Joyce is married to Jack.) Janna mediates between two generations, one quite young, the other quite old, as mentor to Jill and caretaker to Maudie. Her sister selves seem to be divided into stereotypical roles; Georgie has the children, Joyce the career. Joyce is, however, a more complicated figure, for she fights to keep her husband from leaving her for his younger mistress. Part of this fight involves giving up her job with *Lilith* to accompany her husband to America. Janna chose to have neither children nor an emotionally close relationship with her husband, Freddie.

Another aspect of the naming strategies in this novel almost acquires the status of an in-joke. The *Lilith* staff debates whether *Lilith* is right for the girl of "the difficult, anxious eighties." The name *Martha* is proposed: "Arguments for *Martha*. We need something more workaday, less of an incitement to envy, an image of willing, adaptable, intelligent service" (140). As a description of Martha Quest, this is tongue-in-cheek, yet essentially accurate. It is harder, odder, or more amusing to read *Lilith* as a name that represents glamor. Perhaps the omission of Lilith's role as the wife in the attic, the wife who preceded Eve, is deliberate, even slyly comic. The name *Lilith* may sound glamorous because it is exotic; but in her person Lilith was in fact radically disobedient. Or is that part of the comedy?

The name *Lilith* remains on the masthead, but the magazine changes. Under Janna's leadership, it begins to have articles about aged women, about alcoholism and other "hard" issues. The discarded *Martha* remains to amuse readers of the Martha Quest novels.

The world of Jane Somers is not a world concerned with transcendence or last things. Its discourse is not eschatological or religious. It is bare, flat, and without reverberation, yet Janna's relationship with Maudie vibrates with "higher" meanings, for Janna wants to do good and to be good; she wants to atone, to learn to feel, to give, and to love her fellow woman. Janna does change, but her changes are not dramatic. One could be cruel and say that instead of long soaks in her tub, she takes shorter ones and sometimes even skips a soak altogether. Her character, like the overall conception of the novel, has its parodic edge. Yet Janna does travel beyond dirt and smell to the person Maudie is, to the person she herself is.

Janna also learns to experience time differently, as the very young and the very old do. The examples are simple: sitting "on a wall, along a garden" watching birds, sitting at a café, looking, listening (165). This over-busy woman begins to experience pleasure. She can sit still; she no longer fears the old on streets or park benches; instead she waits "for when they trust me enough to tell me their tales, so full of history" (166). Janna can look past the physical impairment of others and understand the fragility of her own good health, of anyone's good health. She is another person, "not at all that Janna who refused to participate when her husband, her mother, were dying. I sit for hours near Maudie, ready to give what my mother, my husband, needed from me; my consciousness of what was happening, my participation in it" (218). The contrast with Martha Quest's behavior to May Quest is striking.

At ninety-two, Maudie still holds on to life—and to Janna. This "sullen, sulking furious old woman" is in constant rebellion against her physical destruction; she rages in her way against the ravages of time. To Janna, "her hand nevertheless speaks the language of our friendship" (220). Her bravery and her spirit of independence are remarkable. She is one of the futures Martha Quest might have had; she is a Lilith figure.

Janna does not abandon her; she stays with Maudie until she dies, for death is an end in this novel. There is no afterlife. Janna will, like Martha Quest and Anna Wulf, go on. Her newfound saintly/secular vocation as a good neighbor, not a Good Neighbour, will not end with Maudie's death. Some Lessing readers thought that Jane Somers was a social worker like themselves ("Doris Lessing Talks about Jane Somers," 4). This aspect of Jane Somers recalls Anna Wulf's years of nonprofessional mediation before she decides, at the end of *The Golden Notebook*, to become a marriage counselor. In her self-appointed selfish/selfless role, Janna will befriend other old women, probably Annie and Eliza, whose names, like Maudie's, repeat earlier Lessing names. These repetitions are one expression of the inevitability, perhaps even the desirability, of circularity in fiction and in life.

ALSI AND THE REPRESENTATIVE(S)

The word "good" is not used ambiguously or ironically for Janna/Jane Somers as it is for Alice Mellings of *The Good Terrorist*. But the word is oddly redolent; it gives to these flatly realistic, often banal, novels a hint of Lessing's larger moral and religious concerns, concerns she can bring to the surface more directly, more fully, and more openly in her Canopus novels. *The Making of the Representative* can be described as her most devotional novel as well as her most eschatological one. It is a contemporary version of Job's struggle to understand apparently arbitrary affliction. Lessing's parable transfers individual struggle to a planetary theater. Its parable elements pointedly relate it to the second novel in the Canopus series, *The Marriages between Zones Three, Four, and Five*, as Betsy Draine has cogently argued. The two are almost mirror images of one another, *Marriages* being "light, warmth and optimism" and *Making* "dark, cold, and pessimism" (Draine, *Substance under Pressure*, 174). The subject matter and time of composition also relate *Making* to the Jane Somers novels in a different way. Both are concerned with last things.

Making is "more elegiac than political," as one reviewer describes it, only if political is narrowly defined (Lehmann-Haupt, 25). It is certainly doctrinal. The elegiac tone is firmly grounded in a Canopean doctrine whose essentials exist in many religions.

Planet 8 is a lovely planet, almost as favored as Rohanda (Earth) was before its fall. It has never known crime or winter or poverty. It has been a model planet in complete harmony with its Canopean mentors. It has been obedient and devout. Canopus descends and tells the Planet 8 population that it must build a wall around the planetary circumference. The people cannot comprehend its function: "A wall. A great black shining wall. A *useless* wall" (4). Yet Planet 8 performs its duty. The building of the wall takes the communal effort of generations, almost as though it were a medieval cathedral. Doeg, the narrator, was an infant when its construction began. The gradual transformation of Planet 8 and its inhabitants that follows is existentially haunting. Temperate climate disappears; ice, snow, and darkness define the new dispensation; theft and murder destroy the Eden that was. At first the wall does hold back the snow and Canopus does airlift food and promise to airlift the population elsewhere at a later time, a not unreasonable solution, since Canopus is always busily shifting populations from planet to planet as part of its mysterious long-range plan for genetic improvement of the galaxy. The Planet 8 population is itself a product of such genetic manipulation; it is a mix descended from native and imported peoples from different planets.

Something goes wrong; Canopus cannot say what. It can only reveal itself as capable of error, as subject to another, greater power. Or is Canopus not entirely truthful? Does it participate in setting up the destruction of Planet 8 as a test of the devotion of its inhabitants? The apparently arbitrary suffering and destruction of the planet and its people inexorably proceed. The "benign" imperialism (Parrinder, 9) of Canopus proceeds on its malignant way. ("Our populations felt as if they were being punished ... yet they had done no wrong" [36].) Those who survive long marches, starvation, unbearable cold, and premature aging achieve a final transcendence which suggests that all their trials have been stages in mystical experience. In effect, they become one with the cosmos. Doeg, Alsi, Marl, Masson, Klin, Bratch, Pedug, Rivalin—even Johor, the Canopean agent who has remained to share their suffering—break into molecular matter as Charles Watkins of *Briefing* yearned to do, as the survivor and Emily of *Memoirs* in effect do when they walk through their wall. Lynda and Mark were their predecessors; their efforts to break through four walls cannot quite be defined as a desire to break through the wall of phenomenality, but in their novel, *The Four-Gated City*, the compulsion to break boundaries does undergo a qualitative leap. It is fair to say that the desire to break through the boundaries of matter has been in Lessing's fiction for a long time, at least since 1969, and that this breakthrough has been most obviously demonstrated in *Memoirs of a Survivor* and in *Making*.

Another way to describe the explosion of the inhabitants of Planet 8 into the cosmos is to say that its "we-ness" at that point reaches its apogee. Johor has flatly announced, "You will not die out" (16), but he does not, of course, say what form the life of the people will take. Later, he says, changing yet imitating Genesis, you will return to the light (not to the dust) from which you came (59). The inhabitants have already traveled far toward we-ness when we meet them. They are all functional creatures. Doeg, the narrator, is the Memory Maker and Keeper of Records; Marl, the Keeper of the Herds; Bratch, the Physician; Klin, the Fruit Maker; Rivalin, the Guardian of the Lakes; and so on. These functions are not necessarily permanent, although Doeg feels that he is always essentially Doeg: "Though I have been Klin and Marl and Pedug and Masson, when needed. But Doeg is my nature, I suppose" (55). There are other Doegs as there were other Ambiens. When Klin, Marl, and Doeg return from a reconnaissance trip to Planet 10, "we were all Doeg" (54). At one point in the narrative three Marls appear.

Characters who duplicate each other, who "'break down' into each other, into other people," are not new in Lessing's fiction, as I have been arguing throughout this study (see the preface to *The Golden Notebook*, vii). In *Making*, shifting, multiple selves have become totally positive. The new element is the identification of the selves with a particular skill, as though we are all potentially poets, herdsmen, doctors, and farmers and can call these selves into existence when they are needed. The Martha Quest who picks at the thirteen layers of wallpaper she finds in a bombed-out house in postwar London announces personality as a thing of layers rather than fragments. In *Making*, societal mores encourage every inhabitant to become a layered entity. If there could be a deviant on Planet 8 in its Edenic phase, he would be a single personality.

Only Alsi's name does not stand for a function, probably because she is too young to have acquired a function. That Alsi (another Alis/Alice?) is the only woman among the several Representatives who are to become the single Representative is a shock for a number of reasons. That she is both the only woman and the only person without a functional name at the final transcendence is disturbing—especially since Lessing takes the trouble to note that the Scott expedition of 1910–13, cited in the afterword as a major source for the novel, had no women. "At that time," she goes on, "the women who were demanding rights were being beaten by policemen, forcibly fed in prisons, derided and jeered at by fine gentlemen, generally ill-treated and often enough by other women. It was simply not possible for women to be on expeditions ... the idea would not have surfaced" (132). Yet women longed to participate in exploration; Lessing cites letters between women of the period who knew they could "'be as brave and resourceful'" as men, of women who lamented their exclusion with "'the bitter tears of unused and patronised and frustrated women'" (132). Lessing further notes that even the "frieze or backdrop" of women "—no, ladies—who stood elegantly about in their drooping fettering garments, smiling wistfully at these warriors of theirs ... did not always see things as their men did" (132). How remarkable that in dealing with a future society aeons away from our own, Lessing chose not to eradicate the exclusions of 1910–13. How remarkable that Lessing's sensitivity to these exclusions is recorded in an afterword and not in the novel proper. From this point of view Planet 8 seems atavistic rather than futurist.

Alsi begins and ends as a token woman even though she becomes a Doeg for a while. Her role as the keeper of the little snow animals who mysteriously and briefly come to life is more memorable than her stint as Doeg. Indeed, given the emphasis on interchanging and multiple personality in *Making*, the male character of the Representatives/Representative is overwhelming. Even the storyteller historian of Planet 8 is male, although he is imagined by a woman author.[3]

The concept of Representation is built into the social organization of Planet 8. Five Representatives govern the entire planet. But Representation means more than it does in our world; it seems to mean almost physical embodiment of those represented in the Five who represent. During one of his catechizing sessions with Doeg, Johor takes the planet's already far advanced we-ness to the point where Doeg, startled, asks: "'You cannot be saying to me that it does not matter if the populations of a whole planet have to die—a species?'" (55)—that is, can Representation be taken to the point where we shall continue to exist as some other form of matter even outside our planet? This concept goes far beyond the kind of essence in multiplicity that Doeg understands.

Doeg can speak of filling "a town with these variations of myself, then a city, then, in my mind, whole landscapes. Doeg, Doeg, Doeg again, and mentally I greeted these non-existent never-to-exist people ... all of whom resembled me more or less, closely or only slightly" (81). His words beautifully evoke the dense population of the artist's imagination, different yet overlapping, partaking of and dependent on the artist for existence, as much as they describe multiple existence. They validate the kind of repetition of names, characters, and events that Lessing's work demonstrates. Doeg is Doeg even though he has "used many names in my life" (81). Doeg, although I, is "the feeling of me that I share with my unknown friends, my other selves" (85). His words also give new shape to traditional mystical doctrines of the one and many.

Sometimes Representation becomes too narrowly, too simply, defined—when, for example, the change of name is merely a way of saying that for a brief time we change roles. When Alsi becomes Doeg, she takes "her turn to remember and to reproduce in words experiences that we all needed to have fixed and set so that our annals would be in order" (86). In the world of Planet 8, "we often enough changed our roles, did different kinds of work; becoming for those times the Representative for whatever it was that was needed" (86). So described, the change in personality seems superficial, too small to contain the larger metaphysical meanings and metaphors Lessing is reaching for. At these times, the proverbial change of hats would do as well as a name change.

Lessing's claim that her ninety-two-year-old friend went into the novel has a more specific referent than the general one that the friend and the novel were both confronting aging, suffering, and dying. Alsi, the only woman in the novel, is also the only figure to display the aging process that we are told all Planet 8 inhabitants are experiencing. She looks down at her body beneath the numberless layers that cover it to see "her rib cage, with the yellow skin stretched tight over it, each bone evident and—where were her breasts?" (88). She probes lower to find "two skinny bags depended, and these bags ended in small hard lumps, and on the skin that held the lumps were brown wrinkles—her nipples" (88). She becomes a kind of totemic figure as Doeg and Johor look at "the old, very old woman's body, shrivelled by starvation, ... displayed there before us, ... her face ... bare to us—gaunt, sallow, with sunken black eyes" (88).

Surely this Alsi is Maudie. The specifics of her description belong to Maudie; they leap out of the page, the only nakedness Lessing chooses to reveal. If this connection is accepted, then the names, with their *A/M* pattern, leap out in another way, as versions of the first use of *A* and *M* introduced so many years ago in *Martha Quest* in the figures of Alfred and May Quest, who are repeated in the many female/female and female/male pairs: Martha/Marnie/Maisie/Alice/Marjorie; Martha/Anderson/Adolph/Anton; Anna/Molly/Mark; Al•Ith/Murti; and so forth. The names of Marl and Masson also belong to this constellation. Names like Bratch, Pedug, and Rivalin are probably concoctions made to sound deliberately strange in the traditions of science fiction. Doeg is different; his is an Old Testament name, belonging to the Edomite chief of Saul's herdsmen who slaughtered eighty-five priests of Nob at Saul's command (1 Sam. 21–22). The parallels with Lessing's Doeg are sufficient to establish his ironic kinship with the biblical Doeg.

Another interesting fact about Alsi is that despite her aged body, "the hollows near the sockets" of her eyes show "vulnerability, something still fresh and youthful" (88). So Alsi seems to be simultaneously both a young girl and an old woman, experiencing that division differently yet in the same way as ordinary mortal women (like May Quest, for example), who find their old bodies in the mirror incompatible with their inner ageless selves.

Alsi's double self suggests another hypothesis. The two parts that constitute Alsi might also have been placed in different bodies, in the bodies we know as Janna and Maudie of *The Diary of a Good Neighbour*. Jane's nickname of Janna only slightly disguises her Anna name, confirming what is clear from her characterization, that she is both the independent *A* female and the *J* child. Thus Alsi resurfaces in somewhat different form in the mother and daughter figures in *Diary*, repeating and altering her character as it reappears in both Janna and Maudie. She does what the people of Planet 8 and its artists do all the time. Lessing functions like Doeg—making, repeating, participating in her creations. Of course, she also disguises and riddles. Her extraliterary hints about the creation of Maudie are in *Making*, not in the novel in which she appears. Her information that Janna is in part based on her mother is not very convincing; it is more convincing to see Janna as a piece of her own self made somewhat younger, as Lessing has often made characters based on her own life.

If the structure of *Marriages* can be described as mimicking "stages of consciousness" (Draine, *Substance under Pressure*, 143–44), then *Making* can be described as mimicking stages of mystical experience. By the end of the novel, Doeg and his people have an extraordinary experience of transcendence. They do not become, like shamans, "specialists in ecstasy" (Eliade, *Myths*, 73), but their single and final experience of ecstasy is unmistakably the apogee of mystical transport. Perhaps it is the unknowable and untranslatable experience that awaits Al•Ith of *Marriages* when or if she reaches Zone One. The Representative can also be described as having undergone "the symbolic return to chaos [that] is indispensable to any new creation" (Eliade, *Myths*, 80). Ecstasy, chaos, and death become almost interchangeable events; in Mircea Eliade's words, "Every 'trance' is another 'death' during which the soul leaves the body and voyages into all the cosmic regions" (*Memories*, 96). In *Making* the body is not left behind; it voyages with the soul. Death does indeed become the ultimate rite of passage (Eliade, *Myths*, 226).

Katherine Fishburn defines the mystical center of *Making* as peculiarly Eastern (Sufi primarily); she daringly argues that the novel must be seen through "the double lens of particle physics and Eastern mysticism" (122). Doeg's vocabulary does make this approach persuasive; words like "pulses," "atom," "molecules," and even "atomic structure" recur during the final explosion of body into cosmos. Furthermore, Lessing has elsewhere (in the preface to *The Sirian Experiments*, for example) indicated her attraction to the romance of the new physics, especially to its extraordinary vocabulary:

> What *of course* I would like to be writing is the story of the Red and White Dwarves and their Remembering Mirror, their space rocket (powered by anti-gravity), their attendant entities Hadron, Gluon, Pion, Lepton, and Muon, and the Charmed Quarks and the Coloured Quarks.
> But we can't all be physicists. [ix]

The new physics may finally be more a graft than an essence in *Making*, but its presence is unmistakably there to buttress older mystical thought and to give it new metaphors.

Let me add another suggestion, one that coexists with rather than excludes the other strands of Lessing's thought and strategies. The concept of the double has been considered both a protection against the fear of death and a sign of the fear of death. This apparent contradiction distinguishes all discourse about the phenomenon. The double appears to be at once one thing and its other. For one recent commentator, doubles fictions "impart experiences of duplication, division, dispersal, abeyance" (Karl Miller, 25). If this interpretation is accepted, the dispersal at the end of *Making* is as much a part of Lessing's doubles talk as her division of opposites and similars into figures like Alsi young and Alsi old, Janna and Maudie, or Martha and May Quest. The protean potential of doubling is amply demonstrated in *Making* and *The Diaries*, as it is in Lessing's entire body of work.[4]

Perhaps guilt is the shape goodness takes in the Martha/May dialectic. The Martha Quest novels were framed outside an ethos that considers questions of the good in traditional religious terms, but if we think of guilt as the negative pole of an ideal of filial and other behavior, then goodness is also at issue in the Martha Quest novels. The shift to direct confrontation with the question of goodness is a feature of Lessing's later novels. That question, applied on a galactic stage, is framed in religious, species terms that only temporarily or superficially resolve problems of mothers, daughters, and aging. These problems resurface in the Somers novels and in *The Good Terrorist*.

Making succeeds despite its central belief in obedience, a belief Lessing had constantly questioned when her gods were Marxist. Coming to terms with undeserved punishment is the framework of her latest parable, one inconceivable to the adolescent Lessing, who rejected her mother's adulation of one of the heroically fallen members of the Scott expedition with the wonderfully astringent retort, "'But what else could he have done? And anyway, they were all in the dying business'" (afterword, 125). Now an older Lessing has become a reverent explorer of "the dying business."

"The dying business" as it is imagined in *Making* removes women from the center of Lessing's narrative. Yet women erupt even within this male-centered eschatological meditation. Their bodies force themselves into the narrative. Alsi's body, like Maudie's or May's or the young Martha's, acquires a haunting particularity rarely achieved or even sought for in the Canopean novels. Thus, though the mother/daughter dialectic appears to be buried or absent in *Making*, it is still there and still connected with questions of aging and dying. Lessing's mirror imperatives still display themselves in this novel about transcendence. Lessing need not envy the imaginative freedom of the new physics, for she has, in her novels about the aging and dying of mothers and daughters, created her own remembering mirrors.

NOTES

1. Mona Knapp, letters to the author, 13 January 1986 and 6 February 1986; the quotation is from an article in *Frankfurter Allgemeine Zeitung*, no. 254, 2 November 1981, p. 21. See also, Mona Knapp, "Lessing on the Continent," 9. Lessing's fictional Anton stayed in Rhodesia amid the white settler community; the historical Lessing returned to East Germany and became, as Murray Steele reports, "East German consul at Dar-es-Salaam in the 1960s" (54).

2. Lessing does mention elsewhere her delayed realization that her mother "could, I think, be something like Jane Somers if she lived now" ("Autobiography: Impertinent Daughters," 58).

3. See Fishburn for an excellent overview of Lessing's use of narrator guides in the Canopus novels.

4. Miller's rich discussion of Joyce's "prodigious doubling," with its "elements both of division and dispersal," has no counterpart discussion of Lessing's (or Virginia Woolf's) "prodigious doubling" (37). Although his *Doubles* has sections on Jane Austen, Charlotte Brontë, Edith Wharton, and Sylvia Plath, Miller notes: "The literature of duality is at once submissive and rebellious. But a male rebelliousness looms large. Comparatively few women are awarded doubles, or write about them" (52). Although *Doubles* was published in 1985, it neglects the feminist analysis of the doubles phenomenon, especially in works by Adrienne Rich (her essay on *Jane Eyre* was originally published in 1973 and was republished in 1979 in *On Lies, Secrets, and Silence*) and Sandra Gilbert and Susan Gubar (their book, *The Madwoman in the Attic*, was published in 1979). This absence is a shock in so omnivorous a work. Lessing is referred to only once as the author of a favorable review of Flora Rheta Schreiber's *Sybil*, a study of multiple personality (339).

GAYLE GREENE

Re: Colonised Planet 5, Shikasta:
"After Long Circling and Cycling"

Things change. That is all we may be sure of.
—Doris Lessing, *Shikasta*

Everything changes in *Shikasta*,[1] and frequently—time and place, speakers, settings, cities, continents, planets, galaxies, eons. Like the planet Rohanda, like the universe itself, this novel is "sizzling with change" (14)— "this is a catastrophic universe, always; and subject to sudden reversals, upheavals, changes, cataclysms" (3). Lessing herself seems to have changed, for neither the form nor the content of this novel is like anything else she has written. She speaks of the "exhilaration" she felt turning to science fiction, at "being set free into a larger scope": "It was as if I had made—or found—a new world for myself" (xi).

Mona Knapp claims that Lessing is no longer using "literature as a consciousness-raising tool," but as an "escape from an altogether imperfect reality."[2] But in fact Lessing *is* still using fiction for purposes of consciousness-raising: what is different is that she has found in biblical history a way of mythologizing and also of defamiliarizing some familiar concerns—our defects of imagination and failure to know ourselves as part of one another and the universe, our "fall ... into forgetfulness" (9). *Shikasta* is a creation myth of Miltonic scale and splendor, an epic that addresses—like

From *Doris Lessing: The Poetics of Change*. © 1994 by the University of Michigan.

Paradise Lost and *Paradise Regained*—the origin of evil and "all our woe":[3] only it combines Christian myth with a history of contemporary times and with future history. It takes dizzying leaps backward and forward in time, offering a perspective of ages and eons, then zeroing in on a few years in the life of one adolescent girl, Rachel Sherban—tunneling in and telescoping out, taking both "the long view" and "the near, the partial views" (170). It offers a mélange of genres and voices, from the impersonal, "objective" records of Canopus to the chatty diary of Rachel, and a range of tones from the detached to the denunciatory, soaring at times into powerfully moving laments for the human condition that resemble Old Testament exhortation. There is no literary precedent for it. There is nothing like it.

Its moves were too disorienting for most reviewers, and Lessing lost many readers over it,[4] but she is in some sense her own harshest critic—she calls it "a mess, but at any rate it is a new mess."[5] But I think it's magnificent—eloquent, inventive, passionate, compelling. Parts of it bring tears to my eyes, sorrow for my ruined planet and race, "creatures infinitely damaged, reduced and dwindled from their origins, degenerate, almost lost" (203). I find its roughness a pleasure and a challenge: the pleasure comes from piecing things together, recognizing the familiar in the strange, the strange in the familiar, as characters and events from biblical history turn up side by side with characters and events from our present time, together with beings from other planets and galaxies. Figuring out the relation of the parts is a "process of imaginative effort" (130), which is what is "needed" if we are to survive these "dreadful last days" (347): the novel puts us through a reading process that works, like the Canopean agents, to "heal [our] woeful defects of imaginative understanding" (349) and make us "*see things differently*" (254).

The "now" of the novel is time present, the "last days" just before the end—the time of *The Four-Gated City* and *Memoirs*. That Lessing feels compelled to return to this dreadful time of ours suggests, again, the need to re-cover this ground until it is recovered, the impulse to repeat in order to revise, to get it to come right. As an epic, *Shikasta* begins *in medias res* and moves back through events that have already occurred; and this epic convention suits Lessing well, for, as in *The Four-Gated City* and the *Children of Violence*, ends work back to beginnings in a circular pattern in which all has already happened. Here, too, the end is foretold in the beginning: the ten-page history of the "Century of Destruction," which recounts how each war brings a new "descent into barbarism" and how the rampant consumption of the planet is "built into the economic structure of every society" (89), points the way to the end of our world that occurs at the end of the novel, in famine, disease, and nuclear holocaust. But it also points the way to a time after the end, when Shikastans are "restored to themselves" and "wondered *why* they had been mad" (93), when, "after long circling and cycling" (202) we reach the end which is also the beginning in a circular return that is Alpha and Omega: the cities are rebuilt, the lion lies down with the lamb—"And here we are all together, here we are."

THE USES OF DISMAY

Shikasta is not an easy novel to read and not an easy novel to take. It teaches some hard lessons about "necessity"—about what is needed in these terrible times—and it's right that it be hard: "Dismay has its degrees and qualities. I suggest that not all are without uses" (3), as Johor tells us early on; later, he says that "the hidden power, or force" that drives Shikastans "nearer to self-knowledge, understanding" is never "'happiness' or 'comfort'" (175). This is a novel that dramatizes what Shakespeare, in *As You Like It*, termed "the uses of adversity," what King Lear terms "true need."[6] Since comfort and security are not what is needed—here, as in Shakespeare's tragedies, "security / Is mortal's chiefest enemy" (*Macbeth*, 3.5.32–33; p. 1124)—it is right that this novel discomfort and unsettle, that it frustrate our attempts to settle in, that, by breaking narrative sequence and requiring us to engage and disengage and readjust our relation to events and the fictional frame, it make us work to construct meaning. Also, since consumption is at the heart of the rot of our civilization, it is right that this novel not be easily consumed but that it require thoughtful and energetic reconstruction.

Also *Shikasta* is also difficult to grasp in terms of its central doctrine, the coexistence of "freedom" with "necessity" and obedience to the whole. In the state of prelapsarian harmony Johor describes,

> everybody accepted that their whole existence depended on voluntary submission to the great Whole, and that this submission, this obedience, was not serfdom or slavery— ... but the source of their health and their future and their progress. (26)

Some critics see such "submission" as "slavery": several object that it makes human beings into "mere pawns of Good and Evil, so thoroughly manipulated by these great abstract powers that human actions have no moral import at all."[7] Some compare Lessing's views unfavorably with

Christian doctrine, seeing Lessing's vision as "morally inferior ... to that of
the Old Testament"—in that "every good development on earth is due to
these heavenly visitants," her "philosophy ... dwarfs the individual."[8] But in
fact Christianity also makes good emanate solely from God and salvation
depend solely on grace, even while it holds human beings accountable for
their actions, and these positions involve it in some contradiction. When
Milton wrote *Paradise Lost* "to justify the ways of God to man" (1.26, p.212),
it was this paradox—the coexistence of man's free will with God's
providential plan—that he was justifying: that God foreknew yet man is free,
"sufficient to have stood, though free to fall." "If I foreknew," God says,
"Foreknowledge had no influence on [human] faults / Which had no less
prov'd certain unforeknown" (3.99 and 117–19, pp. 260–61). The Canopean
doctrine of necessity no more precludes the idea of free will than Christian
doctrine does.

But while Milton writes to justify the ways of God to man, Lessing
writes to justify the ways of man to God: Johor's purpose is to demonstrate
that Shikasta "*is* worth so much of our time and trouble" (3). Critics who
object that the Canopean perspective "dwarfs the individual" overlook this.
It is true that *Shikasta* punctures our inflated "ideas" of ourselves—"This
planet knows nothing of the little scum of life on its surface," "this film of
liquid that the profusion of life depends [on]"; it "has other ideas of itself"
(5);[9] and true also that it posits a geography so radically redescribed as to
reduce England to the status of "the northwest fringe." Nevertheless, this
spectacle of Shikastans as "scuffl[ing] and scrambl[ing] and scurry[ing]
among [our] crumbling and squalid artifacts" also shows us "reaching out"
"to heights of courage and ... *faith*" (203). Such heights are exemplified by
Lynda Coldridge and others of the meek and downtrodden who provide
instruction to Dr. Hebert and inspire his "testament of faith"—

> All these people can take weight, responsibility, burdens,
> difficulties, delays, the loss of hope. As we know, this is essential
> equipment for these hard times.... I want to say something to you
> that I regard as a testament, an act of faith! It is that if human
> beings can stand a lifetime of the sort ... that it has been Mrs.
> Coldridge's lot to undergo ... if we, the human race, have in us
> such strengths of patience and endurance, then what can we not
> achieve? (353)

Lynda demonstrates not only "what ... is possible in a human being," but
what is "essential"—patience, endurance, responsibility. Thus Lessing faces

a challenge similar to Milton's in *Paradise Lost*, a version of his problem of making Christianity heroic, of adapting the conventions of classical epic to dramatize inherently undramatic Christian virtues of humility, obedience, and meekness: Lessing similarly needs to make glorious the inglorious qualities of patience, endurance, and compassion.

The difficulties are apparent from the outset. We enter the world with Johor, a Canopean agent who is, as Draine says, less a character than a "presiding presence" (151). Jeannette King points out the echo of "Yahweh" in Johor and describes the effects of this beginning:

> Instead of beginning with an individual human experience, taking place in a world recognizably our own, this novel confronts us with an alien universe, and a disconcertingly remote narrator.... The reader's perspective is ... wrenched into an unfamiliar alignment with another, by which our own world and its assumptions are made to appear not only lacking but incomprehensible.[10]

We not only enter the world with an alien; we are confronted with a chronology that defies human comprehension: "And so, returning again after an interval—but is it really so many thousands of years?" (4). As in *Paradise Lost*, we first glimpse our world through the eyes of an alien—and Johor's cosmic journeys recall Satan's trips through hallucinatory landscapes[11]—only here the alien is not the enemy of our race but a friend. We are plunged into "a hard place, full of dangers" (5), a limbo or purgatory full of "chimeras, ghosts, phantoms, the half-created and the unfulfilled" (6) pressing against Shikasta to be reborn.

Starting *in medias res*, then, we begin with Johor's third "mission" (6)—the third for him, that is, though the first for us; immediately after which, Johor recalls his first trip, "in the First Time, when this race was a glory," and recounts the evolution of life, hastened by a "blast of radiation" and a Canopean "booster" (14–15), the establishment of the Lock between Canopus and the people of Rohanda, the building of the cities according to "the closeness, the match, between individual and surroundings" (32), the paradise where humans lived in "the strong quiet purpose which I have always found to be evidence, anywhere— ... of the Necessity" (33). Johor then proceeds to describe the disturbance of the Lock by the malalignment of the stars and the invasion of Shammat, the destruction of harmony and the desolation of paradise—"This paradise ... is where now lie deserts and rock, sands and shales .... Ruins are everywhere" (30)—and the ruin of our intelligence, our falling off into the degenerative disease, against which the codification of Canopean knowledge in the form of the Ten Commandments (62) shores up such understanding as remains. After which, we leap forward thirty thousand years ("I now return to my visit in the Last Days" [74]), a leap forward that is also a return to the beginning of the novel and to "now," "these terrible end days" (197). Again the return—again and again—to "now."

We have heard that "Taufiq had been captured" (6), and we now turn to Taufiq, who is, in his Shikastan incarnation, John Brent-Oxford, a lawyer led astray from his Canopean mission by the temptation to prideful involvement in "political" causes; we then move to the ten-page history of the Century of Destruction. Then, in one of the most dizzying leaps in this novel, we return to "penultimate Time" and reports by Taufiq on postlapsarian events—the earth shifting on its axis, the Flood, the Covenant, Babel, the choice of the chosen people—all of which prompts Taufiq's request, "I again apply for transfer from Shikastan service" (101), eloquent in its understatement. We then proceed to Johor's second trip, at the time of Abraham and the destruction of the cities (104–8), including a five-page official history of the "period of public cautioners" or prophets—and again, a spectacle of devastation, the laying waste of the cities: "Deserts lie where those cities thrived" (108). We then leap forward in time, to now, to an account of "individuals who, if Taufiq had not been captured, would have been in very different situations" (113) and a continuation of contemporary records, with "illustrations: the Shikastan Situation," which include a portrait of the artist (114) and a portrait of the father of the artist (the one-legged farmer in southern Africa [160–62]), of Patty Hearst and the Baader-Meinhof gang. Spliced into this is another hallucinatory journey through Zone Six, which turns out to be not another journey but the same journey with which the novel began, a harrowing traversing of "shivering and swirling sands" (147) that coalesce into treacherous whirlpools—"a vast whirlpool, all the plain had become one swirling centrifuge, spinning, spinning ... some appalling necessity was dragging and sucking at this place" (149).

From the suck and swirl of these forces—the most sinister circles in Lessing's fiction—Johor is rescued by an eagle (an eagle also guides Dante out of hell), in whose care he leaves Ben and Rilla. These scenes are interspersed with "Additional Explanatory Information" on the Generation Gap and the most amazing passage in the book, which asks us to bore into the molecular structure of a leaf and contemplate a universe like a "roaring engine" of change in which Shikastans nevertheless rise to heights of dignity and courage—another testimony to faith, this time Johor's. Thence follows another journey through Zone Six, which is again the same journey with which we began, during which Johor picks up Ben and Rilla to take them back to Shikasta. This journey ends as they enter flesh, about to be reincarnated as George, Rachel, and Ben:

> In a thundering dark we saw lying side by side two clots of fermenting substance, and I slid into one half, giving up my identity for the time, and Ben slid into the other, and lay, two souls throbbing quietly inside rapidly burgeoning flesh.... The terrible miasmas of Shikasta close around me. (210)

So by the middle of the novel, we have returned, after long circling and cycling, to the beginning.

But with the double line on page 210, we lose the presiding consciousness of the novel: Johor is reborn as George, though we reemerge not into George's consciousness, but into that of his sister, Rachel, whose journal recounts their growing up. This part of the novel proceeds more chronologically and comprehensibly, but since Rachel's perspective is partial and limited, it presents us with other problems of interpretation: we see things from her perspective, while also bringing to bear on her story the point of view we have learned from the first part of the novel, which means that we have a sort of double vision of her: her dashing off to save George looks different to us than it looks to her, and we are left to find our own meaning in her melodramatic suicide. We also have to piece together Chen Lieu's account of the Trial of the White Races and speculate why the mock trial dispelled the rumor of the extermination of the European populations. Finally, at the end, George disappears, Rachel dies, and we're in the consciousness of Kassim, one of the children rescued by George, from whose point of view we witness the rebuilding of the cities: what has happened is that the Canopean perspective has yielded to the human, as the human perspective—the survivors' and ours—has expanded to encompass the Canopean.

Draine describes *Shikasta* as "a movement without end, an action without climax" and refers to the text's "refusal ... to resolve into unity":

> As the book drifts to an end, with an instruction to consult other volumes of the archive, the reader is implicitly asked not to conclude, not to settle on a single perspective, but to sustain tentatively and simultaneously the appreciation of both the

science fiction saga still in progress and the spiritual fable that has only begun to be developed. (160)

But actually the ending is unusually unambiguous for Lessing: though the evolution is on-going and uncompleted, since "the object and aim of the galaxy ... [is] ever-evolving" (35), there is little doubt about what has happened. The old cities are rebuilt in a way that suggests that the Lock is back in place, that Shikastan minds are back in harmony with the purpose. This is the clarity of "divine comedy," where we emerge from a past that was "a thick ugly hot darkness" (364), into the light and new beginnings: "It is Paradise nowe" (354).

Saving Graces

But if the overall plan and purpose are clear, what is less clear is our part in this scheme—what is to be done, how we should behave in these terrible last days, in order not only to survive but to salvage something of value. This is a message that needs some teasing out, for it is not so simple as that propounded by *Paradise Lost*, "the sum of wisdom" stated by Milton's Adam:

> Henceforth I learn that to obey is best,
> And love with fear the only God, to walk
> As in his presence, ever to observe
> His providence, and on him sole depend.
>   (12. 561–64, p. 467)

While Milton and Lessing would agree that blessed are the meek, their reasons for believing this are quite different.

Lessing has set herself the hardest of tasks, to write a novel that engages without recourse to the usual means of engagement—identification with striking individuals who are brought into dramatic conflict over the things of this world—yet which nevertheless inspires us to feel for the human plight. Her task is to get us to feel deeply, for she knows that human beings do not learn where they do not feel, and to feel differently, to engage us emotionally about "voluntary submission to the great Whole" (26). So far is she from allowing us to "identify" with an individual that she hardly even allows us a human protagonist, for to identify with a striking individual would be to incriminate ourselves, to share the degenerative disease: "To identify with ourselves as individuals—this is the very essence of the Degenerative

Disease, and every one of us in the Canopean Empire is taught to value ourselves only insofar as we are in harmony with the plan, the phases of our evolution" (38). Even what looks like a dramatic situation turns out not to be. "Taufiq's capture," for example, turns out to refer to his descent into mortal oblivion and his lapse from purpose, and lest we derive any suspense from Johor's "search for Taufiq," Johor tells us its outcome:

> I could foresee ... that later in the frightful time in front of us, I, a young man, would confront [Taufiq] and say to him some exact and functioning words. An enemy—for he would be that for a time—would become a friend again, would come to himself. (82–83)

Whatever suspense this situation might hold is further dispensed with when their confrontation takes place off-stage, as it were; though we hear that Johor and Taufiq (George and John Brent-Oxford) meet at the Trial of the White Races and are much seen together (326), we never observe their meeting. Even death does not provide drama, since there is no death, only a movement to another state. Rather than drama and rhetoric, what Lessing offers is—"exact and functioning words": exact and exacting, functioning and functional.

The closest we come to identifying with an individual is with Rachel, and what her brief, unsatisfactory tale illustrates is how disastrous it is to identify with the individual and with the old conventions of heroism and histrionics: these are no longer what is needed. When we meet Rachel after the double line on p. 210, we welcome a human consciousness; as Draine says, "By this point in the narrative, we are starved for characters to follow consistently"[12]—though our hunger is hardly assuaged by the thin gruel of her story. Rachel is keeping her journal at the suggestion of Hassim, one of George's "friends," and that such friends all turn out to be Canopean representatives suggests that the journal will be "functional." And the record she keeps does turn out to be instructive, though more instructive for us than for her, for we have a perspective on it that she lacks, which we've gleaned from the first part of the novel; we read knowing who George is, what his mission is; we read knowing Rachel's history in Zone Six, scrutinizing her story for signs that she is passing or failing her test. We have become informed readers, have learned to see and hear in new ways—to hear double meanings, to see a variety of possible perspectives on an event.

In her efforts to record the truth, the facts, Rachel confronts many of the obstacles encountered by Anna Wulf. Like Anna, she writes to discover "what to think" (254). Like Anna she is dismayed by the unreliability of her thoughts: "If what we think now is different from what we thought then, we can take it for granted that what we think in a year will be different again" (224). Her awareness of the way emotions distort her perceptions, her sense of herself as "a sort of sack full of emotions" (255), recalls Martha's (RS, 226). Her development recapitulates that of earlier Lessing protagonists, only like Emily in Memoirs, she moves through the stages more rapidly and efficiently. She can reject the conventional female roles, partly because she feels them as "a terrible snare or trap" (243) and partly because she realizes that biological motherhood is no longer what is needed: "I don't want it. How could I want to be grown-up and marry and have six kids and know they are going to die of hunger or never have enough to eat?" (244). She is right, what is needed now is a generalized kindness and caring for the children who already exist—which George gives her an opportunity to exercise when he brings home two children for her to "look after" (276), Kassim and Leila, whom he has rescued from the childrens' camps. Like the protagonist of Memoirs, Rachel feels inadequate to the task, but when she draws back from it George warns her to toughen up (267): "If you can't face all this, then you'll have to come back and do it all over again. Think about it" (270).

After George leaves Rachel begins to drift toward death, and it is Suzannah who takes over responsibility for the house. Finally, Rachel rushes off after George to save him, against his command that she stay and care for the children, and is arrested and commits suicide—"theatrical events" (294) that are not only not needed, but disastrous. Comment on suicide has been provided by Olga: "There is evidence to suggest that there is hell to pay. Literally. But in any case, we do not commit suicide" (256–57). "Hell to pay" is one of those clichés that turn out to have an exact and functional meaning. George's words when he hears of Rachel's death, "Well, better luck next time" (300), are also exact and functional—Rachel will have to return to Zone Six and endure another round of Shikasta because she hasn't managed to "toughen up" and work herself free; she has shirked the hard way for the easy way of martyrdom and heroics and has succumbed, again, to the miasma of Shikasta. It is Suzannah who, though more stolid and less intelligent, "more like a servant" (291), is what is needed; Suzannah, who is both "tougher" and "kinder" (and these terms recur in relation to her and recall Milt's description of Anna in The Golden Notebook) and is a "householder," literally, in that she stays behind and holds the house together. The only way to "freedom" is, as in the Children of Violence, "the hard way": "by enduring it, to be free of it forever" (Shikasta, 207, 9).

To identify with Rachel's heroics would be to incriminate ourselves of the degenerative disease, though actually, there is not much chance that we will do this: Lessing has not lavished the dramatic and rhetorical appeal on this character that Milton lavishes on Satan. But Milton enlists our identification with Satan, not because he is "of the devil's party," as some readers have claimed, but rather—as Stanley Fish demonstrates—as a rhetorical device calculated to teach us that we are fallen: insofar as we respond to Satan's histrionics, we demonstrate how ruined our hearts and minds are, how defective our wills and intelligence, how much we need grace.[13] Like Milton, Lessing puts the reader through a series of responses that demonstrate the ruination of our faculties and emphasizes the need to renounce ego, but she deploys her rhetoric on the side she endorses—in Johor's laments for the human condition and exhortations to endurance and faith. Like *Paradise Lost*, *Shikasta* teaches us to feel differently and to strengthen the faculty that is the means to our restoration. But for Milton it is obedience that is the saving grace, our one hope of resisting the devil's snares, whereas for Lessing it is the creative imagination whereby we may repair our defective understanding—and to strengthen this, she appeals to poetry rather than renounces it. It seems to me that her vision confers greater dignity on human beings—it is less humbling, more enabling.

THE USES OF IRONY

King claims that Johor shows no "subjective bias, and seems to have little interest in the usual concerns of the individual"—that he is "too disembodied, too removed from the world and assumptions of the reader" to provide "a focal point for his or her concerns."[14] But in fact Johor does become involved with what he describes, and his involvement is a source of considerable interest. The novel instructs us in the doctrine of "necessity," the governing principle of the Canopean universe (25–26; 33); but Johor devises "additional material"—since "*facts* are easily written down: atmospheres and the emanations of certain mental sets are not," he provides "sketches and notes made in excess of his mandate" (153–54), "setting down thoughts that perhaps fall outside the scope of the strictly necessary" to justify that Shikasta "*is* worth so much of our time and trouble" (3). This "additional material" is the most compelling writing in the novel, and its effects derive from Johor's engagement with his material, from a compassionate involvement with Shikastans that wells up in spite of himself, which is the more moving for his determined restraint and subordination of purpose to the whole. In this sense Johor does become a focal point for our concerns, and as he comes to share our perspective, we align ours with his, stretching our imaginations to attain the vision of Canopus.[15]

Johor's involvement emerges the more powerfully by virtue of its understatement:

> But the ability to cut losses demands a different type of determination from the stubborn patience needed to withstand attrition, the leaking away of substance through centuries, then millennia.
>
> ... Dismay has its degrees and qualities. I suggest that not all are without uses. The set of mind of a servant should be recorded. (3)

No headlong rush to judgment, this, but rather, the caution, the restraint: "Not all the degrees and qualities of dismay are without uses." The ambiguity of "a servant" makes it unclear who Johor is referring to, himself or us: *whose* losses need cutting, *whose* patience is required? And the ambiguity is purposeful and evidence of his identification with Shikastans, for both Johor and we are servants. The need to cut losses is Canopus's but "the stubborn patience needed to withstand attrition" is Shikasta's.

Johor's "Additional Explanatory Information" consists of two powerful, lyrical laments for the human condition which are the emotional center of the novel and are rhetorically in "excess" of what is "needed." Though rhetoric is debunked in this novel—in Ben's account of the political rhetoric deployed at the Trial of the White Races—as it is elsewhere in Lessing, particularly in *The Sentimental Agents* (the fifth of the Canopus novels), Johor's "additions" do not stint on rhetorical appeal.

The first of these passages describes the generation gap, the dislocation in human life due to our drastically shortened life spans (171–74). The sense in this passage is of time speeded up, hurtling toward the end, of a frenzy that makes for a desperate grab and snatch on the part of the young:

> They do not know what their own history is ... they know nothing, understand nothing, but are convinced because of the arrogance of their education that they are the intellectual heirs to all understanding and knowledge. Yet the culture has broken down, and is loathed by the young. They reject it while they grab it, demand it, wring everything they can from it. And because of this loathing, even what is good and wholesome and useful left in traditional values is rejected. So each young person finds himself facing life as if alone. (172–73)

The disruption of natural temporal processes interrupts processes of germination and growth and, above all, of learning: the older generation is left, having "learned so much, so painfully, at such a cost to themselves and to others," unable to teach the young anything (174). George's dream of "a civilization once" that lasted the ages, in which there is time for sane and loving relations between parents and children and men and women, a civilization based on "close links with the stars and their forces" and with "necessity" (285–89), offers an image antithetical to this, the ideal against the actuality.

The second additional explanatory note describes Shikastans' attempts to find "some good or substance that will not give way as they reach out for it" (201), their frantic and failed efforts to find in ideologies (religion, nationalism, politics, science) some purpose larger than themselves, something solid to which the heart can cling, all of which turn out to be transient. Even what was once certain—pleasure in the young, in the nourishment of food and in nature—is now poisoned. Looking for some lasting good or substance in nature, a Shikastan woman and a man look at a tree, then a leaf; and I quote most of this full-page sentence because it is so amazing:

> And this is what an eye tuned slightly, only slightly, differently would see looking out of the window at that tree ... no, not a tree, but a fighting seething mass of matter in the extremes of tension, growth, destruction, a myriad of species of smaller and smaller creatures feeding on each other, each feeding on the other, always—this is what the tree is in reality, and this man, this woman, crouched tense over the leaf, feels nature as a roaring creative fire in whose crucible species are born and die and are reborn in every breath ... every life ... every culture ... every world ... the mind, wrenched away from its resting place in the close visible cycles of growth and renewal and decay, the simplicities of birth and death, is forced back and into itself, coming to rest— tentatively and without expectation—where there can be no rest, in the thought that always, at every time, there have been species, creatures, new shapes of being, making harmonious wholes of interacting parts, but these over and over again crash! are swept away! crash go the empires and civilisations and the explosions that are to come will lay waste seas and oceans and islands and cities, and make poisoned deserts where the teeming detailed inventive life was, and where the mind and heart used to rest, but

may no longer, but must go forth like the dove sent by Noah, and at last after long circling and cycling see a distant mountaintop emerging from wastes of soiled water, and must settle there, looking around at nothing, nothing, but the wastes of death and destruction, but cannot rest there either, knowing that tomorrow or next week or in a thousand years, this mountaintop too will topple under the force of a comet's passing, or the arrival of a meteorite. (201–2)

This is a vision of catastrophic change that goes beyond the merely social and political upheavals of the century of destruction—this is change built into the substance of life, pushing life itself into new substances. Yet it is not depressing, partly because it is so compelling—"The woman may ... think that the laws that made this shape must be, must be, stronger in the end than the slow distorters and perverters of the substance of life"—and partly because it is only "one truth":

The man ... forcing himself to see the tree in its other truth, that of the fierce and furious way of eating and being eaten, may see suddenly, for an instant, so that it has gone even as he turns to call to his wife: Look, look, quick! behind the seethe and scramble and eating that is one truth, and behind the ordinary tree-in-autumn that is the other—a third, a tree of a fine, high, shimmering light, like shaped sunlight. A world, a world, another world, another truth. (202–3)

As in *The Four-Gated City*, the other world is glimpsed fleetingly and fitfully, shimmering just beyond the reach of our senses, just out of sight beyond this one—"Quick, said the bird" (Eliot, "Burnt Norton," 118):

This, then, is the condition of Shikastans now ...

Nothing they handle or see has substance and so they repose in their imaginations on chaos, making strength from the possibilities of a creative destruction. They are weaned from everything but the knowledge that the universe is a roaring engine of creativity, and they are only temporary manifestations of it.

Creatures infinitely damaged, reduced and dwindled from their origins, degenerate, almost lost— ... they are being driven back and away from everything they had and held and now can

take a stand nowhere but in the most outrageous extremities of—
patience. It is an ironic and humble patience, which learns to look
at a leaf, perfect for a day, and see it as an explosion of galaxies,
and the battleground of a species. Shikastans are, in their awful
and ignoble end, while they scuffle and scramble and scurry
among their crumbling and squalid artifacts, reaching out with
their minds to heights of courage and ... I am putting the word
faith here. After thought. With caution. With an exact and
hopeful respect. (203)

Again the restraint, as Johor ventures "the word *faith*," after thought, with
caution, and with an "exact and hopeful respect." Again the ambiguity: the
"faith" is Shikastans', but it is also Johor's, on behalf of Shikastans.

Thus Johor is drawn into a compassionate involvement with Shikastans
that goes beyond necessity, into identification with the race that, though so
nearly lost, is capable of heights of courage and faith. Johor may be an alien
but he is also familiar, an extension of qualities toward which Lessing's
protagonists have been tending—the compassionately observing
protagonists of *Memoirs* and *The Four-Gated City*, who shed their
personalities to blend in with the lives of those they care for. This is now
what is necessary—this identification with the collective, "I" become "we,"
the "we" that emerges triumphant at the last: "And here we are all together,
here we are." The protagonist is finally the human race, about whom we
learn to think and feel differently. Lessing is teaching another kind of
"identification with ourselves" that is regenerative rather than degenerative,
collective rather than individual; she is teaching "kindness"—and the
etymological coincidence that *kindness* derives from *kynde*, *nature* in Middle
English, implies that it is human nature to be gentle. As always it is the life
of society that Lessing cares about,[16] and she makes this identification as
emotionally charged and compelling as the romantic love and flashy heroism
that have long been the mainstays of narrative and that have served us so
poorly in building a better world.

Though the way forward is the way back, to old truths and values, the
novel also moves us ahead to new levels of awareness, to the next step of
evolution implied in *The Four-Gated City* and *Memoirs*. This is what the Trial
of the White Races suggests, in which the white races are put on trial by the
dark races. From one point of view the entire episode, narrated in a letter
from Chen Liu to Ku Yuang, is anticlimactic and unsettling. The issues seem
to evaporate, as it becomes apparent that the dark races have behaved every
bit as badly as the white races; Knapp sees this as "a laconic outcome typical

of these novels' shoulder-shrugging indifference to political issues" (138). But looked at another way, the trial accomplishes something important: it makes it impossible for the white races or the dark races to project enmity onto an "other" and demonstrates (what Martha discovered in her breakdown) that there is no "enemy," that the enemy is always us—the trial makes everyone accountable. Moreover, as we see the participants beginning to understand what is happening, all at the same time and without words, as we see that the young are developing telepathic powers, we realize that the catastrophic events of the century of destruction have pushed life into new forms.

Besides, the traditional values to which the novel refers us—faith, endurance, patience—may be old, but they are also new, re-envisioned in a way that makes them the same but different from the traditional Christian virtues, reimagined in a way that answers the question Lessing's works always ask, how to get there from here? In *Shikasta* the meek inherit because they can tolerate uncertainty, can suspend judgment—which is quite different from the solidly certain "sum of wisdom" that Milton espouses: what is new in Lessing's conception of meekness is this linking of humility with irony. As Dr. Hebert describes Lynda and others who have endured lifetimes of being treated as lunatics:

> These are all people ... who, because of their experience are inured to hardship, misunderstanding, uncertainty, and a capacity for suspending judgement that is the inevitable reward of having to undergo years of suspending judgement on the workings of their own minds. These are most useful qualities! (352)

So too is the reader encouraged to cultivate these "useful" qualities, for the experience of reading forces us to suspend judgment and tolerate multiple viewpoints and develop a capacity for irony like Lynda's, like Johor's: the capacity Johor evidences in his double attitude toward his subject, an ability to hold opposite, even logically contradictory perspectives in tension. The "use of dismay," then, is not only the "stubborn patience needed to withstand," the small painful courage that is larger than anything, but the "courteous irony" that emerges as a saving grace from *The Golden Notebook*.[17]

Irony is "needed" because of what Shikasta is—"This planet is above all one of contrasts and contradictions .... Tension is its essential nature. This is its strength. This is its weakness" (5). These "contradictions" require ability to entertain a multiplicity of perspectives. But irony also has immediately tangible benefits as regards survival, because without it one is vulnerable—

because "it takes one to know one" (343). "It takes one to know one" is one of those gnomic utterances, reiterated in *The Four-Gated City*, that is both utterly obvious and utterly opaque. In *Shikasta* its meaning becomes clearer because it explains why Canopus is continually misjudging Shammat ("that revolting empire") and also why Shammat cannot finally understand Canopus: because "benign and nurturing minds" are unable "to credit the reality of types of minds keyed to theft and destruction" (22) and evil minds are similarly incapable of comprehending good. Yet the principle "it takes one to know one" locks one into one's own perspective and makes one defenseless: so the question becomes, how "to know one" without being one—how to develop understanding of what one is not so that one can defend oneself? How to resist Shammat without being Shammat? This is the question at the heart of Shakespearean tragedy, which asks why the good are so vulnerable to evil, and which also shows evil being obtuse about goodness. Irony, the ability to suspend judgment and tolerate multiple perspectives, is what enables one to know one without becoming one, to defend oneself without succumbing, and so it turns out to be of enormous value in survival.

Like *Paradise Lost*, *Shikasta* puts us through a reading experience that repairs the ravages of the fall, teaching us to see and hear new meanings and reconstruct the world. To read this novel attentively is to learn to hear and see as Canopeans, for when at the last Johor's perspective gives way to Kassim's, our perspective becomes Johor's. Yet Lessing does not teach a simple Miltonic doctrine of obedience. She teaches us, rather, how to realize our full human intelligence and imagination—to reach out amidst the mad scramble for profit to a creative, redemptive irony.

NOTES

1. *Shikasta* (New York: Vintage, 1981), 3.

2. Mona Knapp, *Doris Lessing* (New York: Ungar, 1984), 131. She was not the only one to criticize the novel for being escapist. Karen Durbin describes Lessing's recent fiction as "retreat[ing] not merely from realism but from reality" ("Doris Lessing Inside Out," *Village Voice* 24, Nov. 12, 1979, 41); according to Anthony Burgess, "to posit cosmic aetiologies and galactic cures is an evasion of reality as well as a mockery of terrestrial suffering"; "Creeping towards Salvation," *Times Literary Supplement*, Nov. 23, 1979, 11).

3. John Milton, *Paradise Lost*, bk. 1, 1. 3; *Complete Poems and Major Prose*, ed. Merritt Y. Hughes (New York: Odyssey Press, 1957), 211.

4. "The trouble for me," says Alex de Jonge, "was that the narrative is very dispersed" (review of *Shikasta*, *Spectator* 244, June 12, 1980, 22). According to Mark Ably, "The celestial machinery creaks and grumbles ... a mosaic, a hodge-podge" ("In the Century of Destruction," *Maclean's* 92, Nov. 26, 1979, 62). Ursula Le Guin calls it "earnest and overambitious, badly constructed, badly edited," and refers to its "unshapeliness" and "aesthetic incoherence"—though she acknowledges that Lessing's "creative spirit" redeems "this lurching, lumbering, struggling book" (review, *New Republic* 181, Oct. 13, 1979, 32, 34). *Publishers' Weekly* found it "not so much a novel as a rather cumbersome literary device" whose characters "seem more like ideas on legs than people" (216, Sept. 17, 1979, 140). Others criticized it for its failure to fulfill their expectations about character and plot: "Much of the book is pedantic, turgid, polemical, and lacking in the kind of novelistic tension found in character interaction" (*Choice* 17, Apr. 1980, 221); "There is little character development ... and what characters there are prove difficult to care about" (Durbin, "Doris Lessing," 40). The most imaginative reading is Betsy Draine's, who calls it a writerly text that "provides material for the production of imaginative satisfaction, but leaves to the reader the task of 'writing' the constituent elements into a whole" (*Substance Under Pressure: Artistic Coherence and Evolving Form in the Novels of Doris Lessing* [Madison: University of Wisconsin Press, 1983], 144). Ruth Whittaker also finds its "temporal dislocation" challenging: "It is as if [Lessing] is determined that we should think in cosmic, rather than individual or national, or even merely human terms, and some of the difficulty of this novel lies in coming to terms with this gigantic canvas" (*Modern Novelists: Doris Lessing* [New York: St. Martin's Press, 1988], 100). Katherine Fishburn describes it as "challeng[ing] us not just emotionally but also intellectually and epistemologically" "to join it in redefining reality itself" (*The Unexpected Universe of Doris Lessing: A Study in Narrative Technique* [Westport, Conn.: Greenwood Press, 1985], 59). But generally, reviews of this novel were not welcoming: it was criticized as escapist, incoherent, and even immoral.

5. Interview with Christopher Bigsby, in *The Radical Imagination and the Liberal Tradition: Interviews with English and American Novelists*, ed. Heide Ziegler and Christopher Bigsby (London: Junction Books, 1982), 188–208; quoted in Whittaker, *Modern Novelists*, 103.

6. William Shakespeare, *The Complete Works*, ed. Alfred Harbage (Baltimore, MD.: Penguin, 1975), *As You Like It* (2.2.12, p. 252); *King Lear* (2.4.265, p. 1882).

7. Draine, *Substance*, Le Guin calls it "Calvinist" in its view of humanity as "incapable of doing good on its own" (review, 32). Knapp complains that

Lessing's "requiring [the individual] to submit to the master plan" (*Doris Lessing*, 132), to the "religious ... resignation to the will of the higher-ups," is reminiscent of "the dangers of the Fuhrer principle" (162–63).

8. Hyman Maccoby, "Heaven and *Shikasta*," *Listener* 102, Nov. 22, 1979, 716. Edmund Fuller calls it "a pale shadow of the Judeo-Christian expression of the condition of man" ("Doris Lessing's Imaginative Flight through Time," *Wall Street Journal* 194, Nov. 19, 1979, 22).

9. So, too, apparently do critics have "other ideas" of themselves. George Stade, for example, bristles that "the new unearthly perspective reduces the size of her earthlings" ("Fantastic Lessing," *New York Times Book Review*, Nov. 4, 1979, 1).

10. Jeanette King, *Doris Lessing* (London: Edward Arnold, 1989), 73.

11. Draine objects that Zone Six is radically incongruous with the rest of *Shikasta*, that its fantasy is "out of alignment with the science fiction mode" (*Substance*, 156–57), but I see it as making sense in terms of the novel's intertextuality with *Paradise Lost*.

12. Draine, *Substance*, 158.

13. Stanley Fish, *Surprised by Sin: The Reader in Paradise Lost* (London: Macmillan, 1967).

14. King, *Doris Lessing*, 73.

15. Fishburn also describes a process by which we come to "accept the alien perspective as the normative perspective" and "to question the human perspective for being too limited" (*Unlimited Universe*, 79).

16. Even the messiah is a multiple event, as Draine points out, since there are in *Shikasta* numerous reincarnations rather than one: Johor's incarnation is not "the unique and all-important event in salvation-history" (*Unexpected Universe*, 155).

17. Irony in fact is the initial response of the Giants to learning that they will cease to exist and their work has come to nothing—"not protest," which would be "inappropriate," but "an acknowledgment of the existence of *irony*" (40). This is heroic in the Giants, though it quickly degenerates to self-important posturing, once they succumb to the degenerative disease.

ROBERTA RUBENSTEIN

Briefing for a Descent into Hell

If *The Golden Notebook* and *The Four-Gated City* can be taken as the breakthroughs in Lessing's fiction in both structure and idea, each of the novels (to date) that comes after them carries echoes of the far-ranging nexus of issues, characterizations, and patterns embraced by those two works. Yet, despite the continuity of themes, *Briefing for a Descent into Hell* initiates new formal and narrative shifts in Lessing's fiction. For the first—and only—time, the protagonist of the novel is male.[1] Structurally, the novel is closer in conception to the experimental form of *The Golden Notebook*, with its inversion of chronology and multiple perspectives that reinforce the subjectivity of point of view. In fact, the story itself is adumbrated in the earlier work, in Ella's idea of writing a story about "a man whose 'sense of reality' has gone; and because of it, has a deeper sense of reality than 'normal' people" (*The Golden Notebook*, p. 458).

Like the latter novel, *Briefing for a Descent into Hell* depends on a basic pattern of theme and variations: the "theme" is Charles Watkins's deeper psychic urge to heal the schism of his present condition of self-division; the variations include his nostalgia for union and his recognition of separation, envisioned by Lessing through a series of metaphoric or symbolic journeys. In its paring down of the density of narrative description in favor of a

flowing, more symbolically saturated language, it represents a new shape for
Lessing's central vision.

In its particular exploration of the abnormal consciousness, this novel
poses an even more radical critique of both "reality" and narrative realism
than the novels that precede it. It is worth reviewing here the way madness
itself as a particular manifestation of the abnormal consciousness has evolved
thus far in Lessing's fiction. In *The Grass Is Singing* fragmentation is the
response of Mary Turner's personality to the polarizations of reality along
sexual and racial lines—antitheses that do exist in the phenomenal world and
that are only catalysts for her own inner divisions. The resulting breakdown
emphasizes the disjunction between self and world through the fact that
oppression has both political and psychological modalities, both of which are
divisive. Julia Barr's self-division in *Retreat to Innocence* is primarily
represented through ideological and sexual antitheses. Anna Wulf's
breakdown is the most thorough "working through" of the manifold
implications of unconventional mental experience, with the beginnings of
visionary intuition (adumbrated in the younger Martha Quest of the early
volumes of *Children of Violence*) taken further until they lead to a
reintegration of the personality. Thomas Stern's madness in *Landlocked*
presses that connection between the dissolution of the self common to
certain kinds of psychotic and mystical perceptions still further. Martha
Quest's later incorporation of the meaning of his and of Lynda Coldridge's
schizophrenic visions and her own explorations in *The Four-Gated City* are
thus comprehensible as evolutionary stages in developing the organs of
spiritual perception.

Moreover, as the "inner enemy" or shadow aspect of the self becomes
more conscious and is integrated into the personality beginning with the
character of Anna Wulf, breaking through rather than breaking down
assumes a more central thematic position in Lessing's fiction. At the same
time the emphasis begins to shift from the personal to the collective aspects
of consciousness. For, while Anna Wulf wants, as she tells her therapist, to
be "'able to separate in myself what is old and cyclic, the recurring history,
the myth, from what is new, what I feel or think that might be new ... '" (*The
Golden Notebook*, p. 404), Martha Quest understands her personal
psychological growth as a function as much of those recurring cycles as of
unique events.

The changing function of "madness" thus expresses the author's
conception of both social-political realities and personal development.
Lessing has summarized her long involvement with abnormal consciousness
in her own life, observing,

I have spent nearly thirty years in close contact with mental illness, first through various brands of analyst and therapist and psychiatrist, and then through people who were "mad" in various ways, and with whom I had very close contact. And still have. All this was not by any conscious choice on my part: it happened, presumably because of unconscious needs of my own.

... I have always been close to crazy people. My parents were, mildly, in their own ways. My father was done in by the [F]irst [W]orld [W]ar, from which he never really recovered, and my mother had what is known as an unfortunate upbringing, her mother dying when she was three or so, and she never got over that. Both were acutely neurotic people. But I do not regard this as any personal fate, far from it, I believe that the world gets madder and madder, and when I say that it is not rhetorical or because the words sound attractively eccentric.[2]

As Lessing's protagonists turn away from the Leftist ideological framework for effecting social change, the "revolution" goes inward; the dream evolves from political to psychological alterations of the structures of reality as the novel structure correspondingly incorporates more of the motifs and narrative conventions associated with myth, romance, and speculative fiction. Breaking through one's conventional perceptions remains the primary task, with attendant risks, though even successful accomplishment of that task rarely affects the macrocosm, which continues to poison and fragment itself through self-interest, ignorance, and limited vision.

From the beginning of this next work, Lessing alerts the reader to the dual schema, as well as to the underlying Sufi inflection of its meaning, by providing a context for the novel on the frontispiece: "Category: Inner-Space Fiction—For there is never anywhere to go but in."[3] Two epigraphs—one from the fourteenth-century Sufi Mahmoud Shabistari's poem *The Secret Garden*, and the other from Rachel Carson's *The Edge of the Sea*—describe the macrocosm encapsulated within a raindrop or a sand grain suspended in water. As in *The Four-Gated City*, the part not only represents the whole but paradoxically contains it. By analogy, the unnamed seafarer of the first pages of *Briefing for a Descent into Hell* is Everyman, rediscovering (remembering) through the exploration of the microcosm of his own consciousness the experience of the human race.

Characteristically, the protagonist of this novel is self-divided. As one subsequently learns, the stresses of middle age and personal problems have propelled Charles Watkins, a professor of classics at Cambridge, into a mental breakdown accompanied by a temporary loss of identity medically described as amnesia. The motif of amnesia is a central one in the romance tradition: the series of adventures of the protagonist may be precipitated by "some kind of break in consciousness, one which often involves actual forgetfulness of the previous state.... Such a catastrophe, which is what it normally is, may be internalized as a break in memory, or externalized as a change in fortunes or social context."[4]

In *Briefing for a Descent into Hell* alternating sections correspond to both ways of perceiving the psychic crisis of the central character: from within and without his own consciousness. Accordingly, the first long portion is narrated primarily from the more immediate and subjective focus of the perceiving consciousness, while the remaining portions are composed primarily of letters, dialogues, and more public communications from members of Watkins's milieu and "reminiscences" provided by Watkins himself. In the first section, however, doctors' evaluations juxtaposed with the directly recorded subjective experiences of the protagonist emphasize the perceptual antithesis further.

When the protagonist is most awake and aware within his own mental experience, he is most deeply asleep from the point of view of the medical observers. His being is split into two modes: while his body participates in one, his mind participates in the other; they are complementary and, much of the time, mutually exclusive. "Inner" and "outer" space become metaphors in the novel not only in the sense of the cosmic voyage doubling as the journey of the private self but, more immediately, in the sense of disjunction between the mental and physical spaces that a person simultaneously occupies.

Watkins is Lessing's most identifiably "schizophrenic" character. In fact, a number of parallels can be drawn between the experiences of her protagonist and the existential phenomenology of schizophrenia proposed by R. D. Laing, not the least of which is a ten-day psychotic journey described by one of Laing's expatients, coincidentally named Jesse Watkins.[5] One of Laing's central (and controversial) hypotheses is that the psychotic breakdown manifested in acute schizophrenia is a natural process of mind-healing which, if allowed to run its full course, will be therapeutic rather than destructive. Following Bateson and others, Laing describes the "inner space journey" of the schizophrenic as follows:

The person who has entered this inner realm (if only he is allowed to experience this) will find himself going, or being conducted—one cannot clearly distinguish active from passive here—on a journey.

This journey is experienced as going further "in," as going back through one's personal life, in and back and through and beyond into the experience of all mankind, of the primal man, of Adam and perhaps even further into the being of animals, vegetables and minerals.

In this journey there are many occasions to lose one's way, for confusion, partial failure, even final shipwreck: many terrors, spirits, demons to be encountered, that may or may not be overcome.[6]

However, the inner journey described here is not unique to psychotic breakdown, and Lessing's apparent indebtedness to Laing accounts for only one of the multiple routes to the same archetypal experiences.[7] The comparative mythologist Joseph Campbell has observed that the pattern of experience generated during an acute schizophrenic crisis is "the universal formula also of the mythological hero journey.... Interpreted from this point of view, a schizophrenic breakdown is an inward and backward journey to recover something missed or lost, and to restore, thereby, a vital balance."[8]

As Northrop Frye has pointed out, the motifs of ascent and descent are patterns in the romance tradition in literature, wherein the worlds of idyllic and demonic experience are characteristically polarized as the narrative movement alternates between the psychological representations of wish fulfillment and nightmare.[9] That same journey pattern also appears in esoteric traditions. The Sufis describe man's evolutionary course from the simplest form of matter through vegetable, animal, human, and suprahuman states of consciousness, to the achievement of the "total perception of the external phenomenal world."[10] Further, phenomenologists of consciousness document similar motifs in the classical experiences described throughout the centuries in mystical and occult literature, and in the more recent psychedelic (or psycholytic) drug-induced experiences.[11]

What all of these parallel formulations suggest is that the collective unconscious—whether reached by psychotic, psychoanalytic, psychedelic, or contemplative means—manifests itself in similar archetypal images and symbols. Regardless of the catalyst, the unconscious generates patterns which, under certain but diverse circumstances, become more readily accessible to the other layers of the psyche. That identity is central to the major motifs of *Briefing for a Descent into Hell*, the first movement of which may be read as the narrative of a spiritual, archetypal, psychotic, or even drug-induced inner journey. What determines its fullest symbolic meaning is not so much what stimulates the journey as what is attained through it, and whether or not the change in consciousness has long-reaching effects on the personality of the protagonist.

Throughout the first long portion of the novel, the images resonate on several levels of meaning. The protagonist initially finds himself "at sea," a figurative pun suggesting the nature of his personal crisis as well as the base-element that symbolizes the origin of individual and collective, organic and psychic, life. The protagonist's wanderings express other primary images and rhythms, including heat, light, and circles. His "anti-clock Wise" (p. 38) direction and his need to experience a birth in reverse (p. 33) suggest the circularity of his journey backward both in time and in the development of his own consciousness as he tries to locate the center of his being.[12] He is the archetypal seafarer, alternately Jason, Jonah, Odysseus, Sinbad, adrift in a ship that is inhabited temporarily by a strange unearthly light (called the Crystal) that incorporates his shipmates but leaves him behind. (One learns later in the novel that during Watkins's war experience he was twice the only survivor in a group of buddies; in this section he is twice left behind by the Crystal—an example of Lessing's refraction of events from later in the novel through the protagonist's altered consciousness.)

While the inner space journey traces the narrator's subsequent efforts to reach the Crystal again, it figuratively recapitulates the cumulative history of life on earth. The protagonist is identified with the first living organisms emerging from the slime as they become land creatures (p. 40); the psychological and spiritual parallel is the emergence of human consciousness and its growth toward enlightenment and wholeness. As in *The Four-Gated City*, evolution in *Briefing for a Descent into Hell* is conceived as a dual process, both biological and spiritual; in each context ontogeny recapitulates phylogeny. That progress of human evolution appears in the writings of the thirteenth-century Sufi teacher Jalaluddin Rumi as follows:

> He came, at first, into the inert world, and from minerality developed into the realm of vegetation. Years he lived thus. Then he passed into an animal state, bereft of memory of his having been vegetable—except for his attraction to Spring and flowers. This was like the innate desire of the infant for the mother's

breast....

From realm to realm man went, reaching his present reasoning, knowledgeable, robust state—forgetting earlier forms of intelligence.

So, too, shall he pass beyond the current forms of perception.... There are a thousand other forms of Mind....[13]

Within his existential reality Lessing's protagonist accomplishes the evolutionary step from sea to land, literally and figuratively, with the aid of a dolphin. Once on land, he establishes an intuitive communication with two gentle cat-like creatures who guide him over an apparent impasse in his upward climb. He arrives at what is at first an uninhabited archaic city. Like the mythical four-gated city of *Children of Violence*, it is organized in a circle/square configuration suggesting a sacred dimension. Later the houses are noticeably "turned inwards, to the centre" (p. 77), and the city itself seems to acknowledge the protagonist's presence as if also possessed of consciousness.

At first the archaic Eden-like atmosphere of the surroundings is emphasized, "as if this was a country where hostility or dislike had not yet been born" (p. 42). The protagonist experiences a sense of harmony and unity analogous both to the state of undifferentiated wholeness in the generic individual's personal development, and to the hypothetical primitive pre-ego consciousness in the history of civilization. However, that state is soon interrupted by the appearance of the ubiquitous "enemy" that Lessing has shown consistently as a configuration of the dark side of the mind.

The protagonist accordingly feels himself under a lunar influence, a reference not only to the pull of that dark or irrational side of the self, with its multiple metaphoric meanings,[14] but also an ironic gloss on the "lunacy" that his rambling monologues represent to the medical staff. On the outskirts of the city he witnesses, and feels himself implicated in, a ritualistic blood-letting involving several male babies and three females whose identities are disturbingly familiar to him. He realizes that their rite destroys forever some fundamental innocence in nature by their introduction of carnality into the pure world; like Adam in the Garden, he acquires a knowledge of the flesh, and feels compelled to cover his nakedness. Just as his imagination had "invented" the city itself, "now I understood my fall away from what I had been when I landed, only three weeks before, into a land which had never known killing. I knew that I had arrived purged and salt-scoured and guiltless, but that between then and now I had drawn evil into my surroundings, into me ..." (p. 66). The shadow further manifests itself in two species of ugly, rapacious animals—the negative (and further divided) counterparts of the benevolent beasts that had earlier guided him. From the first appearance of these rat-like dogs and monkeys, the protagonist watches their mutual antagonism build and then break into open warfare, and tacitly acknowledges his own complicity in their violence.

During the time he spends on land, the voyager sees as his task the preparation of a landing pad in the center of the city, in anticipation of the return of the Crystal. Significantly, both the Crystal and the landing area are images of wholeness; in archetypal symbolism crystals and the abstract circle/square configuration often represent "the union of extreme opposites—of matter and spirit."[15] After delays and failures in his effort to prepare himself for this crucial segment of his journey, he finally senses the presence of the Crystal. But, again, he is not ready for it: "Whatever it was that I could not quite see, but was there, belonged to a level of existence that my eyes were not evolved enough to see.... Beating out from that central point came waves of a finer substance, from a finer level of existence, which assaulted me, because I was not tuned in to them ..." (p. 76). The equation of extrasensory perception with the evolving organs of consciousness described by Sufi mystics underlies the formulations of Watkins's experience. The metaphoric language parallels the Sufi chemist Fariduddin Attar's description of inner transformation: "Every fiber has been purified, raised to a higher state, vibrates to a higher tune, gives out a more direct, more penetrating note...."[16] At the same time Watkins's inadequacy makes explicit the difficulty of achieving that elevated level of being.

Thus far the protagonist's journey has been on water or land. His nascent "lighter" state now enables him to move in air, through the assistance of a great white bird, and suggests his further ascent toward enlightenment. Finally, in an event that symbolically condenses the several levels of the meaning of his experience, the Crystal arrives at the center of the circle-in-the-square to receive him. His own body becomes "a shape in light" (p. 102) and the city changes correspondingly, "as if the city of stone and clay had dissolved, leaving a ghostly city, made in light ..." (pp. 102–3). As the boundaries between self and world, inner and outer space, dissolve, the light is simultaneously "inner or outer as one chose to view it" (p. 109). The protagonist's inner being becomes congruent with the macrocosm; he understands that the mind of humanity is also a unified consciousness, of which he is an integral part. Even the war and blood-lust he has witnessed have been essential to his eventual transmutation, providing the "page in my passport for this stage of the journey ... a door, a key, and an opening" (pp. 105, 107).

Formally, the movement toward a higher plane of mystical awareness suggests the ascent motif of romance and myth, in which "escape, remembrance, or discovery of one's real identity, growing freedom, and the breaking of enchantment" shape the narrative; the growth of identity through "the casting off of whatever conceals or frustrates it" typifies the positive metamorphosis of the protagonist.[17] Thus Lessing renders the fundamentally ineffable and self-transcending experience of spiritual illumination—the event that Evelyn Underhill has called the "crystallization" of consciousness at a higher level.[18] The Sufi teachings have it that "when apparent opposites are reconciled, the individuality is not only complete, it also transcends the bounds of ordinary humanity as we understand them. The individual becomes, as near as we can state it, immensely powerful."[19]

In one of a series of lectures given in 1972 at the New School for Social Research, Lessing alluded to her own conversion from the rationalist position to one accommodating the connections among extrasensory perception, elevations of consciousness, and the intensification of personal energy. As she phrased it, "Now the real question is this: Where do you get your energy from? What kind of energy is it? How do you husband it? How do you use it? ... "[20] And, further, concerning the ESP phenomenon—the source of apparent coincidences of like thinking between people (such as the affinity, described later in *Briefing for a Descent into Hell*, of Rosemary Baines's and Charles Watkins's ideas on education)—Lessing added, "What energy is reaching you? We don't know why, do we? There is something there to be explored ... if we don't get upset."[21]

Narratively, the description of this process of exploration unfolding in the consciousness of Lessing's inner space voyager is periodically interrupted by the medical staff's observations on their patient's mental condition, and their disagreements about appropriate treatment. Doctor X (deliberately nameless, like the patient) recommends extensive use of drugs and eventually electro-convulsive therapy (shock treatment), while Doctor Y is more restrained, arguing for a gradual approach with minimal intervention. Watkins perceives the doctors' different sensitivities: while he can scarcely "see" Doctor X, Doctor Y is more "visible," burning with a "small steady light" (p. 162). However, despite their different auras and their conflicting diagnoses, both doctors are primarily concerned to restore their patient to the same orthodox model of "normality." Monitoring his responses to the drugs, they interpret his mental condition through its physical manifestations, concentrating on such behavioral evidence as alertness, coherence, drowsiness, and other physiological signs. The reader, suspended between the image of the protagonist as Everyman journeying through the collective unconscious, and Charles Watkins as amnesiac patient, observes the same experiences as described from internal and external perspectives. To emphasize their radical disparity, Lessing juxtaposes the protagonist's approach to the pinnacle of his vision of unity with the medical records showing that he had "less grasp of reality than when he was admitted" (p. 101). The quintessential spiritual experience is, from the medical point of view, a religious delusion.

Consistent with the paradoxes possible at nonrational levels of consciousness, the protagonist's inner space journey is increasingly conceptualized as occurring in outer space. One recalls Anna Wulf's "game," in which the mind progressively distances itself in the direction of a more comprehensive and inclusive geography, a metaphorical statement of the cosmic perspective (*The Golden Notebook*, p. 469). From deep in inner/outer space the protagonist of this novel has a similar overview of all of the earth, with its petty wars, political schisms, social insanities, divisions. Yet the index of his psychic wholeness is his perception of the fundamental unity of all things, of the interrelatedness of matter and spirit in every dimension of the cosmos. The real madness of humanity, he comprehends, is the failure to remember that unity at the base of all life, instead pursuing the courses of separation and division.

The same identification of microcosm with macrocosm, of inner with outer space, extends still further, as the enlightened protagonist finds himself at a cosmic conference presided over by an illuminated deity (the Sun). There he learns that the troubled planet Earth is in a state of First Class Emergency. The cosmic spirits—including Merk Ury, Minna Erva, and other refractions of Watkins's intellectual familiarity with the Greek classics—are being "briefed" to carry the easily forgotten message of Harmony to its inhabitants once again before it self-destructs. Though the style in this section, occasionally verging on parody of the more classic fabulations of science fiction (and also of conference rhetoric), lightens the novel's tone, the straining after humor is somewhat jarring. While Lessing frequently depends on irony and even parody (as in Anna Wulf's self-parodies in *The Golden Notebook*), humor itself is rare in her work; where it does appear, it is somewhat self-conscious. Thus, of the stylistic variations within *Briefing for a Descent into Hell*, this section and the serious but rather pedestrian verses of the earlier phase of Watkins's journey are the least successful. However, while stylistically awkward, they are nonetheless consistent with the larger design: the creation of verbal equivalents for various kinds of perception and communication, ranging from deeply interior and nearly inarticulable mental experiences to the more public messages (both implicit and explicit) that govern interpersonal relationships. To this point, Lessing has her protagonist repeat several times during his reluctant interchanges with the medical staff, "'I gotta use words when I talk to you ... '" (p. 162).

The Forecast for Earth made by the benevolent overseers echoes the extrapolated future envisioned at the end of *The Four-Gated City* but concludes more optimistically. The "film" of the planetary crisis ends with the appearance of a new breed born with an altered mental structure promoting increased powers of perception; its members are endowed with the heritage of the previous generations, "plus, this time, the mental equipment to use it" (p. 140). Through the apocalyptic perspective, Lessing continues to exploit the narrative liberties of speculative fiction.[22]

If the macrocosm and the microcosm are understood as congruent, then the anticipated cataclysm on earth that Watkins observes corresponds to the psychic crisis in his own personality; like Anna Wulf, he discovers the chaos in the outer world that is a projection of his inner state. Furthermore, for the cosmic beings who seek to revitalize the message of harmony and, analogously, for the vision of wholeness in the unconscious that seeks entry into consciousness, the obstacles are great. Even with the "brain-printed" message, the emissaries face a considerable risk of amnesia during their descent into Hell (earth); Watkins's descent into his own inner hell is manifested as amnesia to the medical observers.[23] Symbolically, though each human being is born ("brain-printed") with the experience of harmony and wholeness, subsequent experience erodes that primary knowledge and substitutes division. As he grows older, he is more and more like a victim of amnesia, increasingly self-estranged and forgetful of the knowledge of original unity as the deepest reality of his being. Literature of the romantic tradition consistently alludes to the transcendental state of innocence (as in Wordsworth's "Ode: Intimations of Immortality"), and all mystical traditions seek the way back (or forward) to that experience of undifferentiated wholeness. Idries Shah notes in the latter case that in the Sufi dervish tradition, "remembering" is an important aspect of psychic development, beginning with "'remembering oneself,' after which the function shifts to one of harmony with the greater consciousness."[24]

The problem given this particular symbolic form in *Briefing for a Descent into Hell* is the characteristic metaphysical one of Lessing's fictional protagonists. As Watkins formulates it, "Each individual of this species is locked up inside his own skull," unable to "see things except as facets and one at a time" (p. 142). Watkins himself is ironically the prime example of that propensity. Unlike Martha Quest, who ultimately fuses the opposites of her personality through diligent "work" on her self, the Watkins of the second part of the novel and the mind-voyaging protagonist of the first part do not constitute a *conscious* integrated whole personality. In his own "First Class Emergency," amnesia is the psychological manifestation of an ontological crisis, a breakdown or disintegration of his life-roles as husband, father, paramour, professor. Forgetting for a time who he "is" for others, he journeys within his own unconscious self in an effort to rescue some deeper knowledge from which his waking ego personality has become severed. Thus the hallucinations, fantasies, and visions of his inner space journey are—from the point of view of his total personality—"unconscious." His larger task is to bring the truths discovered in the collective memory to personal awareness, to fuse the split between the generic Everyman of the inner space journey and the individual self of waking life.

In the subsequent movements of the novel the emphasis shifts from cosmic to biological and social time and their corresponding metaphorical formulations. Formally, the narrative reverses from the pattern of ascent, with its impetus toward unity, to that of descent, with its impetus toward separation. Following the rebirth that expresses his spiritual gnosis, and his cosmic briefing on Harmony, the protagonist "returns to the beginning" again, this time reliving the primary biological separation of his own physical birth experience:

> Sucked into sound, sucked into sea, a swinging sea, *boom*, shhhh, *boooom*, shhhh, *boooom* ... thud thud, thud thud ... one two, and the three is me, the three is me, THE THREE IS ME. I in dark, I in pulsing dark, crouched, I holding on, clutching tight, boooom, shhhh, boooom, shhh, rocked, rocking, somewhere behind the gate, somewhere in front the door, and a dark red clotting light and pressure and pain and then OUT into a flat white light where shapes move and things flash and glitter. (P. 148)

His first "personal" memory following birth is his initiation into the drugging of his awareness and the equation of sleeping with being a "good" baby, an expectation that prefigures the chronic spiritual torpor of adult life.[25] Both literally and metaphorically, sleep is the norm; spiritual awakeness is the abnormal state.[26]

Lessing has noted elsewhere that under the influence of mescaline (in her single experience with the drug) she experienced "both giving birth and being given birth to. Who was the mother, who was the baby? I was both but neither"—surely a resonant image of the creative artist giving birth to her own self. (Lessing emphasizes, however, that drugs are not the most valuable path into the mind; with discipline and patience, "if you can train yourself to concentrate you can travel great distances."[27]) Stanislav Grof, working with psycholytic (psychedelic) drug-induced experiences and extrapolating from the psychoanalytic concept of "birth trauma," has proposed that the universal intrauterine state and the subsequent stages of labor and delivery form biological paradigms for the ecstatic and stressful extremes of psychic experiences at successive levels of consciousness; these may manifest themselves in certain aspects of both drug-induced and psychotic experiences.[28]

Those same extremes of unity and separation permeate the consciousness of the protagonist of Lessing's novel. Each framing of the journey repeats certain patterns in Watkins's split personality, as Lessing illustrates through a variety of contexts the same emotional truths of her protagonist's situation. That the inner journey is itself both a reflection of and an effort to heal the division is the central assumption of the novel. As R. D. Laing has remarked, the "cracked mind of the schizophrenic may *let in* light which does not enter the intact minds of many sane people whose minds are closed."[29] The narrator of *Briefing for a Descent into Hell* describes the mental hospitals that house the "millions who have cracked, making cracks where the light could shine through at last ... " (p. 154).

Like Laing, whose ideology Lessing shares more explicitly in this novel than in any of her other works (despite her own consistent disclaimers),[30] the author emphasizes that "mental illness"—manifested as unconventional behavior or abnormal consciousness—is a cultural label that permits the potential for vision or even self-healing to be drugged and nullified by the very institutions that ostensibly promote recovery. The medical model of psychic disequilibrium prevents doctors (and others) from accepting the possibility that, in Anton Boisen's words,

> certain types of mental disorder are not in themselves evils but problem-solving experiences. They are attempts at reorgan-ization in which the entire personality, to its bottommost depths, is aroused and its forces marshaled to meet the danger of personal failure and isolation.... The acute disturbances ... arise out of awareness of danger. The sufferer is facing what for him are the

great and abiding issues of life and death and of his own
relationship to the universe.

... In some cases the charge of pathology as applied to religious
experience is due simply to the failure to recognize that such
phenomena as hallucinations spring from the tapping of the
deeper levels of the mental life, and that as such they are not
necessarily symptomatic of mental disorder but may be creative
and constructive. But in a large number of cases the association
of the mystical and the pathological is due to the fact that a
fundamental reorientation is a necessary stage in the development of the individual.[31]

If the first major section of *Briefing for a Descent into Hell* shows the
"light shining through" the cracked mind of the protagonist, the remainder
of the novel provides a partial explanation for the crack. As in *The Golden
Notebook*, the scrambling of chronology is essential to the novel's meaning.
Lessing provides the immediate subjective experience of Watkins's abnormal
consciousness first, and only subsequently furnishes its context by showing
the data of his outer world that have been translated into the particular
images of his journey. The literal link between the divided layers of his being
is Watkins's photographic memory (a capacity later reported by one of his
colleagues). The narrative organization thus expresses two kinds of
knowledge: the "information" of the external world of social interaction, and
its imaginative transformations at the unconscious levels of the protagonist's
psyche. Their juxtaposition both invites and expresses the implicit questions
of the novel: which mode is the "real" one? And, is their synthesis possible
within contemporary social and political contexts?

Once Watkins's social identity is established, by means of a photograph
found in his recovered wallet, the doctors attempt to reconstruct his former
identity for him. Watkins, however, categorically rejects the role and name
assigned to him by his former intimates, having found his true center in the
modality of psychic space he has recently circumnavigated. Concurrently, the
testimonies from his wife, mistress, colleagues, and acquaintances to the
doctors contribute a picture of the social persona that Watkins has vacated,
and one that contrasts sharply with the illuminated Everyman of the first part
of the novel. The commentaries of his familiars emphasize the ways in which
Watkins—to *their* perceptions—was always somehow different, abnormal.
Impervious to basic social conventions and feelings, he was "the original
eccentric oddball" (p. 223) who did not even "pay lip service to ordinary

feelings" (p. 227), according to his colleague Jeremy Thorne. His disillusioned former mistress, Constance Mayne, found him "above every human emotion" (p. 232). His wife, Felicity, who might be expected to know him best, seems to know him least, though she does volunteer the fact that he "always sleeps much less than most people" (p. 172). Conversely, Rosemary Baines, a bare acquaintance from one of his lecture audiences, had been so struck by his ideas and his presence that she had written an extraordinary letter, which forms a major section of the narrative (almost to the extent of straining narrative realism), to share with him her ideas on education and other matters.

Though he had initially dismissed Rosemary Baines's remarkable effort at communication, one learns subsequently that Watkins had met with her and her archaeologist friend, Frederick Larson, the night before the onset of his amnesia. Many of the ideas detailed in her letter reappear in altered form as images and events in the inner space journey that he subsequently undergoes (already narrated earlier in the novel). Rosemary discusses the problem of education—the process of indoctrinating children into social norms and thus anaesthetizing their inborn capacity for perceiving wholeness. She describes the psychic wavelength that Watkins's lecture on the topic had struck within her: the feeling of "beings briefly, on a different, high, vibrating current, of the familiar becoming transparent" (p. 183). Her reflections clearly parallel the experience Watkins himself lives out at the climax of his inner journey, which in turn alludes to the elevated awareness of the Sufi mystic.

Moreover, Rosemary Baines reiterates her friend Frederick Larson's archaeological speculations on the forms of life of earlier civilizations. Observations on the roofing materials of archaic houses and the implicit ethnocentric bias of archaeology resonate with Watkins's discovery of the idyllic city with roofless houses; Rosemary's long discussion of Larson's (and others') mid-life crises, precipitated by the questioning of basic assumptions about one's profession and identity, resonates with Watkins's own breakdown. Like Larson, Watkins has suffered from a stammer that is symptomatic of his inner turmoil; like Larson, Watkins is also a student of ancient civilizations, but his intellectual mastery of the heritage of Western thought has failed to develop in him any insight into the larger relationship between the collective past and his personal history. His mind journey of the first part of the novel thus acquires further meaning as a reflection of aspects of the self he has not assimilated into his mundane conscious personality. Ironically, his psychic travels make existentially real his identification with classical mythic figures and motifs from his intellectual discipline.

Though that journey is interrupted by the doctors' efforts to restore him to his pre-amnesiac identity, it is resumed in another form in response to the more sensitive Doctor Y's suggestion that Watkins recall his wartime experiences. Stylistically, this section is one of the novel's most effective passages—almost a set-piece that can be appreciated separately as the representation of an emotionally powerful experience. The sense of immediacy and detail is all the more heightened by the reader's subsequent discovery that it is a pure fantasy—neither "realistic" nor, from the perspective of Watkins's literal past life, "true." His war buddy Miles Bovey, whose death is described in the account, later confirms not only that he is still alive but that Watkins had never seen action in Yugoslavia, the location of his "recollection." Instead, these events are closer to Bovey's own war experience.

Watkins describes a number of events in a political matrix that resonate with those already encountered within a cosmic setting as patterns of his emotional reality: a briefing (this time a military one) followed by a descent (a parachute drop into Yugoslavia), and the experience of belonging to a larger collective whole (participation in the partisan Resistance). Communism is expressed in a pure, ideal form, wherein "an individual could only be important insofar as he or she was a pledge for the future ..." (p. 258). The experience of self-transcendence manifests itself through not divine but earthly harmony and union, in a love relationship with a partisan named Konstantina (an idealized fantasy of Watkins's former real-life mistress, Constance).

Again his (and the author's) nostalgia for Paradise surfaces, as he envisions "the world as it was before man filled and fouled it.... Those vast mountains, in which we moved like the first people on earth.... It was as if every one of us had lived so, once upon a time, at another time, in a country like this, with sharp sweet-smelling air and giant uncut trees, among people descended from a natural royalty, those to whom harmfulness and hate were alien ..." (pp. 256–58). Characteristically, the antithetical shadow emerges. In a variation of the birth-in-death spasm of a rat-dog in Watkins's earlier journey, Konstantina is fatally gored by a threatened doe about to give birth. The cycle of birth and death is the paradigm for the antinomies of human experience; only in the imaginative mythic and spiritual dimensions are they reconciled.[32]

But the more realistic necessity remains of reconciling the divided personality in the social context. In the final movement of *Briefing for a Descent into Hell*, Lessing poses the task one more time. Watkins is by then tenuously balanced midway between the two extremes of his being: the vivid experience of wholeness in its several formulations, and the urgings of his contemporaries to resume his former social identity. He is convinced that he must "remember" something that is crucial to his psychic survival, but what he must remember—the reality of unity—is antithetical to what the doctors urge him to remember—the split identity he has vacated. For a time he preserves his suspension between the two, sharing his intermediate state with a young patient named Violet Stoke. To her he describes the discrepancy in his condition as he and the doctors perceive it: "'They say I lost my memory because I feel guilty.... I think I feel guilty because I lost my memory'" (p. 287). Violet's status as a girl who does not want to grow up emphasizes the ambiguity of Watkins's condition.

In this context, one theory of schizophrenia suggests that the condition is the individual's response to "paradox intolerance," particularly as embodied in the antithetical emotions of love and aggression. Because of the pressure of those conflicting experiences, he seeks a "personal paradise": "a hypothetical life situation where each person can creatively express himself openly, directly, and honestly, and come to fulfillment without double-binds, games, hidden agendas, and complexes.... [T]he person who ends up with the appellation 'schizophrenic' is in some way more imbued with the need to find that paradise for himself, that is, he not only needs to, but has to. Such an archetype is more central to his being...."[33] Mircea Eliade describes the ambivalence inherent in the desire for paradise within the sacred context, noting that "on the one side, man is haunted by the desire to escape from his particular situation and regain a transpersonal mode of life; on the other, he is paralyzed by the fear of losing his 'identity' and 'forgetting' himself."[34] Man must leave Eden in order to grow—but he may spend the rest of his life trying to return to it. The nostalgia for wholeness is his oldest memory, for unity is located, symbolically, at both the beginning and the end of consciousness.

Watkins submits to shock treatment in the hope that it may help him to remember the truth that hovers like a shadow on the edge of his awareness. His final insight before the shock treatment is his explanation to Violet of the phenomenon of timing at work in the level of human evolution and change:

> "It's desperately urgent that I should remember, I do know that.
> It's all timing, you see.... There are lots of things in our ordinary
> life that are—shadows. Like coincidences, or dreaming, the kinds

of things that are an angle to ordinary life.... The important thing is this—to remember that some things reach out to us from that level of living, to here ... all these things, they have a meaning, they are reflections from that other part of ourselves, and that part of ourselves knows things we don't know.... [W]hat I have to remember has to do with time running out." (Pp. 301–2)

As Neumann has observed, in mythology the sense of otherworldly knowledge that must be remembered "is usually projected into a knowledge acquired before birth or after death.... Man's task in the world is to remember with his conscious mind what was knowledge before the advent of consciousness."[35]

In Watkins's long explanation to Violet, Lessing distills a number of the ideas that appear in various forms throughout the novel. In fact, their recapitulation in this segment comes precariously close to didactic excess, given the more inventive shapings of the same ideas earlier in the novel. The "message" intrudes uncomfortably upon the narrative design, and belies the occasional tension in Lessing's work between aesthetic and ideological concerns.

Despite Watkins's various illuminations, the ultimate prognosis is negative; time runs out for him as medical science pre-empts his personal struggle to remember wholeness. The shock treatment works with rather than against the split in his personality, and the amnesia of his earlier life merely reverses itself and becomes an amnesia of his inner journey. Watkins leaves the hospital, presumably fully recovered but in fact as split as before. His wife and friends confirm the Watkins they had known before his breakdown. The tragedy of his medical "cure" is that he has recovered his former identity only to lose, once again, the meaning of his journey.

However, in this novel Lessing suggests that the fault lies not with his choices but with the establishment itself, for its endorsement of that very state of separateness and inner division as the norm. R. D. Laing has enjoined, "Can we not see that *this voyage* [into the self] *is not what we need to be cured of but that it is itself a natural way of healing our own appalling state of alienation called normality?*"[36] Lessing somewhat more pessimistically implies that in society as it is presently constituted, abnormal consciousness is a mixed blessing, for the self cannot exist without reference to a world. If Watkins reflects the schizophrenia of contemporary life, the cure is no better than the disease. Ultimately failing to overcome his self-division, he hovers in the perilous straits between inner illumination and the external manifestations often identified as psychosis, with no certainty as to which is "real," since the definition of reality is established by consensus. By the latter standard, the effort to relinquish the personal ego in order to embrace transcendence is a pathological one. What distinguishes between the schizophrenic and the mystic or enlightened individual, as Lessing has already suggested, is partly the capacity of unique personality to harmonize its own dissonant elements and partly the judgment of the orthodox establishment that labels it.

John Vernon has postulated that Western tradition is fundamentally "schizophrenic" in its very conceptualization of what is "real." The intrinsic dualism of logical thought shapes perception at such a basic level that not only are the patterns discerned in experience split into opposing categories (real/unreal, sane/insane, and so on), but these splits in turn create the further dichotomies in the perception of separation between the self and the world.[37] Accordingly, the politicization of madness leads to the logical paradoxes of either the sanity of insanity, in the form of a retreat into a privately meaningful but ultimately solipsistic awareness, or the insanity of sanity, in the form of capitulation to the division endemic in contemporary life. Both are "schizophrenic," for "each mode of being, the real and the fantastic, the sane and the insane, excludes the other, and each is intolerable because of that exclusion."[38]

Lessing's increasing use of paradox, symbolic imagery, and non-logical frames of reference indicates her attempt to formulate an imaginative way around that logical contradiction. Though the reduction in scope, diversity of characters and events, and density of language (in contrast to the earlier major novels) result in a more schematic work of fiction with occasional stylistic lapses, *Briefing for a Descent into Hell* as a whole is an innovative and effective fusion of form with idea. The suspension between realism and fantasy retains both the metaphysical and formal ambiguity of the whole—a narrative strategy that allies the author with others for whom the "open" ending is the only way to express the uncertainties inherent in the subjective or confessional mode. One thinks of Dostoevsky's divided antihero in *Notes from Underground*, as well as of more contemporary fictions by John Barth, Anthony Burgess, William Golding, Kurt Vonnegut, Thomas Pynchon, and others who have departed from strict representational narrative, adapting conventions from fable, romance, and speculative fiction in order to render "glimmers of a reality hidden from us by our present set of preconceptions."[39] The ambiguous tension between realism and myth, between division and unity, remains the central dynamic of Lessing's fiction. As insistently as her protagonists seek forms of consciousness that can accommodate contradiction and embrace the moment of transcendence,

Lessing seeks fictional resolutions of the antinomies erected by the mind itself.

NOTES

1. Lynn Sukenick hypothesizes that, though *"Briefing* may feature a man's consciousness simply as a preference of imagination [one] suspects ... that a man was chosen in order to give madness its fullest due and its deepest persuasion: the fact that women are more often considered irrational would give a conventional taint to a disordered female and rob madness of the novel authority it possesses in *Briefing.*" She adds that in this novel and the preceding one, "sexuality and gender begin to fade into a transcendent condition and are greatly reduced in stature under pressure of a higher androgynous knowledge." See "Feeling and Reason in Doris Lessing's Fiction," in *Doris Lessing: Critical Essays*, ed. Annis Pratt and L. S. Dembo (Madison: University of Wisconsin Press, 1974), p. 116.

2. From letter from Doris Lessing to Roberta Rubenstein dated 28 Mar. 1977. See Lessing's further comments on madness and on psychoanalysis from the same letter on pp. 80 and 110–11, n. 14, above, and compare with her Stony Brook interview, quoted on pp. 147–48 above.

3. Lessing, *Briefing for a Descent into Hell* (New York: Alfred A. Knopf, 1971), frontispiece (this statement does not appear in the paperback edition of the novel). Subsequent page references will be indicated in the text.

4. Northrop Frye, *The Secular Scripture* (Cambridge, Mass., and London: Harvard University Press, 1976), p. 102.

5. That journey is described in R. D. Laing's *The Politics of Experience and The Bird of Paradise* (1967; rpt. Middlesex, England: Penguin Books, 1970), pp. 120–37. Elsewhere I have identified a number of parallels between Charles and Jesse Watkins's journeys. See Roberta Rubenstein, "Briefing on Inner Space: Doris Lessing and R. D. Laing," *Psychoanalytic Review* 63, no. 1 (1976), 83–93. Marion Vlastos discusses similar, and additional, parallels in her comprehensive analysis of the correspondences between Lessing's and Laing's views of madness and the psychotic experience, in "Doris Lessing and R. D. Laing: Psychopolitics and Prophecy," *PMLA* 91, no. 2 (1976), 245–58.

6. Laing, *Politics of Experience*, p. 104.

7. Without directly acknowledging the origin or degree of her own familiarity with Laing's work, Lessing has identified him as "a peg" upon which intellectuals have hung their need for "a key authority figure who will

then act as a law giver. Laing became that figure." From Lessing's lecture at the New School for Social Research, quoted by Nancy Shields Hardin in "Doris Lessing and the Sufi Way," in *Doris Lessing*, ed. Pratt and Dembo, pp. 154–55.

Moreover, in personal correspondence to me—in response to my suggestion of the strong parallels between her novel and Laing's work—Lessing wrote, "I had not taken Laing as my starting point. I had not read the piece in question by him or the book *Politics of Experience*.

"My book was written out of my own thoughts, not other people's.

" ... It seems almost impossible for people to grasp that people can write from their own experience.

"As for the name Watkins, being used: I took the name out of the telephone book, which is my usual practice ... [because of British libel laws]. I always use the commonest name I can find...." From Letter to Roberta Rubenstein date 17 Nov. 1972.

8. Campbell, "Mythology and Schizophrenia," in *Myths to Live By* (New York: Viking, 1972), pp. 202–3.

9. Frye, *Secular Scripture*, p. 58.

10. Nasrollah S. Fatemi, "A Message and Method of Love, Harmony, and Brotherhood," in *Sufi Studies: East and West*, ed. L. F. Rushbrook William (New York: E. P. Dutton, 1973), p. 59.

11. A particularly striking documentation and synthesis of these several approaches, in which states of altered consciousness are induced with the psycholytic drug LSD, are given in the study by Stanislav Grof, M.D., *Realms of the Human Unconscious* (New York: Viking, 1975). Robert E. L. Masters and Jean Houston, *The Varieties of Psychedelic Experience* (New York: Holt, Rinehart and Winston, 1966), and John White, ed., *The Highest State of Consciousness*, 2nd ed. (New York: Doubleday, 1972), bring together a wide cross-section information on the same broad topic.

12. In an excellent analysis of the themes and patterns of the novel, Robert S. Ryf has similarly described the circle motif as both a structural and a thematic organization within the work. See "Beyond Ideology: Doris Lessing's Mature Vision," *Modern Fiction Studies* 16, no. 3 (1975), 193–204.

13. Rumi, *Couplets of Inner Meaning: Tales from the Masnavi*, trans. A. J. Arberry (London: Murray, 1961), cited by William Foster in "Sufi Studies Today," in *The Elephant in the Dark*, ed. Leonard Lewin (1972; rpt. New York: E. P. Dutton, 1976), p. 127.

Enich Neumann has described the imagery of the parallel courses of the evolution of consciousness in psychodynamic terms: "The fact that the dawn of consciousness and the creation of the world are parallel processes which throw up the same symbolism indicates that the world actually 'exists' only to the degree that it is cognized by an ego. A differentiated world is the reflection of a self-differentiating consciousness." See *The Origins and History of Consciousness*, trans. R. F. C. Hull, Bollingen Series XLII (Princeton, N.J.: Princeton University Press, 1954), p. 329.

14. See Mircea Eliade, *Patterns in Comparative Religion*, trans. Rosemary Sheed (1958; rpt. New York: New American Library, 1963), pp. 157–60.

15. Marie-Louise von Franz, "The Process of Individuation," in C. G. Jung et al., *Man and His Symbols* (1964; rpt. New York: Dell, 1970), p. 221. see also p. 112, n. 33.

16. Cited in Idries Shah, *The Sufis* (1964; rpt. New York: Doubleday, 1971), pp. 122–23.

17. Frye, *Secular Scripture*, pp. 129, 140.

18. Underhill, *Mysticism* (1910; rpt. New York: E. P. Dutton, 1930), p. 195.

19. Shah, *The Sufis*, p. 142.

20. Quoted in Hardin, "Doris Lessing and the Sufi Way," p. 148.

21. Ibid., p. 153.

22. In his incisive analysis of the structure of science fiction, Robert Scholes suggests that "all future projection is obviously model-making, poiesis not mimesis. And freed of the problem of correspondence or noncorrespondence with some present actuality or some previously experienced past ... the imagination can function without self-deception as to its means and ends. Projections can be held tightly to a line of greatest probability, extrapolating from perceptions of current reality according to current notions of what is probable. But it is also possible to project more freely, discarding as many current notions as possible, or accepting as likely things that now seem unlikely." See *Structural Fabulation* (Notre Dame and London: University of Notre Dame Press, 1975), p. 18.

23. In his survey of a variety of occult systems of belief, Colin Wilson observes that many esoteric religious traditions presume an element of amnesia, implying that "life is basically some kind of game, whose precondition is that the players should suffer from amnesia, and then cope as best they can with the series of choices presented over three-quarters of a century.... The founder of scientology, L. Ron Hubbard, teaches that men are gods who invented the world as a game, into which they 'descended,' and then became victims of their own amnesia, so they became trapped in their game." See *The Occult* (1971; rpt. New York: Random House, 1973), p. 102.

24. Shah, *The Sufis*, p. 440.

25. In the context of psychopathology, R. D. Laing points out that "good" babies may become "good" schizophrenics, since the attributes that parents may value as "good" (passivity, conformity to parents' convenience, absence of demanding or assertive behavior) may actually prefigure existential deadness and lack of autonomy in later development. See *The Divided Self* (1960; rpt. Middlesex, England: Penguin Books, 1965), pp. 182–88.

26. The same reversal of meaning of sleep and waking is prominent in certain esoteric traditions. The Russian mystic Gurdjieff (whose teachings derive from Sufism) emphasized that man is typically asleep; only diligent "self-remembering" elevates consciousness to a true waking state. See Kenneth Walker, *A Study of Gurdjieff's Teaching* (1957; rpt. London: Jonathan Cape, 1965), pp. 35 and following.

27. "Doris Lessing at Stony Brook: An Interview by Jonah Raskin" (1969), in *A Small Personal Voice*, ed. Paul Schlueter (New York: Alfred A. Knopf, 1974), pp. 58, 66.

28. Grof, *Realms of the Human Unconscious*, pp. 102–7.

29. Laing, *The Divided Self*, p. 27.

30. In correspondence to me, Doris Lessing wrote, "If I sounded cross about [the Laing matter] [see earlier letter, quoted in n. 7 above] it was because I've had Laing too much—not that I don't admire him for his battles with the British Establishment, which as we all know, is as stuffy a medical citadel as any anywhere.

"It has been my experience again and again—and also that of other writers—that you have only to write something and what you write starts coming true in all kinds of direct and indirect ways. It is as if you bring something towards you if you imagine it and then write it. My new novel [*The Summer before the Dark*], coming out in spring, isn't even in print, and already it starts, the coincidences and the correspondences." From Letter to Roberta Rubenstein dated 31 Dec. 1972.

More recently, Lessing has reiterated, "My view of Laing is that at an appropriate time in Britain, he challenged certain extreme rigidities in psychiatry with alternative viewpoints, and made other attitudes than the official ones possible. That is what he did. No more and no less.

"There was a certain atmosphere abroad in the late fifties and sixties—I mean, of course, unofficially—to do with mental illness. Laing was only part of a much wider movement." From Letter to Roberta Rubenstein dated 28 Mar. 1977.

31. Boisen, *The Exploration of the Inner World* (New York: Harper and Brothers, 1936 [1962]), pp. 59–60, 82.

32. As Frye observes, "Romance ... begins an upward journey toward man's recovery of what he projects as sacred myth. At the bottom of the mythological universe is a death and a rebirth process which cares nothing for the individual; at the top is the individual's regained identity. At the bottom is a memory which can only be returned to, a closed circle of recurrence; at the top is the recreation of memory." See *Secular Scripture*, p. 183.

33. Arthur Burton, "The Alchemy of Schizophrenia," in Burton et al., *Schizophrenia as a Lifestyle* (New York: Springer Publishing Co., 1974), pp. 65–66.

34. Eliade, *Mephistopheles and the Androgyne: Studies in Religious Myth and Symbol*, trans. J. M. Cohen (New York: Sheed and Ward, 1965), p. 123.

35. Neumann, *Origins*, pp. 23, 24.

36. Laing, *Politics of Experience*, p. 136, emphasis in original.

37. Vernon, *The Garden and the Map: Schizophrenia in Twentieth-Century Literature and Culture* (Urbana: University of Illinois Press, 1973), pp. ix–xi and 3–28.

38. Ibid., p. xi.

39. Scholes, *Structural Fabulation*, p. 18.

CATHARINE R. STIMPSON

Doris Lessing and the Parables of Growth

From 1952 to 1969, Doris Lessing published the five novels that were to make up the series entitled *Children of Violence*. Taking on the largest possible obligations that a novel of development might impose upon an author, she wished to dramatize "the individual conscience in its relations with the collective."[1] Her example of the individual conscience, Martha Quest, has become a character whom readers mentally lift from the page and incorporate into their own lives as a reference point. She is a Wilhelm Meister, an Isabel Archer, a Paul Morel, for the last decades of monstrous century and millennium. Martha is also a woman, a possible descendant of Isabel Archer rather than Wilhelm Meister or Paul Morel. However, Lessing would resist, rather than celebrate, the placing of *Children of Violence* in a tradition of a female novel of development.

Naming Martha, Lessing pointed to qualities that all her readers might need during this century. "Martha" refers to one of the two sisters of Lazarus. She leaves home to ask Christ to raise her brother from the dead. Explicitly she states a belief in His divinity and powers. "Yes, Lord: I believe that thou art the Christ, the son of God, which should come into the world" (John 11:27). Martha personifies the principles of activity and faith, and the conviction that history might be redeemed and changed. Christ can both raise Lazarus and raze our sins. "Quest" is, of course, that significant journey

---

From *The Voyage In: Fictions of Female Development*. © 1983 by the Trustees of Dartmouth College.

in which the process of the journey may matter as much as its end. To endure that process, to achieve that end, the quester will need magister figures who may teach benignly, but, in the twentieth century, may prove to be goblins or *idiots savants* as well.

As told by *Children of Violence*, Martha's own story is one of possible redemption and change. She begins as an estranged adolescent of fifteen on a farm in Zambesia, Lessing's composite landscape of the Africa that England colonized, with Dutch aid. She is ostentatiously reading Havelock Ellis. Her father is a failure, an attractive man whom World War I has ruined. Her mother is frustrated and bitter, an energetic woman also scarred by the war. Martha has one sibling, a younger brother whom her mother prefers. Having left school at fourteen, Martha is largely self-educated. She gets a job as a legal secretary in the colony's provincial, segregated capital. Because she thinks too much in a culture that dislikes thought, she must repress herself. To do that, she drinks too much, and plays too hard.

At eighteen, she marries Douglas Knowell, a civil servant running to pomposity and fat. Their wedding takes place in March 1939: Hitler, seizing Bohemia and Moravia, marches toward the war that will help to destroy British colonization. Four years later, the proper Knowell marriage is a disaster. As Douggie wallows in self-pity, and threatens to rape Martha or to kill her and their little daughter, Martha leaves. Her friends and family turn against her; her mother, a betrayer, disowns her, for a while.

Martha, in her own place, has an affair with a Royal Air Force sergeant. She helps to start the Communist party of Zambesia. As an activist to whom the party is an equivalent of self and part of a vanguard group that is central and centering presence, she is both "Red" and "kaffir-loving," characteristics equally abhorrent to colonial society. She marries again: Anton Hesse, a German Communist interned in Zambesia, whose first wife and family are dying in European concentration camps and who needs a more secure immigration status. The marriage is a sexual fiasco. Anton suffers from premature ejaculation, and, ironically, bourgeois domestic values. Both have affairs, Martha with Thomas Stern, a Polish Jew in exile. She embarks upon a Laurentian discovery of the power, joy, and compulsions of sexuality. However, Thomas will leave for Palestine, to fight for Israeli nationhood, and then for a remote African village, in which he dies.

In 1945, with peace, the patterns of Martha's life fall apart. Her father drifts, half-drugged, into death. The party flounders, as its founders move away and postwar politics rush over it. Martha and Anton have a proper divorce. Life has tamed him. Symbolically, he has learned tennis and will doubtless marry the daughter of a rich colonial businessman. Finally realizing an adolescent dream, Martha sails to England and to the London that World War II has devastated, but not destroyed. Her move is much more than a reenactment of the progress to the city by the young provincial man, or woman. For the morally ambitious white, leaving the colonies is a survival act. The women who want to go, but who do not, become what they feared they might become: anxious, emotional, self-conscious conformists who wear masks of bright cheer.

Martha finds a job as live-in secretary to a writer: Mark Coldridge, one of four sons of an elite British family. A brother, Colin, flees to Russia when he is accused of being a Communist spy. Eventually, Martha becomes Mark's lover; a surrogate mother to his son and Colin's son; and a friend of Mark's wife, Lynda, who stays in the basement with female companions when she is not in mental hospitals. At once chivalrous and obsessive, Mark loves her hopelessly. In her basement apartment, Lynda is an obvious sign of buried and ignored psychic energies.

Located in Bloomsbury, the house entertains all of postwar English politics and culture. In the late 1970s, the local government buys it. Martha lives alone, and then goes to a commune in the country to help with the children. However, for years, the inhabitants of the house have prepared for a Catastrophe. Mark has mapped the increase of atomic, biological, and chemical weapons; of fallout and pollution; of war, famine, riots, poverty, and prisons. As Lessing believes it will, the world acts out a logic of homicide and suicide. The Catastrophe does happen. Because authorities lie, and because catastrophes are such chaos, no one knows precisely what has occurred. It may have been a chemical accident, or the crash of a plane with nuclear bombs. Whatever the cause, the effects are clear.

In the brave new shattered world, Mark runs a refugee camp—before his death. He has married again: Rita, the illegitimate daughter of Zambesians whom Martha had once known. Lynda may be dead. Martha has escaped to an island off the coast of Ireland or Scotland. Her last words are in a letter of 1997 to Francis, Mark and Lynda's son. She tells him about a black child, Joseph, who has been with her on the island. In a world in which many children are deformed mutants, he may be a genuinely evolutionary one. He may have paranormal powers, even more effective than those that Lynda, Martha, and Francis have developed. Martha explains:

> He says more like them are being born now in hidden places in the world, and one day all the human race will be like them. People like you and me are a sort of experimental model and Nature has had enough of us. [FGC, p. 648]

Reconstituting itself after the Catastrophe, the world may be breeding a new child, a savior. However, it may also be generating new governments, huge, quarreling, stratified bureaucracies. Joseph is to be a gardener, as Thomas was. Lessing cannot say if he will tend vegetables, or guard our dreams of paradise; if he is to be a serf, or a sage who will, as Marx promised, dissolve divisions between labor of the mind and of the hands.

Such a summary but hints at Lessing's narrative immensities, at the hugeness of her plots and subplots. She asks us to take them seriously, a request at once bolder and less truistic than it seems. Lessing acknowledges that other media—movies, television—are influential. She also assumes that speaking can mean more than writing; that logos may be livelier off than on the page. "Everywhere, if you keep your mind open, you will find the truth in words *not* written down. So never let the printed page be your master" (italics hers).[2] However, she believes, as perhaps only a self-educated farm child can, in the moral and cognitive strength of texts. She does not revel in the postmodern theory that all verbal acts are fictions, language performances, language at play. She pays tribute to the nineteenth-century novel and to the rare book—a *Moby Dick*, a *Wuthering Heights*, a *The Story of an African Farm*—that is on "a frontier of the human mind."[3] Martha may thread her way through literature to revalidate its authority and to reinterpret it, but Lessing also asserts that a writer must be responsible. In essays and in *Children of Violence*, she accosts an "ivory-tower" literature and critics who acclaim it.

The writer must speak *for*, as well as *to*, others. So doing, the writer both serves as a voice for the voiceless, as a witness for the inarticulate, and helps to form a community of the like-minded. Because the writer can reveal that what we thought to be a private hallucination is actually a collective thought, literature can grant us our sanity.

In brief, despite the science fiction she now publishes, Lessing is marvelously old-fashioned, a great traditionalist. *Children of Violence* is an urgent, urging cultural achievement, a composition meant as explanation and guide. Between *A Ripple from the Storm* (1958) and *Landlocked* (1965), Lessing became a public student of Sufi, of Islamic mysticism. A scholar whom she praises has said, "The Sufi teacher is a conductor, and an instructor—not a god."[4] With secular modesty, she seeks to conduct us to and instruct us in truths greater than ourselves. *Children of Violence* is, then, a parable—of epic proportions.

Lessing's primary lesson demonstrates the necessity of growth, particularly of consciousness. Like many moderns, she finds consciousness the precondition of conscience. Understanding must inform our will, perception, judgment. She fears repetition, the active reproduction of social and psychic conditions, and nostalgia, a mental reproduction of the past that longing infiltrates. Martha is frantically wary of "the great bourgeois monster, the nightmare *repetition*" (APM, p. 77). One of the saddest ironies of *Children of Violence* is that Martha, who refuses to be like *her* mother, tells her daughter that she is setting her free. Being left, Caroline will have nothing to imitate. Yet Caroline apparently becomes a well-behaved junior member of Zambesia's elite: what Martha's mother wanted Martha to become and the antithesis of what Martha would have praised, the replication of her fears.

To picture her theory of growth, Lessing consistently employs natural imagery: a tree, a blade of grass. To conceptualize it, she calls on evolutionary theory, not of the Victorians, but of the Sufis. In *Children of Violence*, Lessing uses epigraphs to inform us of her intentions. They are annotations and shorthand exegeses. Significantly, she begins Part IV of *The Four-Gated City*, the last pillar in her blueprint of the architecture of Martha's soul, with passages about Sufi thought:

> Sufis believe that, expressed in one way, humanity is evolving towards a certain destiny. We are all taking part in that evolution. Organs come into being as a result of a need for specific organs. The human being's organism is producing a new complex of organs in response to such a need. In this age of the transcending of time and space, the complex of organs is concerned with the transcending of time and space. What ordinary people regard as sporadic and occasional bursts of telepathic and prophetic power are seen by the Sufi as nothing less than the first stirrings of these same organs. The difference between all evolution up to date and the present need for evolution is that for the past ten thousand years or so we have been given the possibility of a conscious evolution. So essential is this more rarefied evolution that our future depends on it. [p. 448]

Both tropes and theory reinforce the sense that growth has the force of natural law. It transcends individual choice. We may choose to obey or to neglect that law, to dwell within its imperatives or to deny them, but we cannot decide whether or not it exists.

Lessing's commitment to the expansion of consciousness tempts one to call *Children of Violence* an example of Lukács's theory of the novel: "the adventure of interiority; the story of the soul that goes to find itself, that seeks adventures in order to be proved and tested by them, and by proving itself, to find its own essence."[5] She herself has named *The Four-Gated City a Bildungsroman*:

> This book is what the Germans call a *Bildungsroman*. We don't have a word for it. This kind of novel has been out of fashion for some time. This does not mean that there is anything wrong with this kind of novel. [FGC, p. 655]

If the genre groups together tales of "the formation of a character up to the moment when he ceases to be self-centered and becomes society-centered, thus beginning to shape his true self";[6] and if one thinks of Martha as entering into, and then discarding, several societies, then Lessing's label for the last novel holds for her series as a whole. An admirer of Mann, she has produced another twentieth-century *Bildungsroman* in which people and groups are maladjusted and ill. Images of physical, mental, and psychosomatic sickness abound in *Children of Violence*: Martha's pinkeye; Captain Quest's medicine chests; Mr. Anderson's infirmity (he is a retired civil servant who reads government reports and sci-fi pornography); Douggie's ulcers; Lynda's hands, nails bitten until they bleed; babies, after the Catastrophe, born with two heads and fifty fingers. Martha is Lessing's Hans Castorp; Africa and England her sanitorium, her *Berghof*.

Because of the nature and intensity of her sense of social illness, Lessing has grafted the Western apocalyptic tradition to the *Bildungsroman*. For her, we inhabit a period of terrors and decadence. At its best, our age demands a stifling conformity; at its worst, it provokes fear, exploitation, oppression, violence. The End is both imminent and immanent.[7] Like most prophets of the apocalypse since 1945, Lessing is profoundly aware of the splitting of the atom and the origins of atomic warfare. A madman, a fool, a committee—each might bring this dread upon us. In *Ecce Homo*, Nietzsche predicted the rebirth of tragedy when mankind became conscious, without any feeling of suffering, that it had behind it the hardest, but most necessary, of wars. Lessing believes that mankind has before it the hardest, but most unnecessary, of wars, and the suffering of that vision overwhelms *Children of Violence*. The apocalypse we are manufacturing may not permit anyone to survive, let alone a society to enter a reconstituted history.

In the nineteenth-century female *Bildungsroman*, the young woman protagonist often dies—physically or spiritually. Maggie Tulliver drowns, she and her brother clasped in each other's arms.[8] In Olive Schreiner's *The Story of an African Farm*, Lyndall "chooses to die alone rather than marry a man she cannot respect."[9] Martha avoids such a fate. She survives the Catastrophe, and endures until she is an old woman in her mid-seventies. As a *Bildungsroman*, *The Four-Gated City* differs from many of the genre in that Lessing describes far more than her protagonist's maturing years.[10] The novel of development has become the novel of an encyclopedic life, as if the relations between conscience and its collectives were a part of a complex, lengthy process. Yet, Lessing hardly ignores death. Rather, our Cassandra, she broadens the drama of the death of the female protagonist until it becomes that of her culture. She rewrites the female *Bildungsroman* to enlarge the sufferings of a young woman until they become the doom of the collective. The struggle between the woman who would be freer than her society permits her to be also changes to become a struggle between an enlightened group, a saving remnant, that would free society from its self-destruction and the larger group that is in love with its own diseaseful death.

Lessing must obviously reconcile the comic promise of the *Bildungsroman*, that we can within history pass from youth to a semblance of maturity, with the tragic promise of the apocalypse, that history as we know it will explode. She does so through the Sufi belief in "the possibility of a conscious evolution ... this more rarefied evolution that our future depends on." If each of us nurtures consciousness as we pass from youth to a semblance of maturity, if we join with others who are doing the same thing, then we may either avert the apocalypse, or live through it and protect those children whose minds are even more potent than our own. Lessing adapts, from apocalyptic historiography, the myth of individual and collective rebirth. Such myths have consistently attracted her. In 1957, she exulted: "I am convinced that we all stand at an open door, and that there is a new man about to be born, who has never been twisted by drudgery."[11] *Children of Violence* tests and re-tests these myths, to retain them in a grimmer, more shadowed form. In *Landlocked*, Thomas, naked, in bed with Martha, says:

> Perhaps there'll be a new mutation though. Perhaps that's why we are all so sick. Something new is trying to get born through our sick skins. I tell you, Martha, if I see a sane person, then I know he's mad. You know, the householders. It's we who are nearest to being—what's needed. [p. 116]

Since the evolution of consciousness matters so much, Lessing devotes a great part of *Children of Violence* to Martha's own. The narrative is a detailed, subtle account of the methodology of growth, in which Martha is a case study, an exemplary figure, and our potential representative.[12] The fact that she is a woman is less important than the fact that she can give the lie to official lies and ultimately exercise the paranormal psychic powers that Lessing believes are the birth-right of us all. As an excellent critic says, "Ultimately, the deepest task of [Lessing's] characters is to achieve a personal wholeness that subsumes sexual identity or gender under a larger principle of growth."[13]

Such statements embody a complication about Lessing. She is among our most brilliant, persuasive anatomists of contemporary women's lives. She writes compellingly about their friendships: that of Martha and Alice; of Martha and Jasmine, a revolutionary who stays in Africa; of Martha and Lynda; of Lynda and her flatmate Dorothy. She dramatizes the pressures on them to perform and conform. She knows about their disabilities, the need to please, the complicities, the denials and self-denials. Though Martha is incorrigibly heterosexual, Lessing has no illusions about men or male chauvinism, in conservative sets or in the radical sects more dedicated to ideologies of equality. Men exploit, patronize, and ignore women. They demand attention, nurturance, sexual gratification, and service. They seek compliant daughters, willing bodies, or mothers they can possess without complication. They use, abuse, exhaust, and bore women.

Despite all this, Lessing separates herself from the "feminine" and from feminism.[14] She has, I suggest, several motives. Perhaps she has internalized an evaluation of women's activities, especially those of the middle class, as trivial, time-wasting, and private. If so, it might spill over onto her sense of women's politics. Certainly her fear of the apocalypse distances her from them. She has written:

> I don't think that Women's Liberation will change much though—not because there is anything wrong with their aims, but because it is already clear that the whole world is being shaken by the cataclysms we are living through: probably by the time we are through, if we get through at all, the aims of Women's Liberation will look very small and quaint.[15]

In part because of her political history in general, Lessing also distrusts any doctrine, ideology, party, or group that holds a fragment of reality and offers it up as if it were the whole. Consistently, she deplores compartmentalizing the world, separating off those parts, and then fearing the differences we have ourselves created. In her first days in London,

Martha lunches with Phoebe, a left-wing Labourite who will become a noxious combination of Mrs. Quest and bureaucrat. In one of the many scenes in which Lessing insists that privileged moments of vision occur in our daily life, in our walks down an ordinary street, Martha broods:

> There was something in the human mind that separated, and divided. She sat, looking at the soup in front of her, thinking.... For the insight of knowledge she now held, of the nature of separation, of division, was clear and keen—she understood, sitting there, while the soup sent a fine steam of appetite up her nostrils, understood *really* ... how beings could be separated so absolutely by a light difference in the texture of their living that they could not talk to each other, must be wary, or enemies. [FGC, p. 82]

Finally, Lessing writes out of a colonial experience. She has said that to be an African, growing up in that vast land, is to be freer than an Englishwoman, a Virginia Woolf, enwebbed in custom and the city.[16] However, being an African also entails participation in a rigid, hierarchal social structure. Within it white men may dominate white women, but white women dominate all blacks. They have the privileges of class and color. White women subject blacks to their needs, whims, neurotic fantasies, and orders. A Myra Maynard, the wife of a powerful judge, exercises covert political power over colonial affairs and overt domestic power over her "kaffirs." In such a place the progressive conscience must first confront the presence of the "colored" or "native" problem. The treatment of the blacks is the primary structuring agent of a sense of injustice and of public guilt. For Martha, black women have a double symbolic function. Neither entails a sustained mutuality between black women and white. Icons of both a greater imprisonment and a greater spontaneity, they remind her of the injustices against which she must rebel, of the manacles she must unlock, and of a life less arid than her own. In labor in the town's "best" maternity hospital, Martha reveals that duality:

> [Martha] heard the sound of a wet brush on a floor. It was a native woman, on her knees with a scrubbing brush.... Martha tensed and groaned, and the native woman raised her head, looked over, and smiled encouragement.... [She] gave a quick look into the passage, and then came over to Martha.... "Bad," she said, in her rich voice. "Bad. Bad." As a fresh pain came, she said, "Let the

baby come, let the baby come, let the baby come." It was a croon, a nurse's song.... Martha let the cold knot of determination loosen, she let herself go, she let her mind go dark into the pain.... Suddenly ... Martha looked, and saw that the native woman was on her knees with the scrubbing brush, and the young pink nurse stood beside her, looking suspiciously at the scrubbing woman. The brush was going slosh, slosh, wetly and regularly over the floor. [APM, p. 146]

White men and women share more than black subordination: an ambivalent response to the "mother country," a feminized metropolitan center to which a colonial country is tied. It, too, helps to obliterate the resentments gender inequalities breed. Colonials feel physically superior, tougher, stronger. They are also the romantics, the black sheep, the eccentrics who refused to accept the manners of the mother country. Yet they feel blunt, envious, even crude, a sense of dependency and inferiority that Australians call "the cultural cringe." Men and women alike are the stalwart, but crass, younger children in a global family whose power they at once disdain and revere.

As Martha grows, then, she acts out a feminist analysis that Lessing will not extend to an endorsement of a feminist program. Instead, Martha discovers other truths, other principles. They enable her to survive, to continue the process of discovery, and to learn which collectives impede, and which enhance, the self; which citizenships destroy, and which burnish, being. Among her primary tools is a cognitive alter ego, a diligent self-consciousness, the Watcher, a capacity for apperception and self-criticism in her experiments with roles. Even during her first marriage, as she takes "every step into bondage with affectionate applause for Douglas," (APM, p. 250), she is still "secretely and uneasily curious." At its worst, the Watcher devolves into mocking, derisive self-hatred. At its best, it guards against self-deception, wool-gathering, and bad faith. The origins of the Watcher are as obscure as the genes that carry instructions for the child's optic nerves once were, but they include Martha's parents' nagging reminders that she was unwanted and the presence of multiple discrepancies in her life: between reality and what people say about it; between reality and what books say about it; between reality and what her dreams say about it. Each discrepancy stimulates a sense, at once intellectual and emotional, of alienation. Any reasonable child regards gaps between the self, the self-in-the-world, and the world warily—if the child is to stay reasonable.

When consciousness is too watchful to accept the going interpretations of reality, but too fragile to examine its own examinations fully; when consciousness is too vital to permit the will to lapse and collapse into acceptance of the false and the ordinary, but the will is too weak to dictate ruptures from them, then a person, a Martha, learns the value of negation. Saying no, saying I will not, is halfway between submission to the life she despises and one she might actively build for herself; halfway between conformity and authenticity. Negation is inseparable from de-education, from unlearning the formal and informal instructions of a colonial society and of its leaders, a Mr. and Mrs. Maynard.

Martha's most critical act of negation is to leave her first marriage. It proves that she can push her rejections beyond thought and speech. Abandoning Douglas, she walks out on social acceptability; on access to power; on money, comfort, and security; on the pretty, perky, willful daughter to whom she is intricately attached. A particular unfairness of a generally unfair society is the refusal of its petty elite to see Martha's pain over Caroline, which never heals, and its eagerness to rally around Douglas, who so cheerfully plays by their rules. To walk away, Martha must overcome a talent for negating her negations, for repressing her dislike of Douglas, particularly in bed. Only a few weeks before she ends the marriage, he tells her he is going away on business.

> It was a moment when the hatred between them shocked and dismayed them both.

> "Well, perhaps it's just as well we'll—have a break for a few weeks, eh, Matty?" He came over and stood a few inches from her, smiling in appeal.
> She at once responded by rising and kissing him—but on the cheek, for her lips, which had intended to meet his, instinctively moved past in revulsion. This revulsion frightened her so much that she flung her arms about him and warmly embraced him.
> The act of love immediately followed. [APM, p. 279]

Because of the nature of the dominant society, Martha's need for negation will be persistent. A middle-aged woman in London, she will have to say no to Dr. Lamb, the sardonically named psychiatrist, and to the institutional power he conveys; to Jack, once her lover, and to the temptations of masochism he now holds out.

Negation demands something beyond the self to repudiate. Realizing that ego ideal of the modern period, the free and autonomous ego, Martha must also learn that the most stringent self-explorations, the most exacting and fertile meditations, begin in solitude. Her childhood in the awesome African landscape has prepared her for this. She copes with her fear of an empty historical landscape in which she has no patterns to follow. Before she leaves Douglas, she thinks, realistically: "there was no woman she had ever met she could model herself on" (APM, p. 274). She also unravels her dependency on the cold comforts of narcissism. If having a role model means shaping identity through gazing at another's image, being narcissistic means doing so through having another's gaze. Martha has stared at her image in a mirror, or she has waited passively while men watch her. Unhappily, narcissism is as encrusted with guilt as a white dress in a field wet with mud. Guilt oozes from the belief that the recipient of a look has disappointed the onlooker. To have been seen is to be found wanting. Finally, at a Communist party meeting, in a dingy office, Martha regards a new member:

> She's what I used to be; she looks at herself in the looking glass, and she sees how her face and body form a sort of painted shell, and she adores herself, but she is waiting for a pair of eyes to melt the paint and shoot through into the dark inside. [RS, p. 114]

In isolation, however, the naked self is not alone. Through self-analysis, Martha confronts hidden ranges of repressed material: memories, fantasies, terrors, anger, violence—the worst of which the devil personifies. Lessing accepts George Eliot's dictum that no private life has not been determined by a wider public life, a maxim compatible with her early Marxism. That public life means the French and Russian revolutions, World Wars I and II, colonialism, the Spanish Civil War, the cold war, wars of national independence. Breaking down her defenses, breaking into the unconscious, Martha understands that she wants to break up the world as well. This child of violence has internalized the thanatotic rage of global war and the looming apocalypse. Like Freud, Lessing believes we can never wholly purge the past, but seeing the experiences we have battened down helps to shake their spell.

Despite her liberal belief in the individual and freedom, Lessing, writing a *Bildungsroman*, goes beyond the picture of the atomistic self spinning alone atop social space. If Martha rejects the nuclear family, she enters an extended family in which cords of choice replace those of blood and law. If she refuses biological mothering, she becomes a surrogate parent. Lessing is too flexible to feminize wholly the nurturing role and evoke the spirit of a Great Mother to rationalize women as mothers. Mark's son Francis is a paternal/maternal figure.

However, within *Children of Violence* is a sense of the intractability of nuclear family bonds that makes a flight toward a modern extended family necessary. The ties between mothers and daughters, particularly between Martha and May Quest, are especially taut.[17] Martha cannot forgive May her inability to love without demands, complaints, and possessiveness. May cannot forgive Martha her unconventionality, her sexuality, her difference. Yet, because May did bear Martha, and because their disappointments in each other are intense, they cannot forget each other. Their mutual consciousness is so acute that in each other's company, they get sick. They see each other for the last time in London; May is old, Martha middle-aged. Both want to cry:

> As she vanished from her daughter's life forever, Mrs. Quest gave a small tight smile, and said, "Well, I wonder what all that was about really?"
>
> "Yes," said Martha. "So do I."
>
> They kissed politely, exchanged looks of ironic desperation, smiled and parted. [FGC, pp. 286–87]

In *Children of Violence*, irony is a useful tool for digging out sham and cant, but it is treacherous. For the disappointed, it becomes an iron rod, a staff of punishment, a mark of waste.

For Martha, the political party, like the extended family, becomes a community of choice. Deftly, incisively, dryly, Lessing dramatizes the mechanics of the small progressive party: the lobbying, maneuvering of agendas, interplay between insiders and outsiders, the desire for a charismatic leader, the gratifying sense of busyness, the feeding on ideology and hope because of the absence of real power. However, Martha is unable to find a party that fuses a radical ideology and power; vision and efficiency; prophetic zeal and historical wisdom; humanitarian ideals and humane behavior. Though brilliant organizer and analyst, Anton has neither heat, nor heart, nor humor. Martha is too modern, too mobile, too psychological to be like Charlotte Brontë's Shirley Keeldar, but Shirley's cry against a cold sectarianism is the precursor of Martha's progress beyond organized politics:

> Must I listen coolly to downright nonsense ... ? No .... all that *cant* about soldiers and parsons is most offensive.... All ridiculous, irrational crying up of one class, whether the same be aristocrat

or democrat—all howling down of another class, whether clerical or military—all exacting injustice to individuals, whether monarch or mendicant—is really sickening to me: all arraying of ranks against ranks, all party hatreds, all tyrannies disguised as liberties, I reject and wash my hands of.[18]

Significantly, Martha's deepest discoveries about eros—that bond, at once simple and mysterious, that generates a little community—take place outside of the nuclear family and the party. Within them, she has picked up warning signals about repression; about evasive silence about sexual realities; about the sublimation of eros, not into culture, but into violence. She has also succumbed to sexual myths. Science has reassured Martha and Douggie that the rational practice of certain positions will guarantee ecstasy. Romantic poetry has whispered that "love lay like a mirage through the golden gates of sex" (APM, p. 26). The patriarchy has praised her for being deferential, compliant, a Galatea before the Pygmalion of the phallus. A reaction against Victorianism has instructed her to find self-esteem in being good in bed, no matter when, or with what man. Martha begins as a modern to whom sexual competence has the gravity of grace.

Sex with Thomas, a married man, pulls down all such illusions. He is warm, direct, generous. As Martha educates herself in sheer orgasmic pleasure, she experiences both a new simplicity of will, a clarity of action, and a dissolution of the ego that serves, paradoxically, to strengthen that very simplicity of will. As the boundaries of the self blur into the other, Thomas and Martha become each other's histories. Later, with Mark and Jack, Martha will find in sex an even more expansive fusion between self and world, an access to "an impersonal current ... the impersonal sea" (FGC, p. 496). Sadly, Martha's most vital sexual experiences are with men who are flawed prophets: Thomas cannot pass beyond violence and chaos; Jack transmogrifies his knowledge of the body into sadistic domination; Mark, despite his brains and strength and kindliness, cannot transcend Western rationalism. In his camp, after the Catastrophe, he writes: "I can't stand that nasty mixture of irony and St. John of the Cross and the *Arabian Nights* that they all (Lynda, Martha, Francis) went in for" (FGC, p. 652). Martha's most educational prophetic experiences, with a woman, are asexual.

Laying bare Martha's sexual growth, Lessing balances delicate insight and problematic theory. Both maternal and erotic sexuality can threaten freedom. Often cheerfully, the pregnant woman becomes her body. She relaxes into natural time, into the blind impersonal urges of creation. The woman in love is unappeasable, hungry, restless, dependent upon her man.

For Martha, such lapses from liberation are characteristic of a "female self," a simplistic genderizing of identity that Lessing is most guilty of when she talks about female sexuality. To avoid the constrictions of the "female self," and to sharpen her capacity for insights, Martha begins to practice a willed repression of and indifference to sexual claims. She has only one biological child. Later, in London, she decides:

> When a woman has reached that point when she allies part of herself with the man who will feed that poor craving bitch in *every* woman (italics mine), then enough it's time to move on.
> When it's a question of survival, sex the uncontrollable can be controlled. [FGC, p. 301]

Lessing has shown that same mingling of persuasive perception and puzzling theory in an earlier, more poignant picture of repression: the character of Mrs. Van. Highly intelligent, sensitive, tough, she has tutored Martha in the limits and courage of the reformist conscience in Zambesia. She has refused to rebel against her proper marriage and a maternal role. So doing, she has deliberately, if secretly, traded passion for autonomy within the system and political stature. She is a good wife to the husband who does not gratify her and a good mother—to him, her children, grandchildren, servants, clients, and friends. In return, she is an active liberal. In a quick, sad scene, she remembers her wedding night. Lessing wants us to admire her resolve, mourn for her innocence, and dislike a society in which a woman of Mrs. Van's talents must make such compromises. At the same time, she gives Mrs. Van dabs of a sexual rhetoric of swords and soft spots that Norman Mailer, Lessing's lesser and contemporary, also deploys, if far more raucously:

> Cold tears had run down over her cheeks all night ... (an) image ... filled the girl's mind through those long hours while she lay awake by a man who also lay awake, waiting for her to turn to him. The image was of something deep, soft, dark and vulnerable, and of a very sharp sword stabbing into it, again and again. She had not moved ... and so the sword had not stabbed into her never again, the soft dark painful place which she felt to be somewhere under her heart had remained untouched. She had remained herself. [RS, pp. 204–5]

Behind Martha's emerging ego, behind her relations with several communities, are her discoveries of the powers of consciousness. To become a pioneer of the mind, Martha must often crawl through swamps of primordial fear. She first learns to read her dreams. They are both hieroglyphic psychological texts and prophecies. Martha often dreams of:

> "That country" ... pale, misted, flat; gulls cried like children around violet-coloured shores. She stood on coloured chalky rocks with a bitter sea washing around her feet and the smell of salt was strong in her nostrils. [RS, p. 84]

The meaning of the dream will deepen as she grows. The sea is her passage out of Africa to England, but it will become a metaphor for the universal mind and energy in which she will learn to travel, too. Consistently, in Lessing's vocabulary, "shell" is a synecdoche for the mechanisms that protect the self from threatening pain and psychic depths. It evokes armor—of sea creatures and war. "That country" of the dream foreshadows the island on which Martha will die. Although Lessing persistently uses sleep as a metaphor for mindless oblivion, for loss of consciousness, and awakening as a metaphor for new powers of vision, sleep is the site of the dreams that minister to us and that we must monitor. Significantly, Anton refuses to admit that he has nightmares. He tries to banish memory and live glibly in the day.

Martha goes on to listen to, to hear, other people's emotions. Because of her need to know what he is going to do first if she is to react in ways that serve her best interests, and because of their intimacy, she trains herself with Douglas. She does not add new skills, but nurtures an ability that is there. During a bizarre conversation with Douggie about their divorce, she responds: "For a moment she was frightened; then she understood she was not frightened, her heart was beating out of anger. She had become skilled in listening to her *instinctive* responses to Douglas." (RS, p. 24, italics mine) Such a refined empathy tells Martha what is special about other people, but she can also go beyond differences to appreciate a common ground of being. Psychic auditing, in league with the imagination, the ability to see worlds other than our own, can be a basis of a human ecology. Lessing can, then, speak of "colour prejudice" as "only one aspect of the atrophy of the imagination that prevents us from seeing ourselves in every creature that breathes under the sun."[19]

Finally, Martha accepts and explores her paranormal powers, her capacities for ESP, mental telepathy, and sending and receiving messages through the mind. She first hears niggling words, phrases, and bits of music. A feature of *Children of Violence* is the coherence with which Lessing describes shards of consciousness—as if her own style reflected the sense that might lie beyond fragmentation. When Martha stops resisting such signals, she discovers that they are only apparently random: they, in fact, have meaning. Her first guide is her own adventurous spirit, but eventually she finds the "mad" Lynda. In a friendship beyond friendliness, the two "work" together. The word signifies how hard a discipline the expansion of consciousness can be, and how chary Lessing is about ordinary toil, in the home or public labor force, as a field of growth. Martha is not one of the new women whose *Bildungsroman* includes the narrative of a career.

Lynda is Lessing's vehicle for a radical criticism of psychiatry. Rigid, officious, less sure of themselves than they pretend to be, psychiatrists are the policemen of the contemporary mind. Out of several motives, they control our prophets, like Lynda, through calling them schizoid. Though she does not go mad, Martha must experience the sensations of insanity in her rites of passage toward a greater comprehension of the mind. So doing, she lives out a statement of her father, that most defeated of her teachers, who, when he speaks, says too little, too late. As far as he can see, "everyone is mad" (APM, p. 270). For Captain Quest, madness only explains the world. For his more resilient daughter, "the climax of education is insanity," and her *Bildungsroman* is a text in which "madness is moralized into a condition of responsible consciousness."[20]

As Martha's powers enable her to lose the ego but not the world; to shatter barriers but not to slump into violence, nihilism, or infantile regression, she becomes a member of another community: that of her fellow sensitives. She first enters it with Lynda:

> One night, going down to see if Lynda was all right, before she herself went to bed, she asked: "Lynda, do you ever overhear what people are thinking?"
> Lynda turned, swift, delighted: "Oh," she exclaimed, "you do? I was waiting for you to ... " [FGC, p. 371]

Such a society, far more than an esoteric cult, is the basis for a politics of mind. As a party, it transcends hardened theories and harsh practices. As an organization, it abolishes tricks, maneuvers, bureaucracies, and tyranny. It merges the virtues of anarchy and community. Learning to become a sensitive, oscillating between optimism and rage, Francis exults:

> The old right of the individual human conscience which must know better than any authority, secular or religious, had been

restored, but on a higher level, and in a new form which was untouchable by any legal formulas. We quoted to each other Blake's "What now exists was once only imagined"—and did not, for once, choose to remember the dark side of the human imagination. [FGC, p. 623]

Before, during, and after the Catastrophe, the group serves as a survival mechanism, for its members and for the mutants whose evolving consciousness may govern the future.

Lessing's politics of mind are controversial. Critics who otherwise admire her accuse her of bad faith, of sidestepping reality, of a bleak acceptance of the irreconcilability of self and society.[21] *Children of Violence* implicitly answers that we must reread the realities of conscience and the collective. If we do, we will cultivate consciousness and accept certain laws of its evolution. Then, we will grasp what a Sufi master once said:

For him who has perception, a mere sign is enough.
For him who does not really heed, a thousand explanations are not enough.[22]

If we ignore Martha's reminders, we may be heedless, groggily writing out chapters in an inadequate *Bildungsroman*, sleepwalking toward the apocalypse.

In Western culture, beliefs in the apocalypse have been entwined with utopian impulses. Both wish to wipe out time as we have clocked it. For some, the apocalypse is a prelude to a utopian world, to a New Jerusalem. Lessing, despite her belief in the apocalypse, is wary of utopian dreams, of attempts to impose them through violence and of mechanical allusions to them. In *Children of Violence*, Solly Cohen, a childish revolutionary, lives for a while in a commune named "Utopia."

Nevertheless, Martha can summon up a utopian vision, among her other powers. Throughout *Children of Violence*, her picture of the four-gated city has embodied harmony, reconciliation, integration. Her answer to Babel, it speaks against a history that has alternated centrifugal desires to separate with centripetal desires to dominate. It has been her new utopia, "rooted in the body as well as in the mind, in the unconscious as well as the conscious, in forests and deserts as well as in highways and buildings, in bed as well as the symposium."[23] It is a collective of the future toward which the individual conscience might aspire.

Whether or not one likes Lessing's epistemology and her politics of mind in *Children of Violence*, one must respond to the appeal of her stubborn belief in an active, hopeful consciousness; to Martha's returns to a picture of a four-gated city. Lessing, dramatizing the self and society in the twentieth century, tells us what they ought to mean, as well as what they do mean. Martha's visionary rehearsals are goads to growth, that old and aching promise of the *Bildungsroman*.

NOTES

1. Doris Lessing, "The Small Personal Voice," *A Small Personal Voice: Essays, Reviews, Interviews*, ed. Paul Schlueter (New York: Alfred A. Knopf, 1974), p. 14. I will be using and quoting from the following editions of the *Children of Violence* novels: *Martha Quest* (1952; rpt. New York: New American Library, 1970); *A Proper Marriage* (1954; rpt. New York: New American Library, 1970) cited as APM; *A Ripple from the Storm* (1958; rpt. New York: New American Library, 1970) cited as RS; *Landlocked* (1965; rpt. New York: New American Library, 1970); *The Four-Gated City* (1969; rpt. New York: Bantam Books, 1970) cited as FGC. For a recent survey of Lessing criticism see Holly Beth King, "Criticism of Doris Lessing: A Selected Checklist," *Modern Fiction Studies: Special Issue, Doris Lessing*, 26, I (Spring 1980), 167–75.

2. "Introduction," *The Golden Notebook* (1962; rpt. New York: Bantam, 1973), p. xix.

3. "Afterword to *The Story of an African Farm*," *A Small Personal Voice*, p. 98.

4. Idries Shah, *The Way of the Sufi* (London: Jonathan Cape, 1968), p. 31.

5. George Lukács, *The Theory of the Novel: A Historico-Philosophical Essay on the Forms of Great Epic Literature* (1920), trans. Anna Bostock (Cambridge: MIT Press, 1971), p. 89.

6. Roy Pascal, *The German Novel* (Toronto: University of Toronto Press, 1956), p. II. Comment on *The Four-Gated City* as a *Bildungsroman* is common. The most extensive is Ellen Cronan Rose, *The Tree Outside the Window: Doris Lessing's* Children of Violence (Hanover, N.H.: University Press of New England, 1976). Rose, seeing the series as a "novel of development or growth," adapts Erik H. Erikson's psychological theory to it. In "The Limits of Consciousness in the Novels of Doris Lessing," in *Doris Lessing: Critical Studies*, ed. Annis Pratt and L. S. Dembo (Madison:

University of Wisconsin Press, 1974), pp. 119–32, Sydney Janet Kaplan compares Lessing to Dorothy Richardson. She too finds Lessing modifying the *Bildungsroman* through a self-conscious interest in such larger political issues as racism, class conflict, and war. In "Disorderly Company," in the same volume, pp. 74–97, Dagmar Barnouw says that *The Four-Gated City* becomes a collective *Bildungsroman*, its protagonists Mark, Lynda, and Martha. She cannot find the first volume a *Bildungsroman* in the strict sense of the word, for "Matty is neither moving toward a choice, a determining decision she will make at one time or the other, nor is the fact that she is incapable of such a choice integrated into the substance and structure of her developments" (pp. 83–84). I wonder. Matty moves toward the choice of leaving Africa, and her general difficulty of the will is one of Lessing's deep interests.

7. I adapt these terms from Frank Kermode, *The Sense of an Ending* (New York: Oxford University Press, 1967; pbk. 1968), pp. 6, 93.

8. Dorothy Brewster, *Doris Lessing* (New York: Twayne Publishers, 1965), p. 159, correctly compares Maggie Tulliver to the young Martha: "rebellious, adventurous, romantic, chafing against barriers of a narrow provincial society ... and deeply influenced by books."

9. Lessing, "Afterword to *The Story of An African Farm*," *A Small Personal Voice*, p. 107. Of Lessing's critics, only Michael Thorpe has been sufficiently attentive to her African background, though he hurts himself through a programmatic disdain of feminists. He sees the need for a subgenre: *Bildungsromane* about colonized women, be they white, African, Asian, or aboriginal. See Michael Thorpe, *Doris Lessing* (London: Longman Group Ltd., 1973), and Michael Thorpe, *Doris Lessing's Africa* (London: Evans Brothers, Ltd., 1978). For a fine new biography of Olive Schreiner see Ruth First and Ann Scott, *Olive Schreiner: A Biography* (New York: Schocken Books, 1980).

10. Paul Schlueter, *The Novels of Doris Lessing* (Carbondale: Southern Illinois University Press, 1973), p. 75.

11. "The Small Personal Voice," *A Small Personal Voice*, p. 8.

12. Mary Ann Singleton, *The City and the Veld: The Fiction of Doris Lessing* (Lewisburg: Bucknell University Press, 1977), p. 166, makes a similar point.

13. Roberta Rubenstein, *The Novelistic Vision of Doris Lessing: Breaking the Forms of Consciousness* (Urbana: University of Illinois Press, 1979), p. 6.

14. For a fuller analysis, see Lynn Sukenick, "Feeling and Reason in Doris Lessing's Fiction," *Doris Lessing: Critical Studies*, pp. 98–118, and

Elaine Showalter, *A Literature of Their Own: British Women Novelists from Brontë to Lessing* (Princeton, N.J.: Princeton University Press, 1977), p. 313.

15. "Introduction," *The Golden Notebook*, pp. viii–ix.

16. Brewster, *Doris Lessing*, p. 158.

17. "May" is a pun. Mrs. Quest might once have been capable of a quest; she is, after all, the woman whom Martha sees playing Chopin at night on her piano in the mud-and-thatch farmhouse. But she constricts herself. "May" is also Lessing's middle name. That she should assign it to Martha's mother surely reveals some unresolved dilemma. I say this while aware of Lessing's dislike of critics who reduce her texts to a series of autobiographical gestures.

18. Charlotte Brontë, *Shirley* (Baltimore: Penguin Books, 1974), p. 356.

19. Doris Lessing, *African Stories* (New York: Simon and Schuster, 1965), p. 6.

20. Sukenick, "Feeling and Reason," p. 114. Sukenick's tone is more sardonic than mine.

21. Rose, *The Tree Outside the Window*, p. 68. Carol P. Christ, more sympathetic, says that "Women's spiritual quest provides orientation of women's social quest and grounds it in something larger than individual or even collective achievements." See *Diving Deep and Surfacing: Women Writers on Spiritual Quest* (Boston: Beacon Press, 1980), p. 11. Her chapter on Lessing, pp. 55–73, is a fine reading of *Children of Violence* as such a quest, tactfully using Jungian and mythic materials. However, my point is that Martha is meant to represent both sexes. She has some special difficulties because she is a woman: sexuality, the limits of a middle-class role, male chauvinism. She is meant to work her way through this and to act in ways both men and women can emulate. Consciousness is sexless, like angels for Leonardo.

22. Shah, *The Way of the Sufi*, p. 222.

23. Northrop Frye, "Varieties of Literary Utopia," *Utopias and Utopian Thought*, ed. Frank E. Manuel (Boston: Houghton Mifflin, 1966), pp. 48–49.

Chronology

1919	Doris Lessing born in Kermanshah, Persia, to Alfred Cook Taylor and Emily McVeigh.
1925	Family moves to Southern Rhodesia, settling on a farm in the district of Banket. Lessing attends a convent school in Salisbury, the capital.
1949	Lessing moves to London. Until this time, she has earned her living chiefly in secretarial positions. She has been married and divorced twice; Lessing is the name of her second husband.
1950	*The Grass Is Singing.*
1951	*This Was the Old Chief's Country.*
1952	*Martha Quest.*
1953	*Five.*
1954	*A Proper Marriage.* Receives the Somerset Maugham Award, Society of Authors, for *Five.*
1956	*Retreat to Innocence.* After a visit to Rhodesia, Lessing is proclaimed a prohibited immigrant, presumably because of unacceptable views on race.
1957	*The Habit of Loving. Going Home.*
1958	*A Ripple from the Storm. Each His Own Wilderness* performed at the Royal Court Theatre, London.
1959	*Fourteen Poems.*

1960	*In Pursuit of the English.*
1962	*The Golden Notebook. Play with a Tiger* performed in London.
1963	*A Man and Two Women.*
1964	*African Stories. Children of Violence.*
1965	*Landlocked.*
1971	*Briefing for a Descent into Hell* (shortlisted for the Booker Prize).
1972	*The Temptations of Jack Orkney and Other Stories. The Story of a Non-Marrying Man.*
1973	*The Summer Before the Dark. Collected African Stories.*
1974	Essays in Paul Schlueter's *A Small Personal Voice: Doris Lessing: Essays, Reviews and Interviews.*
1975	*The Memoirs of a Survivor.*
1976	Receives the Prix Medici.
1979	*Re: Colonized Planet 5, Shikasta.*
1980	*The Marriages between Zones Three, Four, and Five.*
1981	*The Sirian Experiments* (shortlisted for the Booker Prize).
1982	Receives the Austrian State Prize for European Literature and the Shakespeare Prize (Hamburg). *The Making of the Representative for Planet 8.*
1983	*The Sentimental Agents in the Volzen Empire. The Diary of a Good Neighbor* (published under the pseudonym "Jane Somers").
1984	*If the Old Could* (published under the pseudonym "Jane Somers"). *The Diaries of Jane Somers.*
1985	*The Good Terrorist* (shortlisted for the Booker Prize).
1986	Received the W.H. Smith Literary Award and the Mondello Prize in Italy for *The Good Terrorist.*
1987	*The Wind Blows Away Our Words.* Received the Palermo Prize.
1988	*The Fifth Child* (received the Grinzane Cavour Prize in Italy and was nominated for the Los Angeles Times Book Award). Collaborated with composer Philip Glass on the opera "The Making of Representative for Planet 8" performed by the Houston Grand Opera.

1989	*Particularly Cats and More Cats. The Doris Lessing Reader.* Received Honorary Doctor of Letters from Princeton University.
1991	*Particularly Cats ... and Rufus.*
1992	*London Observed: Stories and Sketches. African Laughter.*
1994	*Shadows on the Wall of a Cave. Conversations. Under My Skin: Volume One of My Autobiography, to 1949.*
1995	*Playing the Game. Spies I Have Known and Other Stories.* Received honorary degree from Harvard. Received James Tait Black Prize for Best Biography and Los Angeles Times Book Prize for *Under My Skin.* On critics' list for 1995 Nobel Prize in Literature.
1996	*Love, Again. The Pit. Play with a Tiger and Other Plays.* On the list of nominees for the Nobel Prize for Literature and the British Writer's Guild Award for Fiction.
1997	Collaborated with Philip Glass for a second opera based on *"The Marraiges Between Zones Three, Four and Five,* in Germany. *Walking in the Shade, Volume Two of My Autobiography, 1949 to 1962* (nominated for the 1997 National Book Critics Circle Award for bio/autobiography).
1999	*Mara and Dann, An Adventure. Problems, Myths and Stories.* Presented with the XI Annual International Catalunya Award. Appointed a *Companion of Honour* by Queen Elizabeth II.
2000	*Ben, in the World. The Old Age of El Magnificato. Mara and Dann* nominated for the International IMPAC Dublin Literary Award.
2001	*The Sweetest Dream* (London Edition). Awarded the 2001 Prince of Asturias Prize in Literature. Awarded the David Cohen British Literature Prize. Received Companion of Honour from the Royal Society of Literature.
2002	*The Sweetest Dream* (American Edition). Won the ST Dupont Golden PEN Award for a Lifetime's Distinguished Service to Literature.

Contributors

HAROLD BLOOM is Sterling Professor of the Humanities at Yale University and Henry W. and Albert A. Berg Professor of English at the New York University Graduate School. He is the author of over 20 books, including *Shelley's Mythmaking* (1959), *The Visionary Company* (1961), *Blake's Apocalypse* (1963), *Yeats* (1970), *A Map of Misreading* (1975), *Kabbalah and Criticism* (1975), *Agon: Toward a Theory of Revisionism* (1982), *The American Religion* (1992), *The Western Canon* (1994), and *Omens of Millennium: The Gnosis of Angels, Dreams, and Resurrection* (1996). *The Anxiety of Influence* (1973) sets forth Professor Bloom's provocative theory of the literary relationships between the great writers and their predecessors. His most recent books include *Shakespeare: The Invention of the Human* (1998), a 1998 National Book Award finalist, *How to Read and Why* (2000), and *Genius: A Mosaic of One Hundred Exemplary Creative Minds* (2002). In 1999, Professor Bloom received the prestigious American Academy of Arts and Letters Gold Medal for Criticism, and in 2002 he received the Catalonia International Prize.

JAMES GINDIN, the late University of Michigan Professor of English, is the author of *Postwar British Fiction* and *The English Climate: An Excursion into a Biography of John Galsworthy*.

PAUL SCHLUETER has been Professor of English at Southern Illinois University. He is the author of *The Novels of Doris Lessing* and the editor of *A Small, Personal Voice: Doris Lessing: Essays, Reviews, Interviews*.

ROBERT BOSCHMAN is an Instructor of English at Mt. Royal College.

BETSY DRAINE is a Professor of English at Temple University. She is the author of *Substance Under Pressure: Artistic Coherence and Evolving Form in the Novels of Doris Lessing.*

GAYLE GREENE is a Professor of English and Women's Studies at Scripps College. She is the author of *Changing the Story: Feminist Fiction and the Tradition,* and the coeditor, with Coppelia Kahn, of *Changing Subjects: The Making of Feminist Criticism.*

ROBERTA RUBENSTEIN is a Professor of Literature at American University, specializing in modern fiction and literature by women writers. Rubenstein's books include: *The Novelistic Vision of Doris Lessing: Breaking the Forms of Consciousness; Boundaries of the Self: Gender, Culture, Fiction; Women in Culture;* and *Worlds of Fiction* (coeditor of anthology of short fiction).

SHEILA ROBERTS is the author of *Johannesburg Requiem, The Weekenders, This Time of Year* and *Dialogues and Divertimenti.*

CATHARINE R. STIMPSON is a University Professor and the Dean of the Graduate School of Arts and Sciences at NYU.

KAREN SCHNEIDER is an Associate Professor of English at Western Kentucky University.

PHYLLIS STERNBERG PERRAKIS is a part-time Professor of English at the University of Ottawa and is president of the Doris Lessing Society.

Bibliography

Bowker, Veronica. "Textuality and Wordliness: Crossing the Boundaries: a Postmodernist Reading Achebe, Conrad and Lessing." *Journal of Literary Studies* (5:1) 1989 55-67.

Brewster, Dorothy. *Doris Lessing.* New York: Twayne Publishers, 1965.

Colakis, Marianthe. "Doris Lessing's New Cupid & Psyche: a Platonic Myth Retold." *Classical and Modern Literature* (12:2) 1991, 153-160.

Contemporary Literature 14, no. 4 (1973). Special Doris Lessing Issue.

Dentith, Simon. "*The Golden Notebook* and the End of History." *Literature and History* (third series, 1:2) 1992, 55-66.

Doris Lessing Newsletter, 1977-.

Draine, Betsy. *Substance Under Pressure: Artistic Coherence and Evolving From in the Novels of Doris Lessing.* Madison: University of Wisconsin Press, 1983.

Fishburn, Katherine. "Back to the Preface: Cultural Conversations with *The Golden Notebook*." *College Literature* (17:2/3) 1990, 183-95.

Fishburn, Katherine. "Wor(l)ds Within Words: Doris Lessing as Meta-fictionist and Meta-physician." *Studies in the Novel* (20:2) 1988, 186-205.

Galin, Müge. *Between East and West: Sufism in the Novels of Doris Lessing.* Albany: New York State University Press, 1997.

Greene. Gayle. *Doris Lessing: The Poetics of Change.* Ann Arbor: University of Michigan Press, 1994.

Hanley, Lynne. "Writing Across the Color Bar: Apartheid and Desire." *Massachusetts Review* (32:4) 1991/92, 495-506.

Hite, Molly. "Doris Lessing's *The Golden Notebook* and *The Four-Gated City*: Ideology, Coherence and Possiblity." *Twentieth Century Literature* (34:1) 1988, 16-29.

Kaplan, Carey, and Ellen Cronan Rose, eds. *Doris Lessing: the Alchemy of Survival*. Athens: Ohio University Press, 1988.

Knapp, Mona. *Doris Lessing*. New York: Ungar, 1984.

Linfield, Susan. "Against Utopia: an interview with Doris Lessing," *Salmagundi: A Quarterly of the Humanities & Social Sciences* (130/131): 2001, 59-74.

Marder, Herbert. "Borderline Fantasies: the Two Worlds of 'Briefing for a Descent into Hell.'" *Papers on Language and Literature* (19) 1983, 427-48. *Modern Fiction Studies* 26, no. 1 (1980). Special Doris Lessing Issue.

Pickering, Jean. *Understanding Doris Lessing*. Columbia: South Carolina Press, 1990.

Pratt, Annis, and L.S. Dembo, eds. *Doris Lessing: Critical Studies*. Madison: University of Wisconsin Press, 1974.

Rigney, Barbara Hill. *Madness and Sexual Politics in the Feminist Novel*. Madison, University of Wisconsin Press, 1978.

Rosner, Victoria. "Home Fires: Doris Lessing, Colonial Architecture and the Reproduction of Mothering," *Tulsa Studies in Women's Literature* (18:1): 1999, 59-89.

Rubenstein, Roberta. *The Novelistic Vision of Doris Lessing*. Chicago: University of Illinois Press, 1979.

Sage, Lorna. *Doris Lessing*. London: Methuen and Company, 1983.

Scanlan, Margaret. "Memory and Continuity in the Series Novel: the Example of 'Children of Violence.'" *Modern Fiction Studies* (26) 1980, 17-30.

Schlueter, Paul, ed. *A Small Personal Voice: Doris Lessing: Essays, Reviews, Interviews*. New York: Alfred A. Knopf, 1974.

————. *The Novels of Doris Lessing*. Carbondale: Southern Illinois Press, 1969.

Singer, Sandra. "Unleashing Human Potentialities: Doris Lessing's *The Memoirs of a Survivor* and Contemporary Cultural Theory." *Text & Context* (1:1) 1986, 79-95.

Singleton, Mary Ann. *The City and the Veld: The Fiction of Doris Lessing*. London: Associated University Presses, 1977.

Sprague, Claire, ed. *In Pursuit of Doris Lessing: Nine Nations Reading*. New York: St. Martin's Press, 1990.

Sprague, Claire. *Rereading Doris Lessing: Narrative Patterns of Doubling and Repetition*. Chapel Hill: University of North Carolina Press, 1987.

Sprague, Claire and Virginia Tiger, eds. *Critical Essays on Doris Lessing*. Boston: G.K. Hall and Co., 1986.

Stout, Janis P. "A Quest of One's Own: Doris Lessing's *The Summer Before Dark*." *Ariel* (21:2) 1990, 5-19.

Taylor, Jenny, ed. *Notebooks/memoirs/archives: Reading and Rereading Doris Lessing*. Boston: Kegan Paul, 1982.

Thorpe, Michael. *Doris Lessing's Africa*. London: Evans, 1978.

Tiger, Virginia. "'The words had been right and necessary': Doris Lessing's transformations of utopian and distopian modalities in *The Marriages Between Zones Three, Four and Five*." *Style* (27:1) 1993.

Tyler, Lisa. "Our Mothers' Gardens: Doris Lessing's Among the Roses." *Studies in Short Fiction* (31:2) 1994, 163-173.

Weinhouse, Linda. "Doris Lessing and the Convention of Self." *Commonwealth Novel in English* (6:1/2) 1993, 94-111.

Wright, Derek. "Thin Iron and Egg-shells: the Wall Motif in the Novels of Doris Lessing." *Commonwealth Novel in English*. (6:1/2) 1993, 69-79.

Yelin, Louise. *From the Margins of Empire: Christina Stead, Doris Lessing, Nadine Gordimer*. Ithaca: Cornell University Press, 1998.

Acknowledgments

"Doris Lessing's Intense Commitment" by James Gindin from *Postwar British Fiction: New Accents and Attitudes* by James Gindin, © 1962 by the Regents of the University of California. Reprinted by permission.

"Self-Analytic Women: *The Golden Notebook*" (originally titled "*The Golden Notebook*") by Paul Schlueter, from The Novels of Doris Lessing, © 1969 by Paul George Schlueter, Jr. Reprinted by permission.

"Briefing for a Descent into Hell" by Roberta Rubenstein from *The Novelistic Vision of Doris Lessing: Breaking the Forms of Consciousness* by Roberta Rubenstein, © 1979 by Roberta Rubenstein Reprinted by permission.

"Doris Lessing and the Parables of Growth" by Catharine R. Stimpson from *The Voyage In: Fictions of Female Development* edited by Elizabeth Abel, Marianne Hirsch, and Elizabeth Langland, © 1983 by Catharine R. Stimpson. Reprinted by permission.

"A Different War Story: Doris Lessing's Great Escape" by Karen Schneider from *Journal of Modern Literature* Volume XIX, Number 2, Fall 1995, © 1995 by the Indiana University Press. Reprinted by permission.

"Excrement and 'Kitsch' in Doris Lessing's *The Good Terrorist*" by Robert Boschman from *Ariel: A Review of International English Journal* 25:3, 1994, © 1994 by the Board of Governors, The University of Calgary. Reprinted by permission.

"Mothers and Daughters/Aging and Dying" by Claire Sprague from *Rereading Doris Lessing: Narrative Patterns of Doubling and Repetition* by Claire Sprague, © 1987 by Claire Sprague. Used by permission of the publisher.

"Sufism, Jung and the Myth of Kore: Revisionist Politics in Lessing's *Marriages*" by Phyllis Sternberg Perrakis from *Mosaic: A Journal for the Interdisciplinary Study of Literature* 25:3, Summer 1992, © 1992 by *Mosaic*. Reprinted by permission.

"*The Four-Gated City*: The Pressure of Evolution" by Betsy Draine from *Substance Under Pressure: Artistic Coherence and Evolving Form in the Novels of Doris Lessing* by Betsy Draine, © 1983 by the Board of Regents of the University of Wisconsin System. Reprinted by permission.

"*Re: Colonised Planet 5, Shikasta*: 'After Long Circling and Cycling'" by Gayle Greene from *Doris Lessing: The Poetics of Change* by Gayle Greene, © 1994 by the University of Michigan. Reprinted by permission.

"Sites of Paranoia and Taboo: Lessing's *The Grass is Singing* and Gordimer's *July's People*" by Sheila Roberts from *Research in African Literatures* 24:3, 1993, © 1993 by the Indiana University Press. Reprinted by permission.

Index